Shakespeare's poetic styles

Shakespeare's poetic styles

VERSE INTO DRAMA

John Baxter

Department of English
Brock University, Ontario

Routledge & Kegan Paul

LONDON, BOSTON AND HENLEY

First published in 1980
by Routledge & Kegan Paul Ltd
39 Store Street,
London WC1E 7DD,
9 Park Street,
Boston, Mass. 02108, USA and
Broadway House,
Newtown Road,
Henley-on-Thames,
Oxon RG9 1EN

Set in 11/12 IBM Journal by
Academic Typesetting,
Gerrards Cross, Bucks
and printed in the USA by
Vail-Ballou Press, Inc.
Binghamton, New York

British Library Cataloguing in Publication Data

Baxter, John
  Shakespeare's poetic styles.
  1. Shakespeare, William - Versification
  I. Title
  822.3'3   PR3085   80-49931
ISBN 0 7100 0581 4

184406

For C. Q. Drummond

Contents

Acknowledgments

This book was written at The University of Alberta, and I was sustained immeasurably throughout the writing of it by the support of the institution and of many students, friends, and teachers associated with it. My first debt is to the successive groups of students who helped me to sort out the issues and who alerted me to what was alive in the topic. I wish to thank Janice Cherewick, Lorraine Baxter, and Jim Young for reading the manuscript and for objecting to points of obscurity and unreason. I am also indebted to Richard Bosley, Linda Fitz, John Orrell, and Thomas McFarland who, as a sympathetic but critical examining committee, proposed a number of changes on matters of tact, fairness and precision. And finally, to Christopher Drummond, whose generosity and judgment give life to the idea of a university, I owe the best part of the book. Mr Drummond suggested many points, refined many others, and left none unimproved. If he will continue to own its merits, I will acknowledge its defects with better courage.

J. B.

1 · Verse into drama

If we can disengage ourselves sufficiently, then, from
the preconception that 16th century poetry is essentially
Petrarchist, to sift the good poems, regardless of school
or of method, from the bad, we shall find that the
Petrarchist movement produced nothing worth remembering between Skelton and Sidney, in spite of a
tremendous amount of Petrarchan experimentation
during this period, if we except certain partially Petrarchan poems by Surrey and by Wyatt, and that the
poetry written during this interim which is worth
remembering belongs to a school in every respect
antithetical to the Petrarchist school, a school to which
Wyatt and Surrey contributed important efforts, perhaps their best, but which flourished mainly between
Surrey and Sidney and in a few men who survived or
came to maturity somewhat later, a school which laid
the groundwork for the greatest achievements in the
entire history of the English lyric, which itself left us
some of those greatest achievements, and which is
almost wholly neglected and forgotten by the antho-
logists and by the historians of the period, even by the
editors, for the greater part, of the individual con-
tributors to the school.[1]

The school of English poetry to which Yvor Winters refers
in this sentence produced what he calls elsewhere the native
plain style,[2] and the 1939 essay from which the sentence is
quoted initiated a radical revaluation of English poetry in
the sixteenth century. Not all subsequent writers on the
subject agree with Winters's emphases, but C. S. Lewis and
G. K. Hunter, using the terms 'drab' and 'golden' to reassert
the eminence of the golden style, agree that there is a distinction.[3] Moreover, Winters's claims for the centrality of
the plain style have been corroborated and refined by a

1

number of scholars and critics including J. V. Cunningham, Wesley Trimpi, and Douglas Peterson.[4] The arguments on behalf of either style now have numerous advocates, and the two styles have been variously called Petrarchan, eloquent, golden, sweet, pleasant, or sugared; and native, plain, drab, flat, didactic, or moral. While there is no reason to suppose that any of the terms on either side is exactly synonymous with any other on the same side, the major distinction is sufficiently secure to support an exploration of a question not yet considered in the debate: namely, the possibility that the style that 'laid the groundwork for the greatest achievements in the entire history of the English lyric' also laid the groundwork for the greatest achievements in the entire history of the English drama. This exploration involves two further questions: first, are Winters, Cunningham, Trimpi, and Peterson right to regard the plain style as the central style and the eloquent style as, finally, an enrichment of it, and second, are the verse techniques developed in writing short poems readily available to the writer of dramatic poetry? Are the two styles that were perfected in the lyric poetry of the sixteenth century germane to the style and form of late Elizabethan poetic drama, especially poetic tragedy?

How does a dramatist make verse into drama? There are certain traps or disadvantages in putting the question in this way. The form of the question suggests that the dramatist must always start with whatever poetic styles are available and then make what he can out of them. It seems to assign an unwarranted priority to style or language. In a related way, the question insists that drama is primarily, even essentially, a form of literature and so minimizes its non-linguistic elements. And finally, to the extent that the model for analysing verse derives from the study of short poems, the question might focus attention on isolated passages without sufficient regard for their interrelationships. In any of these cases, the full complexity of the drama goes unrecognized.

None the less, the question is worth asking, all the more worth asking because of these very objections. However the dramatist begins – whether he begins with elements other than style, such as plot, character, theme, spectacle, or song – the reader, and for the most part the audience as well, recovers the dramatist's intention by attending to the cumulative effects of his styles. The analysis of style leads out to larger questions, whereas the pondering of larger questions seldom stoops to find proof in the minutiae of style. An author may very well be under pressures of an indefinite variety and kind that bear on his work, but if he is a writer, they get expressed in language. Even if there are non-verbal kinds of drama, drama, especially Elizabethan drama, is still essentially a form of literature because of the central place that language holds in the human world. The imitation of human action can hardly avoid a fact so important. For a similar reason, the language of a play should bear close inspection moment by moment. Passages isolated for analysis should return us, finally, to a renewed sense of the meaning and form of the whole.

The relationship of style and form in drama is a question that can be most sharply defined by referring again to the criticism of Yvor Winters. Though he celebrates repeatedly the achievements in the short poem in English, Winters's infrequent discussions of drama offer some challenging criticisms of the form. From early in his career Winters was suspicious of what he called 'imitative form', the doctrine whereby 'the form of expression is determined by the subject matter'. Following this doctrine, an author attempts to express the confusion of his subject matter by making his form deranged and confused – a procedure tantamount to the surrender of form. Since the dramatist seems to be committed to some kind of imitation, the procedure would appear to be an all but inescapable part of dramatic form, unless he restricts himself to the portrayal of characters whose understanding is lucid and firm at all times. Late in his career, in 'Problems For the Modern Critic of Literature,' Winters, using *Macbeth* as his example, challenged the very heart of drama.[5] Since the dramatist must differentiate his characters from one another and differentiate the various stages of growth or decline in individual characters, and since he must do these things directly without the intervention of authorial comment, he will be forced at

times to write badly or to express unworthy ideas or sentiments in order to depict characters inferior to himself in
perception and expression. And such stretches of inferior
writing are not merely an occupational hazard for the dramatist, but an unavoidable part of the medium. Dramatic form
is inherently defective.

The problem that Winters here poses for the modern
critic has not been answered satisfactorily. While Winters's
account of the sixteenth-century lyric has been refined and
extended by several other writers, his discussion of dramatic
form has received scant notice. A. L. French in 'Purposive
Imitation: A Skirmish With Literary Theory' takes up some
of the issues and, after discussing the difficulties involved in
trying to exonerate bad prose by saying that it is *deliberately*
bad, he admits that the difficulties 'become even more
formidable when we think of plays'.[6] But though French
acknowledges at the end of his essay that Winters's 'fallacy
of imitative form' provided the starting point for some of
his reflections, he does not address himself at all to Winters's
comments on drama, and he shies away from exploring that
question very deeply. His essay remains not a sustained
engagement but what he calls it himself, a skirmish.

Jonas A. Barish does attempt a direct and sustained
answer in 'Yvor Winters and the Antimimetic Prejudice',
and Barish does indeed have some valid points to bring
against Winters – most notably the presence of certain
mimetic principles even in the poems that Winters most
admires, such as Valéry's 'Ebauche d'un serpent', and even
in Winters's own poems.[7] Barish, however, damages his own
case by supposing from the outset that the criticisms of
drama are a peculiarity of taste or prejudice. He seems to
find in the criticisms not so much a challenge as an affront,
and in his eagerness to rebuff the affront, he allows Winters
to win the argument by default. He attempts the wholly
legitimate enterprise of trying to win a hearing for the role
of dance, music, ritual, gesture, costume, light, and architec-
ture in drama by the dubious method of denying Winters's
claim that poetic drama is primarily a form of literature.[8]

The most one can say is that at certain epochs, when
language held a central place in culture, the written

4

word acquired a temporary working ascendancy in the theatre also. It acquired it a few centuries back in western Europe, and now seems to be on the point of losing it again; increasingly, playwrights today seem to feel themselves to be working in a nonverbal medium. Winters's definition arrogates an unwarranted despotism to language in drama, and denies the independence of the theatre as an art form in its own right, with its own laws of realization.

It is a superficial view of culture that can with such insouciance displace language from the centre. But quite apart from that complex issue, it is no defence of *poetic* drama to argue that the theatre as an art form in its own right is independent of language. There may well be such an art form, but it cannot be called poetic drama since poetry is by definition something made in words. Through a prejudice in favour of theatricality, Barish fails to confront the real question that Winters asks. What kind of poetry is possible within the form of a play?

One should be able to ask this question and still attend fairly to both of its aspects, verse and drama. It may be true, as Barish, following Andor Gomme, alleges,[9] that Winters is at his weakest when writing about drama. Certainly his comments on the form are comparatively brief and largely theoretical. By comparison, his study of the short poem in the English Renaissance is a matter of complete engagement – the whole man wholly attending – and a model worthy of emulation. There is, then, a kind of tension involved in using Winters's criticism as a way of thinking about Renaissance drama. If we import his methods for analysing verse into the analysis of drama, are we committed to his conclusions about dramatic form?

This question, along with the others raised so far, contains numerous and important implications for the study of Shakespeare. The questions, however, can be set in historical perspective by first considering certain aspects of the work of Sir Philip Sidney and of Fulke Greville, First Lord Brooke. Sidney, in *A Defence of Poetry*, and Greville, in *The Tragedy of Mustapha*, reveal certain crucial ideas concerning form and purpose in Elizabethan drama. Moreover, since both Greville and Sidney fashioned their most impressive achievements in

5

the form of the short poem, and since both contributed materially to the development of English verse, their ideas about drama have a special relevance for a study of the relation between drama and verse. They are among those most responsible for the sophistication of the poetic styles available to Shakespeare.

The plays of William Shakespeare offer a wealth of material, but two, *The Tragedy of Richard the Second* and *The Tragedy of Macbeth*, are particularly well-suited to this study. *Richard II* is one of the few plays of Shakespeare that is composed entirely of verse, and it was probably written during the period that saw the writing of some or many of the sonnets as well. In addition, the play recommends itself because of intrinsic merit: the action is momentous, the characters are nicely drawn, and much of the verse is extremely fine. It is much admired both for its dramatic and for its poetic qualities. The issues raised by the play are historical in origin and are at least potentially tragic in intensity, so that Shakespeare's subject matter here offers full scope to the rhythmical heightening that is a characteristic feature of poetry. Shakespeare in this play makes use of the whole range of poetic styles that could be discovered or invented in England in the 1590s, and *Richard II*, therefore, stands as a kind of summary achievement of Shakespeare's early period and, in addition, as a kind of prognostication of the style Shakespeare brought to maturity in a play such as *Macbeth*. In the study of *Macbeth*, the analysis of verse serves finally to answer Winters's criticisms of drama. In *Mustapha, Richard II,* and *Macbeth* it is possible to see the demands that dramatic form makes of poetic styles and also to see the plenitude produced in the exchange.

2 · Sydney's *Defence* and Greville's *Mustapha*

I

Some of the principles of style and form in tragedy and something of their relationship to poetic style in general are set forth clearly in *A Defence of Poetry* by Philip Sidney and in *The Tragedy of Mustapha* by Fulke Greville. Sidney's own short poems, of course, provide much that is immediately useful to the dramatist. His technical subtlety, especially as developed in *Astrophil and Stella*, provides a means of registering subtle and dramatic shifts in the mental or emotional state of a character. Even more important for the essential purposes of drama, his mastery of the plain style provides a means of registering the moral certitudes within which or against which a character must act out his desires. Greville's similar mastery and, in *Caelica*, his even more pronounced separation of the two styles makes his play a good choice in which to explore the influence of lyric styles on poetic drama. But it is Sidney's *Defence* that most clearly exhibits some of the important tenets of Elizabethan critical theory: it presents both an affective theory of tragedy and a descriptive theory of poetic style.

To begin with, the *Defence* defends each of the two styles. As several critics have observed, Sidney's treatise conforms to the model of a classical oration,[1] and it includes, just before the peroration, a long digression on the state of contemporary English poetry. The main body of the *Defence* is an argument on behalf of the golden style, while the digression argues for the plain style, connecting, as it does so, poetic style with the everyday, practical purposes of oratory.[2]

> For my part, I do not doubt, when Antonius and Crassus, the great forefathers of Cicero in eloquence, the one (as Cicero testifieth of them) pretended not to know art, the other not to set by it, because with a plain sensibleness they might win credit of popular ears (which credit is the nearest step to persuasion,

which persuasion is the chief mark of oratory), I do not doubt (I say) but that they used these knacks [i.e. similitudes] very sparingly; which who doth generally use, any man may see doth dance to his own music, and so be noted by the audience more careful to speak curiously than to speak truly. Undoubtedly (at least to my opinion undoubtedly), I have found in divers smally learned courtiers a more sound style than in some professors of learning; of which I can guess no other cause, but that the courtier, following that which by practise he findeth fittest to nature, therein (though he know it not) doth according to art, though not by art: where the other, using art to show art, and not to hide art (as in these cases he should do), flieth from nature, and indeed abuseth art.

The interest in an art that hides art and in the credit of a 'plain sensibleness' and the objections to using similitudes and to being 'more careful to speak curiously than to speak truly' are all clear demands for the plain style. Alongside this passage can be set Sidney's comments on the difficulty of finding contemporary English poems to commend.

Besides these I do not remember to have seen but few (to speak boldly) printed that have poetical sinews in them; for proof whereof, let but most of the verses be put in prose, and then ask the meaning, and it will be found that one verse did but beget another, without ordering at the first what should be at the last; which becomes a confused mass of words, with a tingling sound of rhyme, barely accompanied with reason. (p. 64)

The concerns for prose meaning and for the supremacy of rational order are once again clear demands for a poetic style that aims to disclose the plain truth, a style that is the instrument of reason.

By contrast, earlier sections of the *Defence* promote the golden style. Against the charge that poets are liars, Sidney replies by claiming that, 'for the poet, he nothing affirms, and therefore never lieth' (p. 52), and a little further on he continues in this vein:

> If then a man can arrive to that child's age to know that
> the poets' persons and doings are but pictures what
> should be, and not stories what have been, they will
> never give the lie to things not affirmatively but allegori-
> cally and figuratively written. (p. 53)

Here allegories and figures (both may be considered as kinds
of similitudes) are defended, and the affirmations of truth
are irrelevant. As Sidney declares very early in the treatise:
'[Nature's] world is brazen, the poets only deliver a golden'
(p. 24).

O. B. Hardison Jr in his essay 'The Two Voices of Sidney's
Apology for Poetry'[3] has seen quite clearly that Sidney is
committed to defending two antithetical schools of poetry,
but Hardison's conjectures about the significance of that fact
are debatable. In the first place, he is mistaken to conclude
prima facie that the first voice, the one heard earlier in the
treatise, is 'the one that speaks the more effectively for the
poetry of the Elizabethan period', when it is in the digression
(the second voice) that Sidney addresses himself specifically
to the question of contemporary Elizabethan poetry. Second,
to stigmatize the second voice as 'incipient neo-classicism' is
to make too easy an equation between the plain style of Ben
Jonson and the neo-classicism of Dryden, Pope and the eighteenth century, especially in view of the work of Cunningham
and Trimpi, who show that Ben Jonson's plain style is the
result of a confluence of the classical plain style and the
native plain style. Sidney's defence of this school, then, is
not necessarily quite the *avant garde* critical outlook that
Hardison suggests.[4] Finally, though one must sympathize
with Hardison on this point, it may not be true that 'the
contradictions of attitude and precept' in the two voices are
so fundamental as to prohibit reconciliation. Curiously,
Sidney's *Defence* in its most famous and oft-repeated formu-
lations, what Hardison calls its first voice, cannot stand on its
own. Against the charge that poems are sinful fancies, Sidney
replies that some poems are indeed infected, but that such
examples are an abuse of poetry and that, like anything else,
poetry must be judged 'upon the right use,' which in this
case presumably means poems of virtuous fancy. In either

9

case, however, poems are the product of fancy, and both the poet and his reader are left with the problem of sorting out the abuse of poetry from the right use of it. Neither will be able to do this without some recourse to a plain sensibleness and a carefulness to speak truly.

Sidney himself does not make this reconciliation in the *Defence* (though he sometimes does in his short poems). Nevertheless, the *Defence* does set out quite clearly two of the styles available to poets in the last part of the sixteenth century. Moreover, tragedy, which does deal in some measure with the truth of accomplished fact, with the truth of history, may well find the affirmations of the plain style suitable to its purposes. But again, Sidney does not say so. In fact, his brief paragraph outlining an affective theory of tragedy does not say anything directly about what styles are appropriate to the genre.

After discussing comedy, he turns to the subject of tragedy.

> So that the right use of comedy will (I think) by nobody be blamed; and much less of the high and excellent Tragedy, that openeth the greatest wounds, and showeth forth the ulcers that are covered with tissue; that maketh kings fear to be tyrants, and tyrants manifest their tyrannical humours; that, with stirring the affects of admiration and commiseration, teacheth the uncertainty of this world, and upon how weak foundations gilden roofs are builded; that maketh us know
>
> > *Qui sceptra saevus duro imperio regit*
> > *Timet timentes; metus in auctorem redit.*
>
> But how much it can move, Plutarch yieldeth a notable testimony of the abominable tyrant Alexander Phereus, from whose eyes a tragedy, well made and represented, drew abundance of tears, who without all pity had murdered infinite numbers, and some of his own blood: so as he, that was not ashamed to make matters for tragedies, yet could not resist the sweet violence of a tragedy. And if it wrought no further good in him, it was that he, in despite of himself, withdrew himself from hearkening to that which might mollify his hardened heart. (p. 45)

The most important remark of this paragraph deals with the emotional effect of tragedy, which Sidney calls 'admiration and commiseration.' J. V. Cunningham, in his book, *Woe or Wonder: The Emotional Effect of Shakespearean Tragedy*, points out that Horatio's phrase, 'aught of woe or wonder', designating the emotional effect of *Hamlet*, 'is simply a translation from Latin to Germanic diction of Sidney's, with the substitution of the more general and more traditional notion of sorrow for the more special and more Aristotelian notion of pity'.[5] Cunningham goes on to demonstrate that, in addition to the famous passage on pity and fear, there are three passages in Aristotle's *Poetics* arguing that wonder is an emotional effect of tragedy; that Plato's *Ion* concurs with Aristotle in associating fear, pity, and wonder; and that the same doctrine is discoverable throughout antiquity and the Middle Ages. As Cunningham remarks, 'whatever appears in the scholastic philosophers and at the same time in Aristotle, as well as in Cicero and Quintilian, is likely to appear any-where in Renaissance literature' (*CE*, pp. 74, 75). Sidney's phrase, then, is almost as traditional as Horatio's and coincides exactly with Horatio's on the subject of wonder.

It is worthwhile to draw attention to Cunningham's argument because many modern students are still in the grip of a misinterpretation of the tradition, and the misinterpretation can cause an insensitive reading of Renaissance literature. For example, Jan Van Dorsten, editor of the Oxford edition of *A Defence of Poetry*, has the following comment on Sidney's paragraph:

> Sidney's only, but important, departure from the main (Aristotelian) line of argument is in calling the 'affects' (emotions) stirred by tragedy 'admiration' (great won-der and reverence) and 'commiseration', instead of 'pity and fear'. 'Fear' itself he reserves for the royal spectator (l. 17), or he relegates it to the tragic theme, as in the couplet 'Qui sceptra etc.'. 'Who harshly wields the sceptre with tyrannic sway, fears those who fear: terror recoils upon its author's head' (Seneca, *Oedipus* 705–6). (p. 94)

Van Dorsten's mistake about 'departure' is perhaps less serious than his notion that the emotion of fear is 'reserved' for the royal spectator, as if the emotion felt by the royal spectator were somehow exclusive and eccentric rather than central, the epitome of what any spectator should feel. Sidney is here paying tribute to the universal appeal of tragedy, to its universal social and political significance, which makes it fit for a royal audience, and to its enormous power to move even the most hard-hearted of tyrants. If tyrants 'fear', and if even the abominable Alexander Pheraeus weeps, of course the rest of us must experience similar emotions. Likewise with wonder, which, Cunningham suggests, was sometimes regarded as a species of fear (*CE*, p. 16).

As emotional effects, admiration and commiseration obviously carry certain implications for the style and structure of tragic drama, so that, while Sidney says nothing directly on this subject, one may at least infer that the tragedian's styles must be capable of producing the appropriate effects. Certainly, in the only other place in the *Defence* where he mentions admiration and commiseration, Sidney is concerned to dismiss such manners as will detract from the appropriate effect of tragedy.

> But besides these gross absurdities, how all their plays be neither right tragedies, nor right comedies, mingling kings and clowns, not because the matter so carrieth it, but thrust in the clown by head and shoulders to play a part in majestical matters with neither decency nor discretion, so as neither the admiration and commiseration, nor the right sportfulness, is by their mongrel tragicomedy obtained. (p. 67)

Like Marlowe after him, Sidney thinks that 'such conceits as clownage keepes in pay' will destroy the effect of tragedy — though his objection to mixed forms is not absolute because if 'the matter so carrieth it' (as the matter of the Porter scene does in *Macbeth*), there is no reason to suppose that Sidney would not approve.

Sidney's *Defence*, then, sets out in a very clear way some of the important principles of Elizabethan tragic drama, and it defends two of the poetic styles available to the tragic dramatist. For an illustration of the principles faithfully worked out and of the poetic styles accommodated to these principles, we may turn to a play by Sidney's closest friend, Fulke Greville.

II

The text of *Mustapha* that is available to the modern reader in volume II of *Poems and Dramas of Fulke Greville, First Lord Brooke*, edited by Geoffrey Bullough,[6] is based on the 1633 collection of Greville's *Workes*. Joan Rees, who in her very useful *Selected Writings of Fulke Greville* prints the play complete,[7] also bases her edition on the 1633 collection. What we read, then, did not appear in print until more than five decades after the writing of Sidney's *Defence*. There are, nevertheless, compelling reasons proving that the play is directly influenced by Sidney's ideas.

The following description appeared on the title page of the 1633 collection: 'CERTAINE / LEARNED / AND / ELEGANT / WORKES / OF THE / *RIGHT HONORABLE* / FVLKE / *LORD BROOKE* / Written in his Youth, and familiar / Exercise with / SIR / PHILIP SIDNEY: / *The severall Names of which Workes the / following page doth declare.*'[8] Moreover, as with almost all of his work, Greville seems to have revised *Mustapha* a number of times over the years. An unauthorized quarto edition appeared in 1609, and at least one manuscript version was probably written many years earlier. Geoffrey Bullough, after sorting out the complicated possibilities with admirable lucidity, concludes that 1594–6 is the likeliest date for the composition of the first version of *Mustapha*.[9] Establishing the exact dates of successive revisions is probably not absolutely essential to a critical understanding of the play because, if anything, Greville's last version is more faithful to Sidney's principles than are the earlier ones.

The plot of the drama revolves around one central, historic event — the murder of Mustapha in 1553 by his father, Soliman the Magnificent, emperor of Turkey. Fearing Mustapha's increasing popularity and having recently married Rossa, a freed bondwoman, Soliman is moved to this action against

his son partly because, as a tyrant, he is inherently vulnerable
to such fears and partly because, as an uxorious husband, he
is susceptible to Rossa's insinuations about her step-son's
ambitions. Rossa plots against Mustapha in order to make
her own son, Zanger, Soliman's chief heir; and she is helped
by Rosten, the husband of her daughter, Camena. But her own
children, Zanger and Camena, as they discover what she intends, are opposed to Rossa. Camena is killed at her mother's
command because she tries to warn Mustapha of his danger,
and Zanger dies by his own hand after learning of Mustapha's
fate. Mustapha himself refuses to heed the warning against
coming to Soliman because heeding it would mean disobey-
ing his father and emperor, thereby introducing a precedent
of disobedience for the entire state. As it is, his murder
nearly provokes riot and general rebellion, and the play
closes as Achmat, Soliman's chief counsellor, despite his
sympathy with the public indignation, decides that he must
try to restrain it in the interest of preserving the state. The
tragedy emphasizes the cost of loyalty to a sovereign who
undermines the ground of loyalty.

The emotional effects at which *Mustapha* aims are set
out most explicitly by Zanger in Act V. As Mustapha's half-
brother, he is, after Mustapha, next in the line of succession,
and it is largely for his sake that Rossa has plotted the murder of her step-son. In other words, he is, in several senses,
the character in a position to be most affected by the murder, and, as well, he has not appeared in the play until this
point. Both of these facts lend the keenest interest to his
initial remarks and to his reaction to Mustapha's death. He
first enters alone.

> Nourisht in Court, *where no Thoughts peace is nourisht,*
> Vs'd to behold the Tragedies of ruine,
> Brought up with feares that follow Princes fortunes;
> Yet am I like him that hath lost his knowledge,
> Or neuer heard one storie of Misfortune.
> My heart doth fall away: feare falls vpon me.
> Tame Rumors, that haue beene mine old acquaintance
> Are to me now (like Monsters) feare, or wonder.
>
> (V, i, 1–8)

Despite great familiarity with actual tragedy and with the stories of tragedy, and therefore supposedly inured to its effects, Zanger, none the less, feels his emotions rising. To have lost one's knowledge, to be beset by the hints and guesses of rumour, is to be in a state of wonder; misfortune is woe. Zanger's forebodings prepare the way excellently for the report of the murder and the confirmation of his fears in the next scene. His actual response to that report is an intensification and a widening of his initial remarks.

> Alas! Could neither Truth appease his [Soliman's] furie?
> Nor his [Mustapha's] vnlook'd Humilitie of comming?
> Nor any secret witnessing remorses?
> Can Nature, from her selfe, make such diuorces?
> Tell on; that all the World may rue, and wonder.
>
> (V, ii, 38–42)

Like Horatio in *Hamlet*, Zanger explicitly designates the appropriate emotional effects of the tragedy, expounding simultaneously his own emotional response and claiming, in the phrase 'all the World', that that response should be universal. As with *Hamlet*, the story is to be recapitulated to that end. For Horatio's phrase, 'aught of woe or wonder', Zanger substitutes 'rue and wonder'; that is, since rue is more nearly a synonym of pity than of woe, Greville follows Sir Philip Sidney's specification of the tradition: commiseration and admiration.

Also, like *Hamlet, Mustapha* facilitates the transfer of the appropriate emotional effects by providing, within the play, a group of silent actors whose function is to convey the proper emotional attitude directly to the larger audience who read or hear the play, 'for emotional effects are directly transferable; indeed, they are much more communicable than ideas'.[10] The equivalent in *Mustapha* of the 'mutes' who 'look pale and tremble at this chance' in *Hamlet* are the 'six slave eunuchs, either taught to colour/ Mischief with reverence or forced, by nature,/ To reverence true virtue in misfortune' (V, ii, 52–3). They exist in the play almost solely for the purpose of expressing wonder and woe at the murder of Mustapha. Achmat's report continues:

> While these six *Eunuchs* to this charge appointed

> (Whose hearts had neuer vs'd their hands to Pittie,
> Whose hands, now onely, trembled to do Murther)
> With Reuerence, and Feare, stood still, amazed,
> (V, ii, 70–3)

and aligns fear, wonder, and pity as they are aligned in Sidney's *Defence*. That the eunuchs are normally callous, irreverent, and pitiless, usually 'not ashamed to make matters for tragedies', and, therefore, in the same class as the abominable tyrant Alexander Phaeraeus, only serves to indicate more strongly the moving power of this tragedy.

Greville, then, is working within the same tradition that Sidney outlines so very briefly in his paragraph on tragedy in the *Defence*. One of the major changes he made in the late revisions of the play has to do with the positioning of Zanger's first speech.[11] In the 1609 quarto and in the manuscript version that was likely composed before this date, Zanger's soliloquy appears in Act IV, scene i. By moving it into Act V, where it appears in the version printed in 1633, Greville underlines his intention to make admiration and commiseration *the* emotional effects of his play by making them conclusive.

III

The obvious concomitant of Greville's allegiance to a traditional theory of tragedy is some sort of connection to a traditional theory of rhetoric. Wonder is the proper effect not merely of marvellous events but also of marvellous eloquence,[12] usually requiring the tragic style or high style of traditional rhetoric. Furthermore, while generations of readers have found *Hamlet* moving, and our interest, therefore, centres on refining our apprehension of that feeling by recovering, as fully as may be, Shakespeare's explicit intentions, few readers have noticed *Mustapha,* and although the observation that Greville and Shakespeare share remarkably coincidental general intentions does have some intrinsic interest, it does not constitute a full vindication of Greville's play. Yet beyond following the theory, Greville explores more deeply than Sidney the problem of a right relationship between the two styles that Sidney defends and the problem of accommodating these to the traditional high style of tragic drama.

Three relevant passages help to explain more fully the principles underlying Greville's dramatic style. The first is from his explicit comment on his own plays in his *Life of Sidney*.[13]

Againe, for the Arguments of these Tragedies they be not naked, and casual like the Greeke, and Latine, nor (I confesse) contrived with the variety, and unexpected encounters of the Italians, but nearer level'd to those humours, counsels, and practises, wherein I thought fitter to hold the attention of the Reader, than in the strangeness or perplexedness of witty Fictions; In which the affections, or imagination, may perchance find exercise and entertainment, but the memory and judgement no enriching at all; Besides, I conceived these delicate Images to be over-abundantly furnished in all Languages already.

And though my Noble Friend had that dexterity, even with the dashes of his pen to make the *Arcadian* Antiques beautifie the Margents of his works; yet the honour which (I beare him record) he never affected, I leave unto him, with this addition, that his end in them was not vanishing pleasure alone, but morall Image, and Examples, (as directing threds) to guide every man through the confused *Labyrinth* of his own desires and life: So that howsoever I liked them too well (even in that unperfected shape they were) to condescend that such delicate (though inferior) Pictures of himself should be suppressed; yet I do wish that work may be the last in this kind, presuming no man that followes can ever reach, much lesse go beyond, that excellent intended patterne of his.

For my own part, I found my creeping Genius more fixed upon the Images of Life, than the Images of Wit, and therefore chose not to write to them on whose foot the black Oxe had not already trod, as the Proverbe is, but to those only, that are weather-beaten in the Sea of this World, such as having lost the sight of their Gardens, and Groves, study to saile on a right course among

Rocks, and quick-sands; And if in thus ordaining, and ordering matter, and forme together for the use of life, I have made those Tragedies, no Plaies for the Stage, be it known, it was no part of my purpose to write for them, against whom so many good, and great spirits have already written.

But he that will behold these Acts upon their true Stage, let him look on that Stage wherein himself is an Actor, even the state he lives in, and for every part he may perchance find a Player, and for every Line (it may be) an instance of life, beyond the Authors intention, or application, the vices of former Ages being so like to these of this Age, as it will be easie to find out some affinity, or resemblance between them, which whosoever readeth with this apprehension, will not perchance think the Scenes too large, at least the matter not to be exceeded in account of words.

Several remarks in this passage bear on the principles of style. The contrast between a poetry that through the strangeness or perplexedness of witty fictions aims primarily at exercising and entertaining the affections and the imagination, and a poetry that aims primarily to enrich the memory and the judgment, is closely akin to the contrast between the golden and the moral style. Such an interpretation of the contrast is reinforced by the opposition, at the beginning of the third paragraph, between the images of wit and the images of life, especially since the former have just been defined by reference to Sidney's *Arcadia*, that monument to the golden style. Furthermore, it should be noted that Greville's well-known description of his own creeping genius proceeds not only by way of contrast with the genius of Sidney (and especially the Sidney of the *Arcadia*), but also proceeds towards an account of the style and intention of Greville's own tragedies. The ordaining and ordering of matter and form together for the use of life is, like the preference for the images of life, an expression of a predisposition for the moral style, and, given his allegiance to the moral and the plain, it is not surprising to find Greville dissociate himself from the public stage. This dissociation however, does not mean that Greville thinks of himself as forgoing any exercise whatsoever of the affections and the imagination. Having already looked at what sort of appeal he makes to the affections, we can also say that in the fourth paragraph of the passage above he appeals emphatically to the imagination of his reader or auditor. In fact, without the intervention of actors and spectacle, a more strenuous exercise of the imagination is called for than would otherwise be the case. The concluding remark, that the reader 'will not perchance think the Scenes too large, at least the matter not to be exceeded in account of words', is a reaffirmation of a stylistic principle, not unlike that of Ben Jonson or Francis Bacon, based solidly on the plain style, but not ruling out the possibility that certain kinds of matter might require a special language.

Similarly, in 'A Treatie of Humane Learning' in four stanzas devoted to a discussion of rhetoric, Greville affirms an essential allegiance to the moral and the plain, without denying the need for metaphor. The discussion follows three stanzas devoted to logic.[14]

107
Rhetorike, to this a sister, and a twinne,
Is growne a *Siren* in the formes of pleading,
Captiuing reason, with the painted skinne
Of many words; with empty sounds misleading
   Vs to false ends, by these false forms abuse,
   Brings neuer forth that Truth, whose name they vse.

108
Besides, this Art, where scarcity of words
Forc'd her, at first, to *Metaphorike* wings,
Because no Language in the earth affords
Sufficient Characters to expresse all things;
   Yet since, she playes the wanton with this need,
   And staines the Matrone with the Harlots weed.

109
Whereas those words in euery tongue are best,
Which doe most properly expresse the thought;
For as of pictures, which should manifest
The life, we say not that is fineliest wrought,

Which fairest simply showes, but faire and like:
So *words must sparkes be of those fires they strike.*

110

For the true Art of *Eloquence* indeed
Is not this craft of words, but formes of speech,
Such as from living wisdomes doe proceed;
Whose ends are not to flatter, or beseech,
Insinuate, or perswade, but to declare
What things in Nature good, or evill are.

The problem is that the mother of invention is often dis-
graced by the harlot of ornate ingenuity. Interestingly
enough, even while expressing his distaste for ornament and
superfluous metaphor, Greville turns out a number of concise
and expressively apt metaphors of his own, the most successful coming at the end of stanza 109. The stanza might be
taken as a fairly simple exposition of a correspondence
theory of language: there is, wholly exterior to language, a
reality, to which language more or less corresponds; words
are thought of, somehow, as an inevitable outgrowth of the
natural (i.e. the real) world, and the problem is simply to
find the words that correspond to, or reflect more or less
exactly and pleasingly, that reality. But sparks are not merely
emanations from fires, they are also capable of striking fires.
In other words, language is responsible not only for giving an
account of reality, but also, at least in part, responsible for
the creation of reality. Actually, the early part of the stanza
is not so simple as I may have made it sound, even though the
emphasis on the word 'like' pushes it in the direction of
correspondence, because in the third line, for example, 'For
as of pictures, which should manifest/The life', the word
'manifest' is indeed not a synonym for 'correspond to' or
'reflect'. But the surprising metaphor of the last line brings
home compactly a more satisfyingly complex understanding
of language and, by being aligned with the metaphor of
'words as pictures,' inserts new life into that very conventional figure. Clearly, Greville is capable of inventing metaphor when need be. To notice this, however, is not to deny
that the main gist of the passage is a plea for the plain style:
'. . . the true Art of *Eloquence* indeed/ Is not this craft of

words, but formes of speech,/ Such as from living wisdomes doe proceed.'

And finally, in an earlier passage from the *Life of Sidney*, Greville explains what he believes is the proper relationship between the moral style and the 'high astounding terms' of the contemporary Elizabethan stage. For Greville the wonder of tragedy need not be as clamourous nor as conspicuous as it was for many of his contemporaries.[15]

> I preferring this generall scope of profit, before the self-reputation of being an exact Artisan in that Poetical Mystery, conceived that a perspective into vice, and the unprosperities of it, would prove more acceptable to every good Readers ends, then any bare murmur of discontented spirits against their present Government, or horrible periods of exorbitant passions among equals.

That is, he declares his moral preoccupations and asserts their superiority to the 'horrible periods of exorbitant passions', a phrase that is surely a near synonym for 'high astounding terms', as well as to the 'bare murmur of discontented spirits against their present Government', a phrase referring to the sort of political allegory that the Essex conspirators, at least, thought they discovered in Shakespeare's *Richard II* or that Greville feared might be construed (or misconstrued) from his own *Antonie and Cleopatra*.[16] His moral preoccupation is something that must hold itself aloof from both the Marlovian attempt at the amoral presentation of an action and from the naive didacticism of political propaganda.

Yet this preoccupation is not necessarily less dramatic than its rivals, even though some readers have thought so; and, in certain ways, it is more dramatic, in a more traditional sense of the term 'drama'. Geoffrey Bullough, for example, misled perhaps by Greville's disclaimers, like the one about not being 'an exact artisan', remarks that:[17]

> The ethical subject is more to him than the dramatic form. Hence he finds it easy to separate the drama from the theatre. . . . He knows something of many kinds of drama, but prides himself on having departed from traditional theme and treatment.

But the ethical subject is traditionally at the very centre of the drama, portraying as it does men faced with the difficulty of making moral choices and living with that difficulty or living out the choices that are made. A willingness to separate the drama from the theatre is not necessarily proof of a disregard for dramatic form. When Greville says of the arguments of his tragedies, 'they be not naked and casual like the Greeke, and Latine', he is perhaps not being entirely fair to Greek and Latin tragedy, but his desire that the argument or form of his own plays 'be not naked and casual' is emphatically traditional: the antitheses of these terms are 'rhetorical' and 'causal'.

And consider, for a moment, the word 'unprosperity' in the phrase expressing his ambition to provide 'a perspective into vice, and the unprosperities of it'. To prosper is to thrive, to succeed, or do well, but also 'to cause to flourish'; 'to be propitious to' (*Oxford English Dictionary*). Prosperity, in other words, is not only the condition of action brought to a successful conclusion, but also the grounds or framework conducive to doing well. Prosperity in this sense is that which makes moral choices possible (one thinks of Prospero in *The Tempest*, or, conversely, from *Richard III*, 'So now prosperity begins to mellow/ And drop into the rotten mouth of death').[18] The unprosperity of vice, then, is not any external punishment that vice brings down upon itself, but simply the elimination of the grounds of moral action. Greville is unquestionably interested in the drama of moral choice, that is, in the causal element in human affairs or in the study of 'men in their causative character' (to borrow a phrase from Coleridge). His intention with respect to the argument or plot of his tragedy is no less traditional than his intention with respect to the emotional effect of that argument. Although it remains to consider the 'rhetoric' with which he clothes that intention and thereby to measure more precisely the success of his achievement, it should be obvious that the advance in English poetry created by the Petrarchan experiment in the sixteenth-century lyric is admirably suited to rendering, in its full complexity, the drama of moral choice, essentially a drama of the human mind.

IV

The purpose of *Mustapha* is not only to appeal to the memory and the judgment, as the *Life of Sidney* explicitly claims a play should do, but at the same time to stir, in an appropriate way, the affections and the imagination. Using the techniques of the eloquent style to portray the intensity and complexity of human desires, Greville assimilates these techniques to a plain style defining the moral imperatives and interdictions within which and against which individual desires acquire meaning. Aristotelian in aiming at the emotional effects of pity and wonder, *Mustapha* achieves the simple grandeur of essential drama.

Greville finds the eloquent style especially useful for portraying characters such as Rossa, Camena and Achmat whose desires are intense and often turbulent. The aspirations of Rossa, in particular, are central to the play.

> O wearysome Obedience, Wax to Power!
> Shall I in vaine be *Mustapha's* accuser?
> Shall any Iustice equall him and me?
> Is Loue so open-ear'd, my power so weake,
> As ought against me to my Lord dare speake?
> Sands shall be numbred first and Motion fixt,
> The Sea exchange her channell with the fire,
> Before my will, or reason stand in awe
> Of God, or Nature, common Peoples law. (III, i, 1–9)

In apostrophizing obedience, Rossa effectively addresses herself, though not at all in the spirit of meditation; Rosten, her son-in-law, is present in any case, and he shares some of her ambitions even though, by contrast, he appears moderate. Rather, her apostrophe is incantatory, expressive at once of her ambition and of her impatience with the existing order of things, an impatience heightened in the succeeding rhetorical questions. The questions here are an efficient means of indicating the pitch and bent of her feelings, as well as of judging those feelings, because the questions that are, from her point of view, rhetorical, are, from the point of view of the play, very much under scrutiny, and the answers given by the play are decidedly at odds with the limited answers she expects.

In both the rhetorical question and the apostrophe, Greville has discovered a means of presenting and at the same time judging bombast. In addition, the antithesis of power and obedience in the opening line lays out one of the fundamental issues of the play, the problem of order. In so far as, in the whole line, Rossa is addressing qualities within herself, the line expresses an impossibility: obedience can hardly wax to power and remain itself, and if no faculties within the individual remain obedient, power is powerless. In so far as the line refers to an external political or domestic order, it discloses Rossa's aspirations, centred as they must be on the emperor, her husband, Soliman, who in this play is power absolute. It is not surprising, then, that from this general but intense opening line the speech moves towards the subject of love and hyperbolic protestations. What is surprising, though not inconsistent, is the audacity of the speech. 'Open-ear'd' love verges on contempt of the very lord over whom she seeks power because it hints at sensual subjection. The hyperboles of lines 6 and 7, which might have been used by a Petrarchan lover to serve as an expression of constancy, are here employed to express inconstancy, much in the same way that Donne uses a similar list of adynata in 'Go and catch a falling star'. Rossa's one fixed resolution is not to stand in awe of fixed resolutions, whether they be those of God or nature. Of course, the inconsistency of her position is obvious since she appeals to received beliefs about the laws of nature in order to assert her superiority to those people who hold to such beliefs. Her avowal is impossible because it attempts to base itself on common notions that sands are innumerable and motion is not fixed, etc., in order to repudiate common notions. In addition, 'Sands', 'Motion', 'Sea', and 'fire' come close to representing the four elements, that is, the order of nature, and by implication, the order of God.

Her repudiation of 'awe' has a direct bearing on the emotional effect of wonder at which the tragedy aims because the repudiation itself evokes the emotion of wonder in the reader or spectator. Wonder is not only the proper emotion in the face of the mystery of God's order; it is also the incitement to inquiry. To wonder is to desire to know, and the emotion is, therefore, the motive to understanding. By dispelling that motive, Rossa makes it impossible that she should ever reach understanding. And from considering love as essentially a means of manipulation, it is no great step for Rossa to countenance, apparently as a rational procedure, the manipulation and eventual murder of Camena, her daughter, as well as the manipulation of Soliman and the murder of her stepson, Mustapha. In this play Greville achieves a good example of what Aristotle calls a 'likely impossibility': 'impossibility' because it seems impossible that a mother should so violate the bonds of natural affection with such an apparent show of reason; 'likely' because once the reason is severed from its moorings, the agent of severance forgoes the possibility of a proper adjustment between emotion and understanding. Furthermore, Rossa's own statement of her intentions, as we have seen, is fraught with impossibility. Here is Aristotle's defence of the method:[19]

> As to the criticisms relating to the poet's art itself. Any impossibilities there may be in his descriptions of things are faults. But from another point of view they are justifiable, if they serve the end of poetry itself – if (to assume what we have said of that end) they make the effect of either that very portion of the work or some other portion more astounding.

For Aristotle, the emotion of wonder has some sort of absolute value (the true end of art) and is not merely permissible, but necessary.[20] The speech by Rossa at the beginning of Act III, a central speech for the analysis of her character, serves just such a purpose, for the character willing to renounce 'awe' is herself appalling, and the renunciation here leads her to commit terrifying deeds in 'some other portion' of the play.

It may seem that Rossa, in her use of 'high astounding terms' and in her declaration of the superiority of her own will, is a good bit like Tamburlaine and that Greville's procedure is indeed Marlovian or, if you like, Senecan. And it must be granted that in several of Rossa's speeches Greville does employ something akin to the Senecan mode; but, even in using techniques such as apostrophe, hyperbole, and rhetorical question, he introduces important differences. For one thing, Rossa's case is presented with a good deal more psychological subtlety than Tamburlaine's, especially in the matter of relating her political aspirations to her sense of love and family connections. Greville and Sidney, in their lyric poetry, show a persistent interest in working out the relationship between love and the Aristotelian faculties. The Petrarchan lover is represented not infrequently in bondage to the power of love, unable to exercise his reason properly (see, for example, *Astrophil and Stella*, XIV and *Caelica*, XIV), and, as a result, in a state of confusion. While Rossa's is not a strictly parallel case, Greville none the less puts his experience to use in exploring the relationship of a certain kind of love (or lust) to political ambitions. That is, while the sonnet sequences offer an analysis of a man in the grip of desire and thereby rendered powerless, the speech portrays a woman employing desire in order to gain power (one kind of desire in the service of another kind). The result is an analysis of character closer to what Shakespeare achieves in Lady Macbeth than Marlowe in Tamburlaine. Second, Greville's moral subtlety is alien to Marlowe. Greville uses a device such as apostrophe not to portray the liberating sense of high spirits and ebullient feelings devoid of moral purpose beyond the celebration of themselves, but to register a precise, even delicate, analysis of the depths of human longings and of the forces that thwart or pervert human feeling.

Compare, for a moment, the apostrophe to the epistle. The latter was often regarded in terms of the three styles of classical rhetoric as the province of the low style (though by the end of the sixteenth century in England, elements of epistolary style had thoroughly invaded all levels of discourse).[21] The epistle addresses another man or woman in reasonable language; an apostrophe often addresses an inanimate object or an abstract quality or feeling. The resulting narrowed focus can lead to heightening or intensification of feeling, but it can also lead to deprivation, if the thing so addressed is regarded as invading the whole being of the speaker. The epistle encourages the speaker to recognize the otherness of the person addressed and to take full cognizance of the whole being of that other; the apostrophe encourages the speaker to abandon himself to his own feelings as they are projected on to an object or abstraction, valued not for itself, but as a vehicle of the speaker's feeling. This is not to condemn, out of hand, the rhetorical device, but to argue that its value for recording elusive or evanescent or even weighty feelings can be appropriated by a certain kind of poet for the purpose of moral evaluation.

Greville uses the apostrophe in this way to evaluate Rossa's speeches when, most like Lady Macbeth, she commits herself to the murder of her child.

> Nay, blacke *Auernus*! so I doe adore thee,
> As I lament my Wombe hath beene so barren,
> To yeeld but one to offer vp before thee.
> Who thinks the Daughters death can Mothers stay
> From ends, whereon a Womans heart is fixt,
> Weighs harmelesse Nature, without passion mixt.
> (III, ii, 39–44)

The first three lines of this passage achieve a remarkable fury of intensity similar to Lady Macbeth's invocation, 'Come, you spirits . . . unsex me here.' Both characters use the apostrophe to suggest that their female sexuality is somehow an extraneous and expendable part of their essential being. Rossa's address to Avernus sets up a horrifying resonance with her reference to her 'barren womb' because together they suggest that the lake Avernus, the mouth of hell, is like, or is in fact, her womb: Rossa is once more using the apostrophe to address a quality within herself. Certainly, the implicit hyperbole of her lament that she has only one to offer up indicates that she is obsessed with her own feelings, to the exclusion of her relationship with others. She commits herself to the murder of one daughter by committing herself to murder in general. And that her general commitment is no more than an abstraction of her own murderous desires is made clear by an apostrophe that appears a few lines earlier, before she learns that Camena stands in her way:

> You vgly Angells of th' infernall Kingdomes!
> You who must brauely haue maintain'd your beings
> In equall power, like Riualls, to the heauens!
> Let me raigne, while I liue, in my desires;
> Or dead, liue with you in eternall fires.
> (III, ii, 10–14)

By showing that Rossa's apostrophe, 'You vgly Angells', and her prayer 'Let me raigne', are no more than a dedication to her own desires, Greville has discovered a method of portraying an intensity of feeling and at the same time judging it to be a state of deprivation: to make desire an end in itself is to deprive it of any object.

The Petrarchan convention, of course, is consistently open to such errors, and the Petrarchan lover persistently vulnerable to the charge that he is more interested in his own feelings than in the lady who is supposedly being complimented. But in its undoubted successes, such as Sidney's 'With how sad steps, O moon', the address allows the poet to present an exquisitely refined, aristocratic feeling, while holding that feeling at a distance. The address creates a slightly unreal, Petrarchan other-world, with the result that, while the poem might seem to be epideictic, celebrating the feeling of melancholy, or judicial, accusing the lady of a lack of feeling, it is, in fact, deliberative, exhorting her to help create a real world where 'ungratefulness' will not be called 'virtue'.

By contrast, Rossa's apostrophes are not arguments of any kind, but incantations to a fixed and reductive purpose. To return to the first quotation, the antithesis of the verbs 'adore' and 'lament' is reminiscent of the Petrarchan situation in which the lover so adores his lady that his only lament is in not having more of himself to sacrifice to her (see, for example, *Astrophil and Stella*, XVIII, 'With what sharpe checkes I in my selfe am shent – '[22]). The Petrarchan convention flirts, rather playfully, with the notion of privation in order to explore the powers and potentialities of love (one might also call to mind, in this connection, Greville's *Caelica*, X, '*Loue*, of mans wandring thoughts the restlesse being'[23]). In *Mustapha*, Greville uses this convention, but reverses it, so that Rossa's only lament is in not having more children to sacrifice to her own fixed purpose. It is this reversal that signals the play's larger purpose, to offer a perspective into the unprosperity of vice. *Mustapha* is not 'naked and casual': it here employs Petrarchan rhetoric in order to investigate the way in which one character relinquishes the possibility of causal action. Moreover, in the last three lines of the same quotation, Rossa shifts from an apostrophe to Avernus to a direct address to the Beglerby, and Greville capitalizes on the dramatic situation to make several points simultaneously. Rossa's assertion that 'the Daughters death' cannot stay 'Mothers' (note that again her contemplation of the relationship between mother and daughter is improperly generalized) from a fixed purpose is meant, from her point of view, as an expression of the resolution and power of her will, including a derisory tone towards the Beglerby for doubting it, while the explicit mention of the relationship between daughter and mother, nature and passion, calls up emphatically the human connections and emotions that Rossa, in the intensity of her own feeling, is excluding and forfeiting.

By contrast with Rossa, Camena understands that making desire an end in itself is self-defeating and finally self-destructive.

> They that from youth doe sucke at Fortunes brest,
> And nurse their empty hearts with seeking higher,
> Like Dropsie-fedde, their thirst doth neuer rest;
> For still, by getting, they beget desire:
> Till thoughts, like Wood, while they maintaine the Flame
> Of high desires, grow Ashes in the same. (II, iii, 1-6)

In the figurative development of 'like Dropsie-fedde, their thirst doth neuer rest' and in the word-play on 'getting' and 'beget', Greville draws on the paradoxes of Petrarchan love poetry to make clear what desire of a mutable fortune is. The antecedent of the analysis in Greville's lines can be seen, for example, in the second stanza of Sidney's 'In vaine, mine Eyes, you labour to amende' from the *Old Arcadia*:[24]

> In vaine, my Hart, now you with sight are burnd,
> With sighes you seeke to coole your hotte desire:
> Since sighes (into mine inward fornace turnd)
> For bellowes serve to kindle more the fire.

Shakespeare, of course, transformed this insight into a strikingly compressed and unforgettable phrase at the opening of *Antony and Cleopatra*: 'His captain's heart/ . . . is become the bellows and the fan/ To cool a gypsy's lust' (I, i, 6–9).[25] In Greville's terms, 'getting' or having one's desire will only serve to 'beget' or generate further desires. In Camena's figure, 'like Dropsie-fedde', there is not even the possibility of momentary satisfaction, whereas in *Antony and Cleopatra,* despite the fact that the soldier obviously finds Antony's effeminate behaviour reprehensible, there is a lingering attraction about being the bellows and the fan to Cleopatra's lust. Greville is much closer to Shakespeare, however, in his use of the figure appearing in the lines: 'Till thoughts, like Wood, while they maintain the Flame/ Of high desires, grow Ashes in the same'. Shakespeare employs the same figure in the third stanza of sonnet 73, 'That time of year thou mayst in me behold'. Both are evocative and emphatic descriptions of mutability.

By means of the eloquent style, Greville portrays Camena as a character who feels caught amidst the complicated problems of fortune and a complicated allegiance to 'sweet Vertue'. Even in dedicating herself to virtue Camena confronts a 'labyrinth' of conflicting loyalties, and she sums up her dilemma in the antithesis: 'Such are the *golden* hopes of *Iron* days' (II, iii, 34). The golden style is here brought impressively to bear on the brazen world, even while the character employing it expresses a yearning for a better world. Camena's virtue is not simple, and it has nothing to do with mere pietism. It is significant that among her admonitions to the important actors in the play is a warning to Mustapha not to presume on his innocence (II, iii, 58). Nor is it out of keeping that her character should be represented as static and without any real outlet in action, for in her we see essentially the drama of the mind. In this respect, she bears an important resemblance to the title character, Mustapha, a point to which we must return later. For the moment, suffice it to say that the golden style, preoccupied as it is with the presentation of feeling, as opposed to the presentation of action, is the right style for capturing a sense of stasis. In iron days, golden hopes have nowhere to go and will seem, at least by contrast with brazen hopes, to be without motion.

Like Camena, caught between the claims of loyalty, on the one hand to her half-brother and on the other to her mother and father, Achmat is also divided in his allegiance to Mustapha and to Soliman. Using imagery very close to the imagery Sidney employs in 'Yee Gote-heard Gods' from the

Old Arcadia, Greville introduces Achmat, in his perplexity, at the beginning of Act II.

> Who, standing in the shade of humble vallies,
> Lookes vp, and wonders at the state of hils;
> When he with toyle of weary limbes ascends,
> And feels his spirits melt with *Phoebus* glories,
> Or sinewes starke with *AEolus* bitter breathing,
> Or thunder-blasts, which comming from the skie,
> Doe fall most heauy on the places high:
> Then knowes (though farther seene, and farther seeing
> From hills aboue, than from the humble vallies)
> *They multiply in woes, that adde in glories.*
> Who weary is of Natures quiet Plaines,
> A meane estate, with poore, and chast desires;
> Whose Vertue longs for knees, Blisse for opinion;
> Who iudgeth pleasures Paradise in purple;
> Let him see me. (II, i, 1–15)

William Empson comments usefully on the effect of the imagery in 'Yee Gote-heard Gods': 'a whole succession of feelings about the local scenery, the whole way in which it is taken for granted, has been enlisted into sorrow and beats as a single passion of the mind.'[26] Achmat, too, enlists a succession of commonplace feelings and assumptions about the landscape and the elements in order to lay out the complex perspective that underlies his perception of the present condition of the state and his position in it. The elaborate pattern of antitheses in: 'humble vallies–hills aboue', 'spirits–sinewes', '*Phoebus–AEolus*', 'farther seene–farther seeing', 'wonders–knowes', '*woes–glories*' serves not merely to contrast the perspective of the lowly and the great, nor is it a sentimental celebration of the simple life in preference to political power. Achmat is well aware of the dignity of his position ('farther seene and farther seeing') even while he expresses his sense of the burden that comes with its responsibilities. As well, the speech keeps the emotional effects of woe and wonder at the centre of the tragedy. Men of high estate will be wondered at in their glory, but as the wonder translates into knowledge it will be largely a knowledge of woe.

Achmat's speech continues with a general analysis of his own case and a narrative summary of conditions in the state, before he is led to a more poignant expression of his own particular paradoxical dilemma.

> Who vtters this, is to his Prince a Traytor:
> Who keepes this, Guilty is; his life is ruth,
> And dying liues, euer denying truth.
> Thus hath the *Fancy-law* of Power ordain'd,
> That who betrayes it most, is most esteem'd:
> Who saith it is betray'd, is Traytor deem'd. (II, i, 52-7)

But the most interesting part of the speech comes as he tries to think his way out of the paradox:

> I sworne am to my King, and to his Honor:
> His Humors? No: which they, that follow most,
> Wade in a Sea, wherein themselues are lost.
> Yet *Achmat* stay! For who doth wrest Kings mindes,
> Wrestles his faith vpon the stage of Chance;
> Where vertue, to the world by fortune knowne,
> Is oft misiudg'd, because shee's ouerthrowne.
> Nay *Achmat* stay not! For who truth enuirons
> With circumstances of Mans fayling wit,
> By feare, by hope, by loue, by malice erreth;
> Nature to natures banckrupts he engageth:
> *And while none dare shew Kings they goe amisse,*
> *Euen base Obedience their Corruption is.* (II, i, 58-70)

Greville here depicts, with subtlety and nice psychological realism, the movement of Achmat's mind. The technique of the first two lines is close to that employed in Sidney's 'Oft have I musde' from *Certain Sonnets*: 'Oft have I musde, but now at length I finde/ Why those that die, men say they do depart;/ Depart, a word so gentle to my minde. . . .'[27] The act of musing, of course, is already very like the dramatic soliloquy, but Sidney's important contribution to the technique of rendering a mind in soliloquy lies in the repetition of words, such as the repetition of the word 'depart' at the end of line 2 and the beginning of line 3, and in the play on meanings and associations, such as the play on the word 'part' in the rest of the sonnet. Neil Rudenstein, commenting on this sonnet, remarks on its similarity to Hamlet's: 'To die, to sleep;/ To sleep: perchance to dream.'[28] In Greville's lines, 'Honor' and 'Humors' are not the same word, but the similarity of sound, the repetition of 'his', and the close connection of honour and humour in the character of Soliman combine to capture the process of Achmat's mental effort. The sense of effort is intensified by the pause at the end of the verse line between the two phrases. And it is this dramatic pause that, among other things, helps to give more weight to the distinction in 'Honor–Humor' than to the play on 'wrest-wrestle', which follows in the next few lines. In both cases, however, the word-play is used to portray a mind confronting a dilemma, though the dilemma is not at the conclusion, but at the beginning of Achmat's reasoning.

And the psychological subtlety in the word-play sets up the more obvious dramatic shifts represented by the lines beginning: 'Yet *Achmat* stay!' and 'Nay *Achmat* stay not!' Even in this dramatic reversal, Greville's technical skill – this time in the question of metre – emphasizes the overriding importance of reasoned distinctions for truly dramatic action. Consider the metre of line 65.

Nāy Ach/māt stáy / nōt! Fór/whō trúth/eñuirōns

That it is a normal iambic pentameter line is surprising only because of the rhythmical variety contained within that norm. The most striking feature is the iambic foot in the third position. The caesura in the middle of the third foot is emphatic, but not unusual, because flexibility in the placing of the caesura is already much in evidence throughout the speech and contributes markedly to the subtlety of psychological presentation. What is unusual is that despite the emphasis of Achmat's denial, summed up in the word 'not', and despite the strength of the exclamation mark pointing the caesura, the foot remains iambic. Considered as an integral unit, the foot forces the accent on the word 'For' and the word 'not' is relatively unstressed; this is so, despite the fact that 'not' has a stronger stress than the accented syllable of the preceding foot. The result is a series of four syllables, in the second and third feet, arranged in an ascending order of intensity. The point is not that Achmat's repudiation of his

33

earlier qualm is unimportant, nor that it is said without feeling, but that the emphasis rests ultimately in the reason given for the repudiation – hence the stress on the conjunction 'For' that introduces the reason. Greville's metrical subtlety makes it possible to combine the excitement of exclamation with the clarity of direct statement. The line cannot be declaimed; it must be said deliberately; yet the deliberation is intensely dramatic. It comes as the culmination of a movement that is clearly dramatic, and it has important dramatic consequences worked out in the rest of the play.

For similar reasons, the first foot is also iambic. Despite the emphasis of the first word 'Nay,' the ultimate focus of the line is on Achmat's realization of his own individual identity and the premises on which that rests, so that the stress in the first foot falls on the first syllable of his name. The normal iambic movement has to be given precedence over the rhetorical pressures of the line. In this way, rhetorical (and dramatic) pressures are felt as the embodiment of thought. Achmat's realization of individual identity entails a corresponding de-emphasis on personal safety (the ethics of character take precedence over the ethics of sensibility),[29] and it is, therefore, fitting that the word 'who' is relatively unstressed by comparison with the word 'truth' in this particular line. In line 61, by contrast, where Achmat *is* preoccupied with his own personal safety, the word 'who' receives the stress. The truth is that, as a counsellor, Achmat must *'dare shew Kings they goe amisse'* or he loses his identity as a counsellor. His identity depends upon an allegiance to truth. If the play demonstrates, in Rossa's speech, that obedience is corrupt when it aspires to become power, it also argues, in Achmat's speech, that obedience is corrupt when it descends to inertness. Even obedience must be a form of action. The complexity of that obedience, or that action, as it is presented in *Mustapha*, is largely a product of Greville's mastery of technical refinements in English verse.

Despite the refinements, however, Greville relies fundamentally on the plain style. In the middle of the play, at the end of the third act, after Rossa has resolved to murder Camena in order to clinch her conspiracy against Mustapha, and just before Soliman resolves to eliminate Mustapha in order, he hopes, to rid himself of fear, Greville places the 'Chorus Tertius of Time: Eternity'. Time speaks first, describing herself and her effects in thirteen stanzas during the course of which she asserts '*I am the measure of* Felicitie' (l. 36). Eternity then speaks, but since eternity is indescribable, it is not possible for Greville to develop the speech by means of the same techniques or techniques parallel to those used in Time's speech. His solution to this problem illustrates the extraordinary dramatic potential of a juxtaposition of the golden style and the moral style.

Of the twelve stanzas in Eternity's speech, the first six continue the description of Time, begun in the preceding speech, with this difference – the description is here made the basis of an analysis, becoming most pointed in stanza four, after Eternity declares that Time is but 'a Minute of my Infinite':

> A Minute which doth her subsistence tye;
> Subsistencies which, in not being, be:
> *Shall* is to come, and *Was* is passed by;
> *Time present* cements this Duplicitie:
> And if one must, of force, be like the other,
> *Of Nothing is not Nothing made the mother?*
> (III, Chorus, 97–102)

The description of Time is here used to support a definition of Time. And since Time has no fixed being, the definition is offered largely in terms of privation: Time is an insignificant particle of infinity. From the metaphysical analysis of what Time is, it is but a small step to the moral analysis of Time's pretensions. Since neither Time nor 'her mortal off-springs' can take or yield 'constant forme':

> But still change shapes to multiply deceipt:
> Like playing *Atomi*, in vaine contending
> Though they beginning had, to haue no ending
> (III, Chorus, 112–14)

Eternity is clearly in a position to dismantle Time's claim to be the '*measure of* Felicitie.'

35

None of these six stanzas is wholly plain in style, but the figurative development is kept to a minimum, and what figures there are are used almost entirely for the elucidation of the abstract analysis. Of the remaining six stanzas, the last five constitute a series of imperatives directed to Time and written in an essentially plain style. In one stanza, stanza seven, however, Greville does attempt a direct presentation of Eternity, and in order to do so, he draws on the resources of the golden style.

> I, that at once see *Times* distinct progression;
> I, in whose bosome *Was*, and *Shall*, still be;
> I, that in the Causes work th'Effects' Succession,
> Giuing both Good, and Ill their destinie;
> Though I bind all, yet can receiue no bound,
> But see the finite still it selfe confound.
>   (III, Chorus, 115–20)

The pattern of this stanza is the same pattern that Greville employs in the love poem, *Caelica*, XXII, 'I with whose colours *Myra* drest her head',[30] though in the first stanza of the poem, the pronoun 'I' is repeated five times, whereas here only four. The difference is significant in that the principal clause here is '[I] can receiue no bound'. That is, the only thing that can be said directly about Eternity is a negative description, and it is, therefore, not accidental that the actual subject of the principal clause is only implied, not stated. The pattern, in other words, offers the poet a means of implying what is, in fact, indescribable. As Sir Walter Ralegh, in 'The Passionate Man's Pilgrimage' (ll. 11–39),[31] uses the golden style to describe heaven (that is, not an ordinary world of plain men and plain language), so Greville here uses Petrarchan patterning to define the indescribable.

The mellifluous flow of stanza seven, caused largely by the pattern of repetition and by the comparatively smooth metre, creates a sense of other-world serenity and sets up a dramatic contrast with the plain blunt language of the following stanzas.

> *Time*! therefore know thy limits, and striue not
> To make thy self, or thy works *Infinite*,
> *Whose Essence only is to write, and blot*:

Thy Changes proue thou hast no stablish't right.
  Gouerne thy mortall Sphere, deale not with mine:
  Time *but the seruant is of Power Diuine.*

Blame thou this present State, that will blame thee;
Brick-wall your errors from one, to another;
Both faile alike vnto *Eternitie,*
Goodnesse of no mixt course can be the mother.
  Both you, and yours doe couet states Eternall;
  Whence, though pride end, your pains yet be
    Infernall.

Ruine this Masse; worke Change in all Estates,
Which, when they serue not me, are in your power:
Giue vnto their corruption doomes of Fate;
Let your vast wombe your *Cadmus*-men deuoure.
  The Vice yeelds scope enough for you, and hell,
  To compasse ill ends by not doing well.

Let *Mustapha* by your course be destroy'd,
Let your wheeles, made to winde vp, and vntwine,
Leaue nothing constantly to be enioy'd:
For your Scithe mortall must to harme incline,
  Which, as this World, your maker, doth grow old,
  Doomes her, for your toyes, to be bought, and sold.

Crosse your owne steps; hasten to make, and marre;
With your Vicissitudes please, displease your owne:
Your three light wheeles of sundry fashions are,
And each, by others motion, ouerthrowne.
  Doe what you can: Mine shall subsist by Me:
  I am the measure of *Felicitie.* (III, Chorus, 121–50)

Greville's plain style is nearly always more complex and sophisticated than the early native plain style employed by such writers as Googe, Gascoigne, or Tichbourne; but in these stanzas he comes closest to that style described by J. V. Cunningham as 'this particular and quite limited tradition . . . : a heavy-handed seriousness, a scorn of urbanity, a deliberate rejection of that delicacy which would discriminate shades of white and of black. It is a morally ruthless, secure, and overpowering style' (*CE*, p. 315). In terms of rhythm, the style is blunt and emphatic, characterized by heavily end-stopped lines, by the regular placement of the caesura after the fourth or sixth syllable in the decasyllabic line, and by a strong differentiation between accented and unaccented syllables. The last five stanzas of Eternity's speech obviously derive a good deal of their energy from the resources of this style. The heavy-handed imperatives to Time are delivered in a series of short emphatic sentences. By contrast to stanza seven, which has only one full stop at the end of the stanza, the succeeding stanzas often have strong pauses, coming at the end of the line and sometimes after the fourth or sixth syllable. And finally, the marked difference between stressed and unstressed syllables offers an emphatic metre in itself and sets up the possibility of the most emphatic metrical variations, the spondee. As Yvor Winters argues, it is only in verse 'in which the rhythm is strongly and obviously marked by a great and regular distinction between accented and unaccented syllables that the true spondee can occur; in a smoother and subtler type of structure, . . . two syllables of nearly the same degree of accent will be absorbed into the iambic pattern and will not stand out as approximately equal to each other'. 'The introduction of this variation into the newly acquired iambic pentameter line' is, Winters argues, Barnabe Googe's 'principal contribution to the technique of English verse'.[32] Greville clearly understands the technique and is capable of putting it impressively to use. There are a number of instances, in the five stanzas under consideration, that could be read successfully as spondees, but it is stanza nine that provides three undeniable examples in the first foot of each of lines 127, 128, and 129: 'Blame thou', 'Brick-wall', and 'both faile'. The spondaic reading is also encouraged by the presence of alliteration and by the fact that each line repeats the same idea under a different aspect. Each opens up the meaning of the last line of stanza seven: '[I] see the finite still it selfe confound.' The spondee is especially useful for highlighting the coinage 'Brick-wall', a strikingly compressed statement of the proverbial notions that time's errors will rebound and that dependence on error leads to a dead-end.

It is his mastery of such verse techniques that enables Greville to unleash the full power of the native plain style, a style whose central feeling may properly be characterized as moral indignation. The castigation of Time is saved from being merely flat didacticism because it follows upon the analytical definition and description of Time and because, especially in the last three stanzas, it is accompanied by a certain amount of descriptive figurative development in phrases such as, 'your *Cadmus*-men', 'your wheeles', 'your Scithe', 'your toyes', and 'your three light [i.e. insubstantial] wheeles' (past, present, future). More important is the juxta-position of the mellifluous style of stanza seven and the abrupt style of stanzas eight to twelve by means of which Greville achieves a clear definition of two opposed ranges of feeling. The repose or tranquillity with which Eternity states her own case stands in marked contrast to the energy with which she presents the turbulence of Time's case. And this tension in the chorus is a good general illustration of the attitude towards which the tragic hero traditionally aspires: that is, *in* this world, but not *of* it. If *catharsis* is to be re-tained as a workable artistic concept, it must surely refer to this sort of tranquillity, achieved not by ignoring the turbu-lence of time, but by perceiving the repose of eternity in the midst of the turbulence. Greville's chorus, then, is intensely dramatic, both on its own terms and in the sense that it is a general choric illustration of the more particular drama represented in the action of *Mustapha*.

For portraying Soliman and Mustapha, the two most important characters in that action, and for delineating the crisis in the plot, Greville employs a fusion of the two styles. Soliman is represented, at the beginning of Act IV, moving towards the decision to execute his son – this, despite con-fronting a vision that presents him with a clear and rational reflection of the nature of his course of action.

> Visions are these, or bodies which appeared?
> Rays'd from within, or from aboue descending?
> Did vowes lift vp my soule, or bring downe these?
> *God's not pleas'd with vs, till our hearts finde ease.*
> What horror's this? *Safetie, Right, and a Crowne,*
> *Thrones must neglect that will adore Gods light.*
> *His will, our good:* Suppose it plucke vs downe;

> Reuenge is his. *Against the ill what right?*
> What meanes that Glasse borne on those glorious wings,
> Whose piercing shaddowes on my selfe reflect
> Staines, which my vowes against my children bring?
> My wrongs, and doubts, seeme there despayres of Vice;
> My Power a Turret, built against my Maker;
> My danger, but disorders preiudice.
> This Glasse, true Mirror of the *Infinite*,
> Shewes all; yet can I nothing comprehend.
> This Empire, nay the World, seemes shaddowes there;
> Which mysteries dissolue me into feare. (IV, i, 5–22)

The imagery here seems meant to perform a logical function, and not merely to clarify and explain, but to move to virtuous action. But, quite obviously, from Soliman's point of view, it fails. Like Macbeth apostrophizing the dagger, he experiences a doubt about whether he is hallucinating or not, but unlike Macbeth, he is not incited by the vision, in any way, to commit the crime. He is presented neither with an instrument for performing the crime, nor with a rationale for continuing to contemplate it. Although the images of the inscription, the mirror, the glorious wings, piercing shadows, stains, and turret are potentially strong invitations to the reader to project sensory constructions,[33] the sensory content of the imagery is held to a bare minimum and is made the occasion of moral reflection.

The notion of a logical function of imagery, despite the effort of Rosemond Tuve in *Elizabethan and Metaphysical Imagery*,[34] remains an obscure concept. It is not clear that imagery is capable of performing a logical function by itself, and it seems better to say, as Winters suggests,[35] that the forms of reason are the forms of syntax. Sir Philip Sidney, talking about similitudes, makes a kindred point:

> the force of a similitude not being to prove anything to a contrary disputer, but only to explain to a willing hearer, when that is done, the rest is a most tedious prattling, rather over-swaying the memory from the purpose whereto they were applied, than any whit informing the judgement, already either satisfied, or by similitudes not to be satisfied. (p. 71)

Clearly, Soliman's judgment, at least, is not any whit informed by the similitudes and imagery applied to it; but before we take Greville to have set out to prove Sidney's point, there are other causes, not far to seek, to consider. The hint may be picked up from the last word quoted from Soliman's speech: 'feare'. It is not for nothing that Rossa, consistent with her repudiation of awe in Act III, has been busy throughout Act I, especially, provoking Soliman's fears and perverting normal expressions of wonder, admiration, or puzzlement into the less reputable emotions of neurotic apprehension and contemptuous disbelief (see I, ii, 109, 119, and 239). J. V. Cunningham, summarizing the Aquinian interpretation of the six traditional species of fear, mentions especially the three whose source is external, wonder (*admiratio*), amazement (*stupor*), and shocked surprise (*agonia*):

> a man who wonders does fear at the moment to give a judgment, fearing that he will fail, but . . . he looks into the matter in the future; the amazed man, however, fears both now and in the future; hence wonder is the beginning of philosophizing, but amazement an impediment to it. (*CE*, p. 74)

Soliman's fear is just this kind of amazement, and it is the antithesis of religious awe. His speech continues:

> I that without feele no Superior power,
> And feele within but what I will conceiue,
> Distract; know neither what to take, nor leaue.
> (IV, i, 23–5)

And concludes:

> If God worke thus, *Kings must looke upwards still,*
> *And from these Powers they know not, choose a will.*
> Or else beleeue themselues, their strength, occasion;
> Make wisdome conscience; and the world their skie:
> So haue all Tyrants done; and so must I. (IV, i, 39–43)

His fear, really not much more than fear for his own personal safety, induces a kind of paralysis or deadlock. He is an enclosed ego, lacking connections with God and with other human beings, with the result that the argument against

Mustapha's execution finds him curiously inaccessible even though, in a sense, he presents the argument himself. By portraying that argument almost strictly in terms of imagery, Greville manages to suggest that it is somehow outside of his person. In the first part of the soliloquy (ll. 7–12), the inter-locking rhyme and the exchange of question and answer maintain the ambiguous sense that Soliman is conducting a debate within himself, but the glass, the true mirror that he finds incomprehensible, is obviously wholly external to him. The mind thus represented no doubt exhibits a kind of mad-ness, but it is difficult to conceive how the wilful persistence in murder, voluntarily denying the directives of reason, can ever be represented as anything but madness. Soliman is one of those unable to choose a will *'from these Powers they know not'*; that is, he is unable to exist in a state of not-knowing, a state of wonder. The murder of Mustapha, there-fore, is not the issue of action, but the issue of distraction; not the issue of thought, but of stupor.

By contrast, Mustapha is presented as capable of the most vigorous thought and unflinching honesty, as Greville em-ploys a fusion of the two styles to portray the assimilation of range and urbanity to moral probity. Though the title charac-ter of the play and the centre of attention for almost every other character in the drama, Mustapha does not appear until late in Act IV and even then his appearance is relatively brief. Like Camena, he is in an essentially static position. But his repose results less from the tension of paradox than from the resolve of a profound understanding. In a world of misguided or unguided commotion, the ability of the tragic hero 'to live in a continual equipoise of doubt'[36] may be regarded as in-action, whereas it is, in fact, the most fully human action possible. The breadth of Mustapha's understanding is sugges-ted in his first two speeches, as Greville introduces him offer-ing spiritual counsel to the priest, Heli:

> Whence growes this sudden Rage thy gesture vtters?
> These Agonies, and furious Blasphemings?
> *Man then doth shew his Reason is defaced,*
> When Rage thus shewes it selfe with Reason graced.
>
> (IV, iv, 56–9)

The antithesis of rage and reason expounds the proper relationship between reason and will (since rage is an extremity
of wilfulness) and indicates the emotional force that works to
subvert that relationship. The couplet, then, contains implicitly the answer to the opening two questions. And since
the questions are answered so immediately, so emphatically,
and with such generalizing power, they have the feel, that is,
the emotional intensity, of rhetorical questions. Yet Heli
obviously needs to learn the lesson, and the questions are
simultaneously real questions. The inherently metaphorical
content of the word 'defaced', normally inert, is here invoked,
quietly but effectively responding to the metaphorical hint in
'thy gesture vtters', as Heli's powers of articulation are called
into question. And the words 'graced' and 'Blasphemings'
summon the larger spiritual issues involved in maintaining a
proper demeanour.

Mustapha's second speech is also both moral and eloquent.

> Horror, and Pride, in Nature opposite;
> The one makes Error great, the other small:
> Where rooted habits haue no sense at all.
> *Heli*! iudge not thy selfe with troubled minde,
> But shew thy heart: *when Passions steames breath forth,*
> *Euen woes we wondred at are nothing worth.*
>
> (IV, iv, 65–70)

Horror, it should be noted, is related to wonder; it is closely
aligned to what St Thomas calls amazement or *stupor*: an
impediment to philosophizing. In the opposition of horror
and pride, Greville investigates the forces that work against
the common pursuit of true judgment. A few lines later, in a
line that is a triumph of simplicity and subtlety, Mustapha
says: 'What shall I doe? Tell me. I doe not feare' (l. 84). That
is, he recognizes and overcomes the paralysing sort of fear that
has defeated Soliman. Yet, to want to know what to do is to
continue to exist in a state of wonder. The simplicity of the
phrasing and the symmetrical balance of the caesuras crystal-
lize the antithesis of wonder and fear; 'Tell me' is the inspiration of wonder and the subjection of horror. In addition, it
should be obvious that Mustapha is now asking Heli's advice.
He is truly the inhabitant of a human community (cf. 'rooted

habits' l. 67 and 'shew thy heart' l. 69), and the 'we' of line
70, *'Euen woes we wondred at are nothing worth'*, is genuinely communal. Heli's predicament is Mustapha's. Thus,
despite the fact that Mustapha is presented, from the moment of his first appearance, as understanding and aiming at
that *catharsis* of woe and fear that is the end of tragedy,
Greville represents, mostly by means of a powerful series of
antitheses, the range of human experience out of which that
understanding has grown. Mustapha is neither sanctimonious
nor filled with the pride of martyrdom, though he envisions
and aspires to the serenity postulated by the chorus of Act
III, Eternity. The convincing portrayal of such an aspiration
is a triumph of the fusion of the two styles.

And the play is a triumph of its kind. It is a thoughtful
and moving investigation of the human condition. It draws
on the resources of an ancient and fully traditional theory of
tragedy, and, in fact, it clarifies that theory by offering one
of the most thoroughly worked out examples, in English, of
drama written according to principles of the theory. Furthermore, the play is exploratory. It makes flexible use of the
liveliest experiment in English verse in the sixteenth century.
In consolidating the gains of that experiment and in bringing
them to bear on a solidly traditional structure lies the origin-
ality of *Mustapha*. Here too, in all probability, lies the reason
for its neglect. Since the traditional intentions of some of
Shakespeare's tragedies have scarcely been admitted – despite
the excellence of Cunningham's book on Shakespeare, his
views do not appear to have circulated widely – it is not surprising that the traditional intentions of Greville's play have
scarcely been entertained. And although there is scholarly
agreement that there were two clearly defined and widely
understood styles available to the lyric poet in sixteenth-
century England, only a few writers, mostly under the
influence of Yvor Winters, have recognized the plain style
as central and the eloquent style as an enrichment of it.
Hence, the implications of this recognition for the study of
drama have hardly been suspected. In any case, *Mustapha*,
with its customary label, would not readily present itself as
the first item of investigation. 'Senecan closet drama' suggests
that it is both non-theatrical in form and declamatory in

style. As to the first objection, in the words of Aristotle, 'The tragic effect is quite possible without a public perform- ance and actors; and besides, the getting-up of the Spectacle is more a matter for the costumier than the poet.'[37] As to the second, Greville himself, as we have seen, was anxious to avoid the coarse and imperceptive rhythms of bombast. Where else to look for an alternative than in the verse tech- niques that he himself helped to pioneer and perfect? For the moving and serious undertaking of *Mustapha*, Greville needed the style that Sir Henry Wotton, commending his own epi- gram to the attention of Queen Elizabeth, called a 'passionate plainness'.[38]

3 · Tragedy and history in *Richard II*

Like Greville, Shakespeare needed an equipoise of styles. And like Greville, Shakespeare discovered some of the groundwork for this balance in the interplay and in the integration of the two styles from lyric poetry: the golden and the moral. In fact, in Shakespeare the tension between opposed ranges of feeling or attitude, and the need for reconciliation, both become more acute, because the range of human experience he explores is much broader, and because his appeal is at least as intellectually profound and, at the same time, a great deal more popular than is Greville's. Since the terms of sixteenth-century poetic technique do not fully comprehend Shakespeare's stylistic mastery, two additional categories are needed: the metaphysical and the Shakespearean. Both of these terms suggest important movements in the English tradition: the poetic styles of the sixteenth century are absorbed and transmuted into the greater complexity of the early seventeenth century. Nevertheless, the interaction of the golden style and the moral style remains central even in Shakespeare's most accomplished apprentice work, *The Tragedy of King Richard the Second*.

Since few will doubt the presence of the golden style, especially in Shakespeare's early work,[1] it is best to begin by considering why, for Shakespeare, as well as for Greville, the moral style remains dominant. As the full title of *Richard II* suggests, Shakespeare aspired to write tragedy.[2] Although the actual title may have been supplied by Andrew Wise, who was responsible for publishing the play in 1597, there is enough evidence in the play itself to corroborate the suggestion. Yet the relationship between historical drama and tragic drama is an obscure one, and the obscurity may be the cause of critical imperceptiveness of the importance of the moral style. Elucidation is offered by an astute commentator on the relationship, Samuel Taylor Coleridge, in some general remarks that are usually placed as a preface to his

particular discussion of *Richard II.* Coleridge's remarks
will serve to advance a traditional concept of tragedy, to
clarify the relationship of tragedy and history, and to pro-
pound the close correspondence of drama and poetry. The
following *Notes on the History Plays of Shakespeare* were
written about 1810:[3]

> The first form of poetry is the epic, the essence of
> which may be stated as the successive in events and
> characters. This must be distinguished from narration,
> in which there must always be a narrator, from whom
> the objects represented receive a coloring and a manner;
> – whereas in the epic, as in the so-called poems of
> Homer, the whole is completely objective, and the re-
> presentation is a pure reflection. The next form into
> which poetry passed was the dramatic; – both forms
> have a common basis with a certain difference, and that
> difference not consisting in the dialogue alone. Both are
> founded on the relation of providence to the human
> will; and this relation is the universal element, expressed
> under different points of view according to the difference
> of religions, and the moral and intellectual cultivation of
> different nations. In the epic poem fate is represented as
> overruling the will, and making it instrumental to the
> accomplishment of its designs:
>   – Διὸς δ᾽ ἐτελείετο βουλή.
>   [That the will of Zeus might be fulfilled]
> In the drama, the will is exhibited as struggling with
> fate, a great and beautiful instance and illustration of
> which is the Prometheus of Aeschylus; and the deepest
> effect is produced, when the fate is represented as a
> higher and intelligent will, and the opposition of the
> individual as springing from a defect.
>   In order that a drama may be properly historical, it
> is necessary that it should be the history of the people
> to whom it is addressed. In the composition, care must
> be taken that there appear no dramatic improbability,
> as the reality is taken for granted. It must, likewise, be
> poetical; – that only, I mean, must be taken which is
> the permanent in our nature, which is common, and
> therefore deeply interesting to all ages. The events

47

themselves are immaterial, otherwise than as the clothing and manifestation of the spirit that is working
within. In this mode, the unity resulting from succession is destroyed, but is supplied by a unity of a higher
order, which connects the events by reference to the
workers, gives a reason for them in the motives, and
presents men in their causative character. It takes,
therefore, that part of real history which is the least
known, and infuses a principle of life and organization
into the naked facts, and makes them all the framework
of an animated whole.

The 'relation of providence to the human will' and the will
'exhibited as struggling with fate' are both explicit references
to the traditional concept of tragic destiny. What is not so
explicit is the last part of the first paragraph. 'The opposition
of the individual . . . springing from a defect' may be equivalent to Aristotle's 'tragic flaw', but not in any crude sense.
If fate is a higher and intelligent will, then the individual is,
by definition, lower and less intelligent, and to that extent
deprived or defective. 'Tragic flaw', in other words, is not a
pathological item in the character of the protagonist, but the
inevitable disparity between whatever intelligence and will
the tragic hero can muster and the intelligence and will
demanded of him by his circumstances. That is, tragedy is
inevitably and irrefutably religious. The effort to ascertain
and act in accordance with the dictates of absolute truth is
the universal element of tragedy, whatever the differences
in moral, intellectual, or religious cultivation of different
nations.
    This emphasis on 'the permanent in our nature' has con-
sequences for the structure of drama. 'In this mode, the
unity resulting from succession is destroyed, but is supplied
by a unity of a higher order. . . .' Coleridge's claim may be
compared with what Aristotle says in chapter 8 of the
Poetics.[4]

The Unity of a Plot does not consist, as some suppose,
in its having one man as its subject. An infinity of things
befall that one man, some of which it is impossible to
reduce to unity; and in like manner there are many

actions of one man which cannot be made to form one action.

If we make a distinction between character and personality, we may say that unified action is not to be derived from the development of a personality. In tragedy, character equals tragic impersonality. 'Character', to quote Aristotle once again, this time from chapter 6,[5]

> is that which reveals the moral purpose of the agents, i.e. the sort of thing they seek or avoid, where that is not obvious – hence there is no room for Character in a speech on a purely indifferent subject. Thought, on the other hand, is shown in all they say when proving or disproving some particular point, or enunciating some universal proposition.

As Coleridge goes on to open up what he means by 'unity of a higher order', not only is his agreement with Aristotle apparent, his list is a near paraphrase of Aristotle's description of the most important elements of tragedy. That which 'connects the events by reference to the workers' is plot or what Aristotle sometimes calls character in action; giving 'a reason for them in the motives' is what Aristotle calls thought; and 'men in their causative character' explicitly names character, while asserting, in the word 'causative', the fundamental relationship between thought, character, and action. 'Presents' strongly implies what for Aristotle is diction (or style), since the presentation is obviously done in language. The fifth and sixth elements, song and spectacle, are pleasing ornaments, but, for Aristotle, less important than the first four. It is, perhaps, worth recalling a similar sentiment in Coleridge: 'Shakespeare, in place of ranting, music and outward action, addresses us in words that enchain the mind, and carry on the attention from scene to scene.'[6] Coleridge, in other words, in his remarks about historical drama, is very close to the traditional view of tragedy.[7]

But, it might be argued, if tragedy presents a unity of a higher order, history is certainly tied to the unity resulting from succession. And it may be that the claims of the two modes are ultimately irreconcilable. In another fragment from Coleridge's notebooks, however, he expounds a closer alignment of tragedy and history than is customarily thought and makes a fundamental distinction between history and historical drama.[8]

> In my happier days, while I had yet hope and onward-looking thoughts, I planned an historical drama of King Stephen, on the plan of Shakespeare's historical dramas. Indeed it would be desirable that some man of dramatic genius. to which I have no pretensions, should dramatize all those omitted by Shakespeare, as far down as Henry VII. inclusive. Henry VII. and Perkin Warbeck would make a most interesting drama. A few scenes of Marlowe's *Edward II.* might be preserved. After Henry VIII., the events are too well and distinctly known to be, without plump inverisimilitude, crowded together in one night's exhibition. Whereas, the history of our ancient kings – the events of them, I mean – are like stars in the sky: whatever the real interspaces may be, and however great, they seem close to each other. The stars, the events, strike us and remain in our eye, little modified by the difference of their dates. An historic drama is, therefore, a collection of events borrowed from history, but connected together in respect to cause and time poetically, by dramatic fiction. It would be a fine national custom to act such a series of dramatic histories in orderly succession every Christmas holidays, and could not but tend to counteract that mock cosmopolitism, which under a positive term really implies nothing but a negation of, or indifference to, the particular love of our country. By its nationality must every nation retain its independence – nationality *quoad* the nation. Patriotism is equal to the sense of individuality from each individual. There may come a higher virtue in both – in the just cosmopolitism . . . (?) but never is this *possible* except by antecedence of the former. Better thus: nationality in each individual, *quoad* his country, is equal to the sense of individuality *quoad* himself – i.e., subsensuous, central, inexclusive, etc.

Notice that while Coleridge's earlier remarks are surprisingly congruent with what Aristotle says about tragedy, he does indeed mean them to refer to historical drama. The latter, no less than tragedy, is a dramatic fiction, investigating the relation of action ('a collection of events') and thought ('connected together in respect to cause and time') by means of poetic techniques. History that is too recent or too well known is intractable to the purposes of drama because the unity resulting from succession is too crowded and too familiar to 'strike us and remain in our eye'; that is, it fails to arouse wonder in the audience and is, therefore, an impediment to thought. Coleridge means no disrespect to history *per se*, nor does 'dramatic fiction' entail anything like irresponsible poetic licence. On the contrary, historical drama 'borrows' events from history in order to investigate better the connection of those events by means of poetic heightening.

In fact, the whole tenor of Coleridge's defence of historical drama is that it promotes thought about nationality and the significance of national history. And just in case the emphasis, such as we find in the earlier passage, on the permanent or that 'which is common' in our nature leads us to a too facile notion of universality, his gibes at 'mock cosmopolitism' remind us that the universal is not a negation of or a cancelling of the particular. The 'just cosmopolitism' is never possible except by the antecedence (that is, not supersedence) of individuality and nationality. T. M. Raysor's note on the lacuna following 'the just cosmopolitism' is: 'the words omitted seem to be "the latter in deity".' If his editorial surmise is correct, it shows that Coleridge's ideas about the relationship between individuality or patriotism and the true or just cosmopolitism are perfectly consistent with his earlier remarks on the relation of providence and the human will. The relation of individual to nation exists in the same continuum as that between individual and divine providence. As well, the emphasis of his remarks on the place of patriotism in historical drama accords well with the traditional notion that tragedy involves heads of state whose personal actions have immediate and profound implications for a whole people or nation.

The complexity of the whole relationship is summed up in the compendious, but partly obscure, triad with which the quotation ends: 'nationality in each individual, *quoad* his

country, is equal to the sense of individuality *quoad* himself –
i.e. subsensuous, central, inexclusive, etc.'. This enigmatic, but
compelling, list of qualities offers something very close to
tragic impersonality. The aim of historical drama is to make
the individual understand the nationality of his country as he
understands his own individuality, that is, as something central and subsensuous (operating below the level of sense perception) but not exclusive – to make him feel that he is part
of something larger, and other, than himself, without forfeiting his own central integrity. To achieve this understanding
and this feeling, it seems to me, is an essentially religious recognition. I say this realizing that Coleridge's concept of universals (as stated here) is fundamentally Aristotelian; universals
are not transcendent, but subsensuous; universals subsist in,
and only in, individuals. Thus the discovery of universality,
even if it leads ultimately to deity, must proceed irrevocably
by way of the human community. But the really puzzling
aspect of Coleridge's triad is that individuality itself is treated
as a universal. This treatment is, perhaps, not faulty logic
(since, in one sense, it is easy to see that individuality is a
trait of character held by many individuals in common), but
it is psychologically foreign to modern habits of mind. Those
habits insist that the individual is self-enclosed, exclusive, isolated and even alienated; they further insist on the pre-eminence
of sensory experience and on the delights of eccentricity
(consider the modern meaning of character in 'he' or 'she' is
'a real character'). This attitude, the incapacity to understand
individuality as a universal, is simultaneously the probable
explanation for why tragedy seems so impossible in modern
literature and the likely sign of what is ailing in contemporary
life. It is also the compelling reason for a renewed (and
renewing) study of tragic drama and of tragic impersonality.

The best definition of tragic impersonality that we have
to date is offered in an essay printed originally in *Scrutiny*
in 1944 by F. R. Leavis, called 'Tragedy and the "Medium"'.
Leavis's definition is not readily extractable from his whole
argument, but a series of three excerpts, basically congenial
and coherent, should be enough to demonstrate emphatically his essential sympathy with what Coleridge postulates as
the end of historical drama.[9]

The tragic experience, however it is to be defined, is certainly not anything that encourages, or permits, an indulgence in the dramatization of one's nobly-suffering self.

. . . it is an essential part of the definition of the tragic that it breaks down, or undermines and supersedes, such attitudes. It establishes below them a kind of profound impersonality in which experience matters, not because it is mine – because it is to me it belongs or happens, or because it subserves, or issues in purpose or will, but because it is what it is, the 'mine' mattering only in so far as the individual sentience is the indispensable focus of experience.

The sense of heightened life that goes with the tragic experience is conditioned by a transcending of the ego – an escape from all attitudes of self-assertion. 'Escape', perhaps, is not altogether a good word, since it might suggest something negative and irresponsible. . . . Actually the experience is constructive or creative, and involves a recognizing of positive value as in some way defined and vindicated by death. It is as if we were challenged at the profoundest level with the question, 'In what does the significance of life reside?', and found ourselves contemplating, for answer, a view of life, and of the things giving it value, that make the valued appear unquestionably more important than the valuer, so that significance lies, clearly and inescapably, in the willing adhesion of the individual self to something other than itself.

The willing adhesion of the individual self to something other than itself offers a way of subduing wilfulness without denying the energy of the will. In so far as the implied comparison in 'to something other than itself' refers to divine providence, it probably succumbs to the criticisms brought against Anselm's ontological proof of the existence of God. Namely, that a comparison is set up, with one of the terms of the comparison missing, in order to prove the existence of the very term that is missing. But if we take 'something other than itself' to refer to the nation or the human community, it might just be easier to bring the implied term of the comparison into view. The historical drama, then, impelled by the same basic concern as the tragic drama, brings that concern to a slightly more manageable framework (the obvious framework for an apprenticeship in tragedy). It might be necessary to say what should be plainly evident: that Coleridge's championing of patriotism is the antithesis of the repugnant sort of nationalism much in evidence, especially in the past century; it is as fair to expect the same conquest of self-assertion and egotism, the conquest, that is, of solipsism, in countries and in leaders of countries as in individuals.

In some respects the paradigm of tragic impersonality is the way that language itself is continually created and re-created in individual speakers. Language is spoken only by individual speakers, it is the creation and the responsibility of individual speakers, and it is in language that the individuality of human beings is most profoundly realized; but it is the exclusive property of no one individual. Poetry, as 'measured language', is simply the most inclusive and subtlest instrument for registering and exploring that kind of impersonality. Implicit in the passages from Coleridge are several important considerations for the connection between drama and poetry and for the study of Shakespeare. Leavis comes to a similar conclusion and states it more explicitly near the end of his essay: 'No theory of Tragedy can amount to more than a blackboard diagram, a mere schematic substitute for understanding, unless it is associated with an adequate appreciation of the subtleties of poetic (or creative) language – the subtleties that are supremely illustrated in the poetry of Shakespeare.'[10] Coleridge and Leavis together, then, provide considerable justification for approaching Shakespearean drama through a close inspection of the poetry. In summary: it is the best way to avoid novelistic criticism that concentrates on the accumulation of incident and on the interplay of personalities. Close attention to the verse allows us better to perceive the wider implications of individual actions – to perceive, when it occurs, the tragic impersonality. In a related way, an approach by way of the poetry will facilitate the perception of Coleridge's 'unity of a higher order'. It will enable one to see the unity of a dramatic plot, as well as its conflicts and tensions. It remains to bring to bear, on the insights of Coleridge and Leavis, the most

perceptive analysis of Renaissance poetry in English, the analysis pioneered in the critical work of Yvor Winters and J. V. Cunningham. The moral style will be essential to the presentation of 'men in their causative character' since the attempt to determine, as well as possible, the causes of action and to proceed according to one's best insights into those causes is a moral pursuit. In the words of Samuel Johnson in the *Preface to Shakespeare*, 'he that thinks reasonably must think morally'.[11] The moral style, in other words, is germane to both thought and diction (as these are in turn germane to plot and character). In fact, the moral style, if we may appropriate Coleridge's terms, is itself subsensuous, central, and inexclusive: central, because interested in every aspect of human action; subsensuous and inexclusive, because it attempts to generalize from particular sensory experience. When it fails, of course, it is sentimental or platitudinous because it attempts to be too inclusive on the basis of too little experience. This failure is the besetting vice of the early native plain style, and, correlatively, the overcoming of it is the abiding accomplishment of the Petrarchan enrichment of that central style. The closer rendering of sensuous particulars provided by the eloquent style makes possible a finer adjustment of tone and a more refined apprehension of reality, but for the presentation of an understanding of human action, the moral style remains invaluable and, indeed, inescapable. *Richard II* is a precursor of Shakespeare's great tragedies, not because it discovers the melancholic character (Richard) confronting the necessity of action, or the character of amoral efficiency (Bolingbroke) confronting the necessity of moral and spiritual sanctions, but because it discovers an adequate style or range of styles for presenting 'men in their causative character'; it discloses a range of stylistic mastery, unprecedented in Shakespeare's career before 1595, that is capable of encompassing, without falsifying, a full complexity of human experience; it offers a clear prognosis of the mature and urbane style of Shakespeare.

4 · The standard: the moral and the golden

Though studies of imagery and, more recently, studies of rhetoric have opened up our understanding of Shakespeare's artistry, they seem persistently vulnerable to the distorting preconception that for each play there exists one item of style, or a small group of items (images, metaphors, certain grammatical or rhetorical constructions) that characterize that play and, therefore, provide the 'key' to understanding it. They are too often ways of evading the task of attending, as fully as possible, to every aspect of style in every utterance; of attending, that is, as fully as possible, to Shakespeare's intentions and holding our own intentions in abeyance. A difficulty that is more serious, because more widespread, is the inadequacy of modern notions of what poetry is and does. One is the idea of poetry as the product solely of the imagination, and the other is the notion of poetry as organic form.

Two observations may serve to clarify things. The first is that for the Elizabethans, poetry is an activity of the whole being; the notion that it is limited to one faculty may be glimpsed in Francis Bacon,[1] but a clear theoretical statement cannot be found until Hobbes's 'Answer to Davenant' in 1650: 'Fancy, when any work of Art is to be performed, findes her materials at hand and prepared for use, and needs no more then a swift motion over them . . . her self being all she seeks.'[2] Invention, the seeking and finding of one's subject matter, was repeatedly discussed by classical, medieval, and Renaissance theorists in association with logic or rhetoric (that is, in association with the art of finding the truth and/or persuading others of it). In Hobbes, invention is sprung loose from all such attachments; Fancy is responsible to nothing but itself. The view of poetry implicit in this theory is, to say the least, highly suspect, but that complex issue aside, it is enough merely to observe that, applied to Shakespeare, it is anachronistic. The second observation is that organic form, if it is thought to be an inherent property of poetry, begs the essential question for the critic or reader and isolates (improperly) poetry from all other forms of human discourse. The question is, 'What sense does this work make of the world?' If the reader asks this question and waits for an answer, he must be prepared for the possibility that the work could make several different senses, could impose or discover several different forms (not all of them necessarily mutually conformable), just as well as it could present something that might plausibly be called organic form. And it could do this with varying degrees of success. Works of art may undertake very different kinds of things in different stretches, and even where the kinds are auspiciously the same, the achievement may still be better or worse.[3] It is necessary to register these doubts at the outset because for the case in point, *Richard II*, both of these attitudes have been at work to inhibit critical thought. The play does indeed present us with poetic strengths, but those strengths are not quite what many readers of the past century have been claiming they are. Similarly, with respect to the question of dramatic unity, at least since Walter Pater,[4] readers have asserted, reasserted, and even given elaborate descriptions of the unity of *Richard II*. That unity is an illusion. To say so is not to disparage Shakespeare's achievement. Quite the contrary, it is precisely because the pressure of the experience and understanding that Shakespeare attempts to deal with in the play is so great that its unity is disrupted. It is genuinely apprentice work. It is only the complex and far-reaching implications of the material that show the maker to be, as yet, imperfect.

To make this judgment is not a matter of importing external standards to Shakespeare's play. The standards with which to assess *Richard II* do not come from an analysis of Greville's drama nor from a discussion of Aristotle's (or Coleridge's) theory, though the investigation of these writers does make it easier to see what Shakespeare is doing. Neither do the standards come from other Shakespearean dramas, though there may well be a continuity of themes, methods, and achievements among the plays; nor from the tradition of the two styles in the short poem of the sixteenth century, though there is undoubtedly a connection between the successes of that tradition (including some of Shakespeare's own sonnets) and Shakespeare's use of it in the play. The standards with which to measure the achievement of *Richard II* are discoverable in the play itself. To explain, in a general way, how it is possible to hold this view and still hold the notion of organic form at arm's length, I wish to appropriate some remarks by Erich Auerbach in *Mimesis*. Auerbach's comments are meant to apply, in part, to *2 Henry IV*, but the *Henry IV* plays are close in time to *Richard II*, and, more important, that time (1595-7) is customarily agreed to be a watershed in Shakespeare's career. For this reason, the appropriation may be especially illuminating. If the remarks are brilliantly true for *Henry IV*, how do they accord with *Richard II*?[5]

Within a specific theme there is still another type of evidence of perspective consciousness. Shakespeare and many of his contemporaries are averse to completely detaching a turn of fortune which concerns a single person or a limited number of persons from its general context of events and presenting it on a single level of style, as the tragic poets of antiquity had done and wherein their sixteenth and seventeenth century imitators even outdid them at times. This isolating procedure, which is to be explained through the religious, mythological, and technical premises of the antique theatre, is out of keeping with the concept of a magical and polyphonic cosmic coherence which arose during the Renaissance. Shakespeare's drama does not present isolated blows of fate, generally falling from above and involving but a few people in their effects, while the milieu is limited to the few persons indispensable to the progress of the action; on the contrary, it offers inner entanglements which result from given conditions and from the interplay of variously constituted characters and in which not only the milieu but even the landscape, even the spirits of the dead and other supernatural beings participate. And the role of these participants often contributes nothing at all or at least very little to the progress of the action, but instead consists in a sympathetic counterpoint – a parallel or contrary motion on various levels of style.

If 'cosmic coherence' in drama sounds perilously close to 'organic form,' it should be noted that it is concomitant with 'perspective consciousness,' and that that in turn is a consequence of the presentation of an action on several levels of style. The actions of single persons may have far-reaching political and social implications. If the *Henry IV* plays are Shakespeare's skilful management of perspective consciousness focused on very definite political and social problems, *Richard II*, less perfectly executed, brings perspective consciousness to bear on matter potentially more profound because the spiritual difficulties that underlie those problems are faced more directly. And though the absence of prose restricts the range of *Richard II*, the interplay of various styles is, for the same reason, more intense, in some ways, and more fluid. Most of the verse in the earlier play is admittedly inferior to the verse of the later plays,[6] but it shows occasional flashes of brilliance and, in at least one stretch, a pressure of experience and an effort at understanding that clearly anticipate the great tragedies. The standard by which to measure the achievement of *Richard II* is found most fully and most cogently in the first 146 lines of Act II. This stretch of the play establishes a depth of perspective consciousness in comparison to which even the best passages elsewhere appear a trifle thin. At the heart of the various levels of style that create this perspective consciousness are the golden style and the moral style, separated out quite distinctly at first, then fused and transmuted into the metaphysical style and the Shakespearean style. In this passage Shakespeare is clearly exploring his poetic talents.

This important passage may be considered in four stages: first, the first thirty lines.[7]

> *Gaunt.* Will the king come that I may breathe my last
>   In wholesome counsel to his unstaid youth?
> *York.* Vex not yourself, nor strive not with your
>   breath;
>   For all in vain comes counsel to his ear.

5 *Gaunt.* O, but they say the tongues of dying men
    Inforce attention like deep harmony.'
    Where words are scarce they are seldom spent in vain,
    For they breathe truth that breathe their words in
      pain.
    He that no more must say is listened more
10 Than they whom youth and ease have taught to glose;
    More are men's ends mark'd than their lives before.
    The setting sun, and music at the close,
    As the last taste of sweets, is sweetest last,
    Writ in remembrance more than things long past:
15 Though Richard my life's counsel would not hear,
    My death's sad tale may yet undeaf his ear.
   York. No, it is stopp'd with other flattering sounds,
    As praises, of whose taste the wise are fond,
    Lascivious metres, to whose venom sound
20 The open ear of youth doth always listen,
    Report of fashions in proud Italy,
    Whose manners still our tardy-apish nation
    Limps after in base imitation.
    Where doth the world thrust forth a vanity –
25 So it be new, there's no respect how vile –
    That is not quickly buzz'd into his ears?
    Then all too late comes counsel to be heard,
    Where will doth mutiny with wit's regard.
    Direct not him whose way himself will choose:
30 'Tis breath thou lack'st and that breath wilt
    thou lose. (II, i, 1–30)

Here are clear confrontations between native plainness and
Petrarchan eloquence. York's moral indignation is placed
emphatically in opposition to Richard's exotic excesses. His
denunciation is a wholesale critique of the preoccupations of
the golden style: flattery (or compliment), 'lascivious metres'
(that is, 'love' poetry), exotic manners, and novelty. The
source of these preoccupations is very largely Petrarch's
homeland, Italy. And, as Peter Ure notes in the Arden edition, 'the specific references to Italian fashions are characteristic of the 16th century rather than the 14th.'[8] In terms of
style, it should be noted that the attack is not on Petrarch

himself, but on the sixteenth-century English Petrarchans, 'our tardy-apish nation'. As well, despite the obvious broader meanings of 'fashions' and 'manners', the attack remains focused on matters of expression – 'report' and 'buzz'd'. The consequence of such preoccupations is just what the English Petrarchans explored over and over again in lyric poetry, the conquest of the reason by the will (l. 28). York's solution to this dilemma is, of course, no solution at all, but an attempt to disregard it, to remain aloof. The moral style turns away from the sweet style to the enrichment of neither.

By contrast, Gaunt, whose attitude is certainly not less moral than York's, who has more reason to feel estranged from Richard because of the banishment of his son, and whose purpose in desiring to offer 'wholesome counsel' is more clearly didactic, employs a vigorous mixture of the two styles. In the opening part of his speech, especially lines 5–8, his use of the native plain style verges on the proverbial – if his formulation is not exactly proverbial, the ideas none the less are unquestionably proverbial. Then by juxtaposing the notion that plain truth is to be expected from a man in pain and dying with the notion that eloquent deceit may equally be expected from 'youth and ease' ('to glose' is to veil the truth with smooth and specious talk) and by indicating a decided preference for the former, Gaunt shows himself capable of the same extreme attitudes that we have just seen in York. But Gaunt's perspective consciousness is a great deal more complex. As his speech continues it evokes some of the loveliest imagery of the play.

> The setting sun, and music at the close,
> As the last taste of sweets, is sweetest last,
> Writ in remembrance more than things long past.
> (II, i, 12–14)

These lines, made more poignant by the analogy with 'men's ends,' exploit, to the full, an elaborate pattern of balance and antithesis in order to heighten the feeling appropriate to the meaning: the experience of closure is dependent upon the perception of a pattern. And it is no accident that the important preceding line, 'More are men's ends marked than their lives before', gives us a brief statement of Shakespearean tragedy: the word 'ends' and the word 'marked' refer implicitly to the tragic effects of woe and wonder, to which Shakespeare draws attention by means of alliteration, of monosyllabic diction, and by trochaic substitution in the third foot. Finally, the first two lines appeal to sight, hearing, and taste, so that the appeal to memory, when it comes in the next line, has an exquisite feeling of sensuous immediacy. This brief passage from *Richard II*, one might add, is much more powerful and cogent than is sonnet 30, 'When to the sessions of sweet silent thought', for the main reason that the character presented here actually *is* thinking. Gaunt modulates from a moral style to a sweet style, which however lovely is not valued merely for itself, but for the 'lesson' it helps to enforce. The sweet style is subservient to the moral style – to the enrichment of both. Gaunt's perspective is a good deal more urbane than York's, and without relinquishing his concern for the truth (what Aristotle in the *Rhetoric* calls 'logos'), he shows himself capable of entertaining considerations of 'ethos' and 'pathos', that is, of selecting, from those feelings appropriate to his own person, the feelings most likely to move his auditor, in this case Richard.[9] The character of Gaunt, as presented here, is certainly no less alive than is Richard to the attractions of sensory detail. In sum, he possesses the necessary talents (in contrast to York) to be a truly good counsellor.

The next section, continuing to elaborate some of the same points – the juxtaposition of styles is, if anything, even sharper – picks up the hint of tragic issues implicit in Gaunt's earlier remarks and opens out into an exploration of something closely akin to tragic impersonality. It is, therefore, crucial to a proper understanding of the play.

> *Gaunt.* Methinks I am a prophet new inspir'd,
>   And thus expiring do foretell of him:
>   His rash fierce blaze of riot cannot last.
>   For violent fires soon burn out themselves;
> 35 Small showers last long, but sudden storms are short;
>   He tires betimes that spurs too fast betimes;
>   With eager feeding food doth choke the feeder;
>   Light vanity, insatiate cormorant,

Consuming means, soon preys upon itself.
40 This royal throne of kings, this scept'red isle,
This earth of majesty, this seat of Mars,
This other Eden, demi-paradise,
This fortress built by Nature for herself
Against infection and the hand of war,
45 This happy breed of men, this little world,
This precious stone set in the silver sea,
Which serves it in the office of a wall,
Or as a moat defensive to a house,
Against the envy of less happier lands;
50 This blessed plot, this earth, this realm, this England,
This nurse, this teeming womb of royal kings,
Fear'd by their breed, and famous by their birth,
Renowned for their deeds as far from home,
For Christian service and true chivalry,
55 As is the sepulchre in stubborn Jewry
Of the world's ransom, blessed Mary's son;
This land of such dear souls, this dear dear land,
Dear for her reputation through the world,
Is now leas'd out – I die pronouncing it –
60 Like to a tenement or pelting farm.
England, bound in with the triumphant sea,
Whose rocky shore beats back the envious siege
Of wat'ry Neptune, is now bound in with shame,
With inky blots and rotten parchment bonds;
65 That England, that was wont to conquer others,
Hath made a shameful conquest of itself.
Ah, would the scandal vanish with my life,
How happy then were my ensuing death! (II, i, 31–68)

Even in only a slightly larger context that it is usually given, Gaunt's famous set piece in praise of England can be seen to be the reverse of simple nostalgia or jingoistic nationalism. Although at the beginning lines 31 and 32 seem to promise vatic afflatus, the lines immediately following are more purely native plain style than any in the first part of the scene. Lines 33 to 37 offer proverbial folk wisdom – home truths available to every man – in the metre and phrasing characteristic of the early native style: heavily end-stopped lines, the exact congruence of the syntactic unit with the metrical unit, regular use of alliteration, a strong differentiation between accented and unaccented syllables. In line 35, if the word 'showers' is regarded as monosyllabic, the first and second feet should probably be read as spondees, a metrical variation almost unique to the native plain style. In lines 38 and 39, the style undergoes a shift. The figure 'insatiate cormorant' presents an example of what we think of as characteristically Shakespearean metaphor. Whereas in a proverb, general or abstract meaning takes clear precedence over concrete imagery, to the extent that the imagery often goes unnoticed, Shakespeare's metaphor, without any lessening of proverbial feel and force, insists upon recognition of the concrete detail. Line 38, in fact, is at once more general ('light vanity') and more specific ('insatiate cormorant') than any of the preceding lines. Moreover, in the preceding, each repeats what is essentially the same idea in units of one line, while the figure here expands into two lines. It is, thus, a summary of the preceding lines and a transition from the plain style opening to the eloquent style of the set piece. The first observation, then, to make about the context of Gaunt's famous panegyric is that it is introduced by an appeal to time-honoured truths expressed in the emphatic accents of the native plain style, an appeal, that is, to truths which, spoken by Gaunt but not his unique property, demonstrate his essential connection with a community of speakers.

The set piece itself is a *tour de force* of the eloquent style. Building up momentum by means of a series of appositives, the lines retain something of the emphasis of the paratactic structure evident in the earlier lines. But the paratactic elements here are held together by a powerful syntactic thrust beginning at line 40, 'This royal throne of kings', and reaching a climax in line 59, 'Is now leas'd out', with an extra line and a half for denouement. In between is a good deal of rhythmical variation as the appositives are expanded in lines 43–4 and 46–9 and then sharply contracted in line 50. The appositives, in other words, are not simply a piling on of compliments or enthusiastic encomiums, but a means of description and definition, suggestive or elaborative as need be. A similar poise and discretion is observable in the handling of imagery: golden style diction is used to create the sense of a golden world, that is, a world of supreme but elusive value. The 'precious stone set in the silver sea', for example, not only describes something of England's independence, but defines, by analogy, something of the value of that nation as it is enhanced by its independence. Furthermore, the images of the fortress and of the moat gain a particular propriety from the urgent sense that that value is under attack. There is a striking juxtaposition of the eloquent style and the plain style as the elaborate series of epithets stress repeatedly the integrity of England; the simple (plain) sentence a loss of integrity: 'This land . . . Is now leas'd out.' The pleasant style gives us a vision of what we would like to be the case, the image of our desires; the flat style, the flat truth. But again, the two styles interinanimate each other. The celebration of England is no mere egregious piece of embroidery on a set theme, but the elaboration of the understanding and feeling that give the moral utterance its point. And the moral point is no mere homiletic lesson tacked on to an otherwise aesthetically pure or serene vision as an anticlimax but the culmination of a series of truly human perspectives in the moral insight that animates and gives shape to human lives. In the syntactical movement of the whole sentence (ll. 40–60), Shakespeare has discovered a means of enactment, for the uttering of the whole sentence requires just the sort of expenditure of breath that York counsels against (l. 30), and the true anti-climax of the speech '– I die pronouncing it –' acquires peculiar force. For one thing, the first person singular pronoun is introduced here for the first time in the sentence as Gaunt presents both himself and his intention to persist in a certain kind of action (despite York's advice) in a position of anti-climax or subordination to the general well-being of England. None the less, the force of his parenthetical remark is truly peculiar in that it is a powerful asseveration of his own individual integrity; it is, in fact, a tragic pronouncement. Not only does the expenditure of breath contribute to Gaunt's death, his recognition of the disintegration of the entity that is England entails the recognition of the concomitant diminution of all individuals (including himself) who make up that entity. And yet this recognition has a positive side. It represents a positive choice of a moral attitude. To choose a moral attitude in the face of death is to give allegiance to a moral order on the side of life. ' – I die pronouncing it – ': the first person pronoun and the indicative form of the verb represent the mutability of individual lives and the absoluteness of death; the participle and the indefinite pronoun, the continuing process of life and the values that give it meaning. Only a master of the plain style could instill such life into a phrase so near cliché, could make, largely by means of subtlety of cadence, 'the valued appear unquestionably more important than the valuer'.

As well as these refinements in the plain style, Shakespeare introduces certain modifications into the eloquent aspects of the speech. To begin with, Gaunt's speech differs from at least two of its most prominent analogues, from *Ortho-Epia Gallica* by John Eliot and from *Deuine Weekes and Workes* from Sylvester's Du Bartas,[10] in not being an extended apostrophe, even though it may seem to carry some of the same swell of feeling we normally associate with the apostrophe. This modification has an important bearing on the quality of imagery and its degree of realization in the speech. For a representative twentieth-century understanding of the imagery of this speech we may turn to Richard D. Altick's article, 'Symphonic Imagery in *Richard II*.'[11] Published in 1947, Altick's essay has been regarded as seminal by a large number of commentators for the past thirty years. Despite additional suggestions, adjustments, or shifts of emphasis, there has been basic agreement about the validity of his approach. But his approach can also mislead because it assumes the presence of organic form without proving it, and it relies too much on statistical tabulations of imagery. Based on the notion that poetry is solely the product of the imagination, the approach regards the image as the unit of meaningful utterance, and it draws on some rather dubious musical analogies. Altick observes that the words 'earth,' 'land,' and 'ground' occur 71 times in *Richard II*, but adds:[12]

> No two persons, doing the same counting for the same purpose, would arrive at precisely the same numerical results. But I am confident that independent tabulation

would enable anyone to arrive at my general conclusions. Statistics here, as in all critical exercises, are merely grounds upon which to base a judgment that must eventually be a subjective one.

Altick's view is that although criticism is unfortunately not an exact science, we can at least ground our ultimately subjective judgment on the precision of statistics. But for one thing, some sort of act of judgment is inevitably entailed in the initial decision about which statistics are relevant to a particular discussion and about how they are to be assembled. For another, the notorious dichotomy of the subjective and the objective simply does not apply to language. Language is neither exclusively subjective nor objective, but both at once. A word may be regarded as an object, but it exists, or has meaning, only in an individual speaker, only in a subject. Any attempt to ignore that subject or that speaker and his intentions, any attempt to treat his words as purely empirical, quantifiable data can only result in a reductive interpretation. Altick comments on the speech by John of Gaunt.[13]

Above all, *earth* is the symbol of the English nation. It is used by Shakespeare to connote those same values which we find in the equivalent synecdoche of *soil*, as in 'native soil.' It sums up all the feeling inherent in the sense of pride in nation – of jealousy when the country is threatened by foreign incursion, of bitter anger when its health has been destroyed by mismanagement or greed. 'This earth of majesty,' John of Gaunt calls England in his famous speech, ' . . . This blessed plot, this earth, this realm, this England' (II, i, 41, 50). And a few lines farther on: 'This land of such dear souls, this dear dear land . . .' (II, i, 57). Having once appeared, so early in the play, in such lustrous context, the words *earth* and *land* forever after have richer significance. Whenever they recur, they are more meaningful, more powerful. Thus Richard's elaborate speech upon his arrival in Wales – [Altick quotes III, ii, 8–11, 23–6] – undoubtedly gains in emotional splendor (as well as dramatic irony) by its reminiscences of John of Gaunt's

67

earlier language. The two men between them make the
English earth the chief verbal theme of the play.

Altick is surely right to insist on the close association of
Gaunt's patriotism and his love for the English land, but in
the realm of statistics, it should be obvious that the most
important word in Gaunt's speech is not 'earth' or 'land' or
'ground' but 'this.' And not only is the word numerically
far ahead of its nearest competitors in this passage, its insis-
tent presence radically qualifies the meaning of the words
Altick chooses to focus on. By contrast, Richard's elaborate
speech upon his arrival in Wales (in Act III, scene ii) repeatedly uses the possessive pronoun, 'my earth' (l. 10), 'my
gentle earth' (l. 12), and like the analogues that might have
influenced Shakespeare's invention of John of Gaunt's
speech, Richard's speech is comprised of a series of apostrophes. Far from there being a unity of tone between the
two speeches, there is a marked disparity in tone.

In music, tone refers purely to a quality of sound. In
poetry, however unquestionably important sound is, it is subordinate to meaning. In language, tone is surely a matter of
the depth and resonance of meaning, even when, as is the case
with poetic language, that meaning is intensified or accented
by careful attention to the sound of words. John of Gaunt's
speech, then, is radically different in tone because its meaning is profound and vigorous. Richard's tone is indulgent and
languorous, essentially shallow. In Gaunt we hear of his feeling for 'this' earth. The feeling is mature, rational and full-
bodied. Richard fancifully supposes the earth ought to have
feeling for him. His emotion is insecure, self-indulgent, and
only half-believed. His use of the apostrophe is a means of
sentimental and shallow projection, and his recourse to the
first person singular pronoun betrays a radical incomprehen-
sion about the nature of his relationship to his kingdom. It
is, perhaps, acceptable for a monarch to speak of 'my earth'
(though the first person plural would be more accurate). But
though the land is Richard's, it is not simply his. It is a 'royal
throne of Kings'. Gaunt uses the plural in both cases where
he mentions the monarchy (l. 40 and l. 51). By contrast,
Gaunt's use of 'this' is a means of stressing, at once, a sense

of intimacy and a sense of otherness. The demonstrative adjective indicates the nearness of England, felt as an immediate present reality by Gaunt, a reality that is of supreme value to him, a reality in which he is himself an important ingredient, but a reality that is also outside and other – ultimately larger than himself. It is for this reason that Gaunt's tone is resonant and profound, for although his suffering is certainly no less personal than Richard's, his vision of its larger implications is as full as can be imagined. His speech is a model of passionate, disinterested attachment – a model, that is, of tragic impersonality. Richard's speech, by comparison, far from gaining in emotional splendour by its reminiscences of John of Gaunt's earlier language, appears self-regarding and even uncomprehending. His emotion seems a little shabby in comparison because sentimental, proceeding as it does by way of posturing or attitudinizing rather than from a clear understanding of his predicament. We have reason to suspect, then, at least on some preliminary evidence of early speeches, that Richard's character is not truly tragic.

As for the 'dramatic irony' mentioned by Altick, though he goes on to explain something of critical importance, its primary effect may also be to disrupt the play's unity of tone. By pointing out that *'earth*, while it emblematizes the foundation of kingly pride and power, is also a familiar symbol of the vanity of human life',[14] Altick raises an idea that E.H. Kantorowicz treats at length in *The King's Two Bodies.* As Kantorowicz puts it, 'The king is "twin-born" not only with greatness but with human nature.'[15] Richard's address to the earth is undoubtedly a piece of dramatic irony, so little able is the earth to sustain his hopes and so imminent is his own abasement. But if in working out the irony involved in his misunderstanding, Richard never achieves the mature view of Gaunt's speech, the major effect, for the audience or reader who compares the two characters, will be the discrepancy of understanding – and hence of tone.

Finally, with respect to Altick's last claim that the two men between them make the English earth the chief verbal theme of the play, it must be said that Shakespeare's subdued treatment of the golden style in Gaunt's speech and the interaction of the golden and the moral styles make this claim doubtful, even if we concede that 'imagery' might refer to figurative language in general, as well as to particular invitations to sensory constructions. The oddness of the phrase, 'the chief verbal theme' results from regarding the individual word (or image) as the unit of meaning and from pursuing the musical analogy. Thus, because there are musical themes, there must be verbal themes. But there is little justification for thinking that uttering the words 'earth', 'land', 'ground', 'blood', for example, is anything like sounding in the appropriate rhythm the first four notes of Beethoven's Fifth Symphony. The individual words have their meaning in the unit of utterance traditionally called (not entirely satisfactorily) the sentence. But whatever description of that unit is offered and however small the unit may be (there is no reason why the unit is not *sometimes* as small as one word, though it is customarily larger), the one presiding consideration in determining its character is the particular intention of a particular speaker. The paramount question is 'what does *he* mean?' In music, as far as I can discern, the question of meaning, in the same sense, is hardly relevant. Still, we might take seriously the claim that the earth as the symbol of the English nation is the chief theme of the play. And we might also grant that Altick is right in directing our attention to the importance of the earth as an image, and a metaphor, for most of the major characters including Gaunt.

But there is a great deal more at stake. To begin with, the sensory content of most of the diction in Gaunt's speech, with the exception of the 'precious stone' image, is not high, despite the obvious elevation of style. The elevated style, as we have seen, is a product of the syntactic movement of the speech. There is, as well, its metrical movement. By filling out his pentameter line with balanced half-lines, often in the pattern of adjective–noun, adjective–noun, Shakespeare alludes to the swelling rhetoric that Howard Baker describes in the early Tudor and Elizabethan tragedians.[16] Gaunt's speech, in fact, repeatedly comes surprisingly close to the bombastic blank verse line – I say 'surprisingly' because the speech does not seem, and indeed is not, bombastic. How does Shakespeare employ the tricks of bombast without succumbing to its crudities? The first answer, which we have already explored somewhat, is the moderating influence of Gaunt's moral diagnosis. A second answer is that, in some ways, Gaunt has a subject worthy of bombastic, or at least oratorical, development and that the oratorical flourishes, coming as they do near the beginning (ll. 40-2) and end (ll. 51-6) of the speech, only serve to intimate its potential weight; the impression is of weighty matter and powerful feelings held in check. The final answer is that Shakespeare in order to balance the bluff of the bombastic style and the subtlety of the golden style uses the plain (and truly human) moral style.

Consider, for a moment, the opening line of the part of Gaunt's speech that is most often quoted and celebrated.

This royal throne of Kings, this scept'red isle

The line clearly involves a reference to the English earth, though the reference is neither strongly visual nor notably symbolic. The 'royal throne' is actually less metaphorical than it seems to a modern sensibility because to a more thorough-going monarchical society a significant part of the meaning of 'throne' is equivalent to the dead metaphor (and therefore literal) 'seat of state'. 'Scept'red isle' is, no doubt, partly metaphor, but it is not the extremity of metaphor that provokes personification. Rather, it suggests an implicit set of correspondences: as the king is in possession of the sceptre, a symbol of authority, so the island is in possession of the king, a symbol of authority. The bombast latent in the repeated adjective-noun development of 'royal throne' and 'scept'red isle' is held in check by the complexity of thought present in the idea of reciprocal possession. The king possesses a throne, the island a king. Altick is certainly right to see that an important part of the play is the way that individual life, as well as the life of the nation, is rooted in the earth; but the play doesn't stop there. The point is not that the island is like the king in possessing a people (either metaphorically or literally) or in having authority over subjects. The hero of the play is not 'England', as E. M. W. Tillyard claims.[17] Both island and king are referred to something other and larger, and the notion of reciprocal possession is merely a hint of this more fundamental fact. Notice that the chiasmic

ordering in line 40 is picked up and elaborated in the subsequent line. 'Earth' echoes 'isle' as 'seat' echoes 'throne'.
C. H. Herford glosses 'earth of majesty' as 'this land, which
is the proper domain of "majesty"',[18] but 'domain' itself
can mean either heritable property or sphere of activity. That
is to say, the exploration of reciprocal relationship between
king and country continues. The self-assertion of the bombastic style is modified by the technical graces the golden style
invented in order to explore the complexities of mutuality.

And those complexities are, in turn, referred to a world of
spiritual value before being referred back to the world of
human attitudes and human action. The whole exercise is
essentially moral, the effort to conduct oneself according to
one's fullest vision of the complexity of things and their
relationships. The references to 'this other Eden' and to 'the
sepulchre in stubborn Jewry' are not merely ornamental gestures toward Christianity, but an attempt to lay out the
fundamental spiritual values that are the basis of all human
value. They are the reasons that support the epithet 'dear
dear land', which would otherwise be jingoism. Notice again
that the balancing half line to 'dear land' is 'dear souls'.
Extracts of John of Gaunt's speech frequently omit the
reference to the crusades, perhaps because of certain embar-
rassment about the historical value of the crusades or perhaps
because of a hesitation about its relevance to Gaunt's line of
thought. But it is not primarily an historical reference, and
it is central to his thoughts. As the king is referred to something other and larger than himself, in an important sense,
his land, so the land is referred to something 'as far from
home', as far from itself, 'as is' that land 'in stubborn Jewry'.
And that land is merely the 'sepulchre' of 'the world's ransom, blessed Mary's son'. Christ is the embodiment of the
spiritual value that redeems the values of the world; he is
the standard of Christian moral values. There can be no
doubt that Gaunt's attitude (and Shakespeare's too at this
moment) is fundamentally Christian. But it is not simply
Christian. It is, in context, a thorough exploration of the universal religious principles that make for the integrity of human
individuals and yet bind those individuals into a larger whole
that is greater than the sum of its parts. The dissolution of

72

England that is presented in the phrase 'now leas'd out' is thus a tragic recognition for the character who perceives its truth, for the clear implication or corollary of the recognition is 'and, therefore, will have to be ransomed again.' It is not that England itself has supreme value, but that the full integrity of the individual and the nation is a necessary pre-condition of the supreme value that gives meaning to life. The just cosmopolitanism is only possible by the antecedence of individuality and nationality.

Perhaps another way of enforcing the point is to return to Gaunt's repeated use of the word 'this.' The word is an important one for the purposes of ostensive definition and for accurate description, but just what is it that Gaunt is pointing to in this speech? As an adjective, of course, the word is attached to a noun. But Gaunt moves rapidly through a whole succession of nouns, all apparently presented in apposition to one another, but none wholly satisfactory for conveying Gaunt's complete intention. I do not propose to introduce the problem of haecceity or, more simply, the problem of saying what a thing is, nor do I mean to suggest that such metaphysical tangles are insoluble, but only to point out, as against the large claims sometimes made for Shakespeare's imagery, that the demonstrative adjective is at least as responsible as the imagery for the emotional power in Gaunt's speech, that that emotional power is in large part the energy of thought (as Cunningham puts it, an intellectual experience 'is not without emotion: otherwise it would not be experience'[19]), and that 'this' is no image but a pure abstraction, to which the closest approximation we might give in this context is 'Englishness'. Gaunt's speech also has 'its own absolute value as "thought" as the accomplished saying of something very much worth saying'.[20] It is the spirit of England (and more) that Gaunt eulogizes, and this *earth* is only an aspect of it. The final proof of this assertion is to note the fluid transitions between the major parts of Gaunt's speech. The metaphor of the insatiate cormorant, consuming means and preying upon itself, facilitates the movement from the proverbs of the first part to the eloquent elaborations of the famous middle section. But more important, though there is a juxtaposition of styles, there is no fundamental disjunction of intention. The spirit of England that the middle section attempts to delineate or define is the same spirit out of which issues the proverbial folk wisdom of the first part of the speech. It is also the same spirit to which Gaunt reverts at the close of his speech and to which he dedicates his allegiance.

> That England, that was wont to conquer others,
> Hath made a shameful conquest of itself.
> Ah, would the scandal vanish with my life,
> How happy then were my ensuing death!

These lines are once again fairly plain, stating as economically and simply as possible the clear antitheses of 'conquer-conquest' and 'life–death'. The dynamic shift from 'this' of the middle section to 'that' in line 65 is a compact representation of his lament for a nation. The contrast is more than a simple contrast of present and past, though the England for which Gaunt feels allegiance did indubitably exist in the past; otherwise it could not be known. The lament is more than simple nostalgia for a particular way of life; it is an expression of anxiety over the very disappearance of nationhood itself, a value that, as the last two lines make clear, continues to be Gaunt's major preoccupation for the present as well as the future. It is hard to imagine a plainer declaration of adherence to the notion that the valued is unquestionably more important than the valuer. The last two plain sentences, the first in the indicative, the second in the subjunctive mood, serve to consolidate the insights of the heuristic middle section.

To take stock, then, of the important first 68 lines of Act II in *Richard II*, it is clear that Shakespeare has mastered and understands the dramatic potential of the two styles of the sixteenth-century lyric. L. A. Cormican in his excellent essay, 'Medieval Idiom in Shakespeare', argues that about 1600 Shakespeare's style achieves a new depth, pliability, and range resulting[21]

> to a great extent from an increased power to make effective dramatic use of a number of medieval convictions and attitudes. . . . [Shakespeare] very probably felt that the literary modes set in operation by Petrarch

and Lyly culminated in *Twelfth Night*; polish, neatness, refinement, urbanity of language, the feeling of a whole aristocratic culture behind a writer — these things could hardly be developed much further; he could not, in the meantime at least, improve on *Twelfth Night* as *Twelfth Night* improved on *A Comedy of Errors.*

Like Auerbach, Cormican believes that the growth of Shakespeare's dramatic art is co-extensive with the development of 'a very complex language, with several levels of intelligibility',[22] and like Auerbach, he sees intimations of this development in the prose speeches of Shylock and in the 'low life' of the histories. 'What this meant in practice for Shakespeare was particularly that he succeeded in the tragedies in avoiding any impression of giving a few hours in the private lives of a few individuals – Shakespeare is conscious, as is the Bible, of the continuing presence of the human race as a whole.'[23] The only adjustment that I propose to these fine general observations is that the intimations come earlier, at least as early as *Richard II* in 1595, because they are not wholly dependent either on the perfecting of prose techniques or on Shakespeare's developing that metaphoric skill capable of investing commonplace objects with mystery. The differentiation of levels of style is clearly possible within the strictly poetic modes that antedate the mature Shakespeare, and if the plain style has not been widely recognized as a poetic mode, that is only because in part it aims at being a styleless style. At any rate, it is clearly the style to which Shakespeare resorts in order to bolster his drama with the normative influence of 'what his fellow countrymen had been thinking for centuries'.[24] In terms of characterization, the native plain style sharply delineates the character of York and, while connecting him to Gaunt, stresses his narrow limitations. The multiplicity of styles present in the utterances of Gaunt characterizes the complexity of his attitudes and the range of his intelligence. The two styles imported from lyric poetry serve to polarize that range from the abrupt security of the native plain style to the exploratory testing of the Petrarchan style. As well, the stability of these poles allows Shakespeare to allude to the self-assertion of the bombastic style and the centrality of a moral style enriched by Petrarchan experiment in mutuality. By these means Shakespeare represents an intense sense of individual life as it really is, that is, radically qualified by the continuing presence of the human race as a whole. But Gaunt's language is not only a means of characterization. It represents a standard of thought and diction against which the actions of other characters can be measured. Throughout the first 68 lines, at least, Gaunt is presented as a master of both the old style, weighty with medieval conviction, and the new style, flashy with Renaissance urbanity. And the consummate ease with which he moves between the styles and molds them to serve his own purposes suggests that he is captivated neither by fashion nor by received opinion, but is capable of controlling language for the purpose of discovering reality.

5 · The standard: the metaphysical and the Shakespearean

Seldom in *Richard II* are the plain and eloquent styles separated out so distinctly as in II, i, 1–68. The next stretch, II, i, 69–146, involves the crucial confrontation between Gaunt and Richard, and it serves as a prelude to the two most perplexing and momentous actions of the play: Richard's seizure of Gaunt's estate and Bolingbroke's (announced) intention of returning to England. For the moment, however, our attention is directed not towards the significant action of the two principals, but towards the quality of language in the exchange between Gaunt and Richard. As might be expected from the pressure of complex meanings and feelings evident in Gaunt's panegyric, Shakespeare's thought is straining against the limits of established poetic modes. In the stretch under consideration, those modes give way to two distinctly new poetic styles, the metaphysical and the Shakespearean, which are yet intimately related to the older poetic conventions, the plain and eloquent styles.

However, before offering a description of the metaphysical style and of the way it influences dramatic action, I will attempt a word of clarification about a notoriously controversial subject. When Dryden introduced the term 'metaphysical' to literary criticism, he referred, albeit pejoratively, to the presence of metaphysical propositions in poetry.[1] When Johnson popularized the term, he referred primarily to outlandish comparisons: 'The most heterogeneous ideas are yoked by violence together.'[2] Subsequent criticism has generally followed one or the other of these two precedents. Metaphysical poetry is thought to be any poetry that elaborates, adheres to, or even merely alludes to, a metaphysical system; or it is thought to be poetry that characteristically exhibits metaphorical ingenuity or even incongruity. In 1933, in 'On Metaphysical Poetry', James Smith made an admirable attempt to reconcile these two critical traditions, reclaiming for metaphysical poetry a meaning not wholly disreputable from the point of view of philosophy, while directing attention to certain aspects of poetic style. Discounting allusions to metaphysical systems, he claims that metaphysical poetry, properly so called, has, as a result of viewing the world in a certain way, something of the same air of puzzlement that characterizes the work of metaphysicians; and further, that this puzzlement is often embodied in a 'metaphysical conceit.'[3]

> Metaphysics is 'puzzling', if I may retain the homely word, in a peculiar way. It is not that, to the matters it studies, there is an abundance of clues, so that the mind is lost among them; or that there is a shortage of clues, so that the mind is left hesitant; but rather that such clues as there are, while equally trustworthy, are contradictory. And again, I do not mean that they are contradictory as are, say, pleas in a law-court. A judge is puzzled if he has before him two chains of evidence, one tending to prove that a certain person was in a certain spot at a certain time, the other that he was not. In cases like this, the contradiction rests upon accidents merely: it is compatible with the nature of the person whose movements are being considered, either that he was, or that he was not, at the given spot. The contradictions in metaphysics, on the other hand, spring from essence. The very nature of things brings them forth. It seems impossible that the nature of things should possess either the one or the other of a pair of qualities; it seems impossible that it should possess both together: it seems impossible that it should not possess both. Concern with problems of this kind gives a quite peculiar air of being puzzled; it is only in possession of this air, and not of any other, that I wish to say Donne and Thomas resemble each other.
>
> I should like to give this air a name – say, the 'metaphysical note'; to describe it generally, as that it is a note of tension, or strain; and merely affirm that it is to be found in Donne.

From this general position Smith proposes an economical definition of metaphysical poetry: 'verse properly called metaphysical is that to which the impulse is given by an overwhelming concern with metaphysical problems; with problems either deriving from, or closely resembling in the nature of their difficulty, the problem of the Many and the One'.[4] And from this definition he proposes to deduce 'some of the characters of metaphysical poetry in general', the most prominent of which is the 'metaphysical conceit' described as startling, but also plausible, satisfying or natural and therefore not startling. The heterogeneous elements of this kind of metaphor may originally have been yoked by violence, but they stay yoked. 'Once made, the figure does not disintegrate: it offers something unified and "solid" for our contemplation which, the longer we contemplate, only grows the more solid. . . . Such strangeness as it has is only that of the world in which it is embedded.'[5] Two of the most famous of Smith's examples are Donne's 'her body thought' and Marvell's 'green thought'.

Now, acute as this analysis is, and admirable as is the intention of offering workable guidelines for the use of a difficult term, there are two objections to be raised. The first, perhaps less an objection than a warning, is that there are certain obvious dangers in attempting to define a style by reference to subject matter. Even if we concede that certain styles are customarily aligned with certain kinds of subject matter (the eloquent style is frequently dedicated to psychological matters – eloquence, after all, is intimately connected with the art of moving people, and the knowledge of what is moving is what we call psychology; the plain style is not infrequently preoccupied with morality), the poet is always free to play off such customary expectations. To give an obvious example, the high oratorical style is repeatedly used on trivial matter for satirical effect. Yet this objection is not damaging, and we may well be glad to have a descriptive term for a style dedicated to passionate intellectuality. The second objection has more pressing ramifications. To begin with, despite the clarity and economy of the definition, the attempt to describe the style largely in terms of metaphor is more restrictive than it needs to be, or indeed should be. There is a good bit of poetry that comes within the scope of Smith's definition, but escapes the terms of his description.

Fulke Greville, for example, achieves, on a number of occasions, the 'metaphysical note' as Odette de Mourgues, for one, recognizes by including a brief discussion of him near the beginning of her book, *Metaphysical, Baroque and Precieux Poetry*, and pointing particularly to *Caelica*, LXXXVII, 'When as Mans life, the light of humane lust'.[6] The poem is preoccupied with the necessity of perceiving the presence of eternity in time. Another interesting example is *Caelica*, LXXXIII, 'Who grace, for *Zenith* had, from whom no shadowes grow', a poem that is 'possibly an appeal to Queen Elizabeth, to restore [Greville] to favour.'[7] It has a special interest because the 'metaphysical note' is attained in what is perhaps the most old-fashioned metre of the native plain style, poulter's measure.[8]

> The Ship of *Greece*, the Streames and she be not the same
> They were, although Ship, Streames and she still beare their antique name.
> The Wood which was, is worne, those waues are runne away,
> Yet still a Ship, and still a Streame, still running to a Sea.
> She lou'd, and still she loues, but doth not still loue me,
> To all except my selfe yet is, as she was wont to be.

Theseus's ship, every plank of which had often been replaced, represents a famous metaphysical puzzle from antiquity. If this were all, Greville's lines would be no more than an allusion to metaphysics. But the allusion is by way of clarification of the central problem, the relationship of the poet and the 'she' of the poem, and that problem is presented in metaphysical terms as puzzling as anything in Donne; it is the problem of identity and difference in love. Can 'she' change and still remain the same? Can the poet suffer change and still remain the same?

> Let no man aske my name, nor what else I should be;
> For *Greiv-Ill*, paine, forlorne estate do best decipher me.

The pun on Greville's own name in the last line of the poem offers a condensed expression of the central problem, for his name refers to what he is, to his essential being, his individual integrity, and simultaneously by means of the pun to his disintegration and loss of identity. If the poem is addressed to Queen Elizabeth, the last line is at once a signature and a beseeching, and it involves a pun on the word 'decipher' as well. Grief, ill, pain, and forlorn estate deprive him of a name, a cipher (*Oxford English Dictionary, s.v.* 6), but if the Queen chooses to recognize Greville, he will no longer be a cipher, a nonentity (*Oxford English Dictionary, s.v.* 2). Greville's name is present merely in potentiality, as it were. It is in the nature of a monarch to have the power to call courtiers into being. The metaphysical note, the note of tension or strain, is not incompatible with the note of elegant compliment; nor are these incompatible with the rustic manners of an old-fashioned verse form.

That James Smith should overlook earlier anticipations of the metaphysical style is perhaps explained by the general account he gives of the distinction between the earlier and the later style.[9]

> The Elizabethans start with an opposition between the intellect and the senses, fail to keep a balance between them, and come down heavily on the side of the senses. Hence they tend to exuberance or to a stolid quality; whereas metaphysical poetry is always alert, and is rarely exuberant, but rather elegaic.

The 'Elizabethans' referred to in the first sentence are pretty clearly limited to the golden stylists (in lyric or in drama) of the late sixteenth century, and while 'exuberant' and 'stolid' leave some room for the distinction between eloquent and plain that we wish to maintain, they do not make sufficient allowance for the alert vigour of poets like Gascoigne, Greville, or Ralegh, nor for an important aspect of Shakespeare.

There is, in fact, no more metaphysical poem than Shakespeare's 'The Phoenix and Turtle'. And Smith's account of metaphysical poetry can be adjusted by bringing it into conjunction with J. V. Cunningham's discussion of Shakespeare's enigmatic poem. 'The material of courtly love in Shakespeare's *Phoenix and Turtle*,' Cunningham demonstrates, 'is treated in terms of scholastic theology' (*CE*, p. 196), specifically in terms of the doctrine of the Trinity – the 'one model in the tradition for the notion that distinct persons may have only one essence' (*CE*, p. 207). The poem is an example of the religion of love carried to its logical extremity; it is the last word in Petrarchan hyperbole. In a sense, we might call it the last word in the golden style, an assessment with which many readers allowing for a difference in terms, might well concur. M. C. Bradbrook, for instance, concludes that 'This great poem, Shakespeare's one work in the Platonic mode, might alone be taken as the justification of courtly poetry.'[10] And F. T. Prince claims that 'What we see in effect is Shakespeare's capacity for "pure" poetry.'[11] Prince, in fact, explicitly denies any suggestion of the metaphysical manner in the poem.

> Nothing could in fact be further from the methods of Donne's love-poetry than the method of this poem. Shakespeare's use of analytic terminology here is free and rhapsodic, a kind of ethereal frenzy; in using it so lavishly, he may well have been influenced by fashion, and by the manner of his fellow-poets writing on this theme, which evidently to them suggested abstract sublimities and verbiage.

Like Middleton Murry and Wilson Knight before him, Prince is baffled by the air of impenetrability in the poem: 'the beauty of the poem consists in a marriage between intense emotion and almost unintelligible fantasy. It is inexhaustible because it is inexplicable, and it is inexplicable because it is deliberately unreasonable, beyond and contrary to both reason and nature.'[12] No one will deny the intense emotion or the air of mystery, but to attribute that air to 'almost unintelligible fantasy' or to the 'free and rhapsodic' use of an analytic terminology is to mistake the source of Shakespeare's invention and to underestimate the intellectual vigour of the poem. As Cunningham demonstrates, the idea that distinct persons may have only one essence is not Neo-Platonic, for, despite the fact that Christianity absorbed a good deal of Platonism, in Neo-Platonism the identity of the soul is lost in the act of union with the One; nor does the idea derive from the scholastic doctrine of love or from the doctrine of the Beatific Vision, for in each of these there is no absolute identification and the persons remain distinct. The middle section of the poem (stanzas 6 to 13) is, as Cunningham carefully documents, a point by point exposition of the scholastic doctrine of the Trinity; that is, it is not an 'ethereal frenzy' nor 'free and rhapsodic' nor a 'fantasy'; it is expository and disciplined and traditional.

> 'The Phoenix and Turtle', whatever its merits, is not a gracious and charming trifle, and could not have been intended as such. One half of the poem consists of a grimly reiterated paradox, stated with the minimum of decoration and the maximum of technical exactitude. The inference is that the poet was trying to say something precisely, and this lays on us the obligation, if we wish to read the poem at all, of trying to find out precisely what he was saying. (*CE*, p. 206)

Or, to translate Cunningham's point slightly, one half of the poem is developed in a rigorously plain style.

> So they lov'd, as love in twain
> Had the essence but in one:
> Two distincts, division none;
> Number there in love was slain.

The diction is abstract, there is no imagery, the syntax consists largely of a series of emphatic declaratives, the rhythm is not mellifluous (there is little enjambment and meaning takes precedence over sound), and the theme is doctrinal. If the poem is beyond reason, that is not because it is contrary to reason, but because it takes us step by step to the very limits of scholastic reasoning, and the sense of mystery is, in large part, the creation of the fully extended and ultimately stymied effort of reason to comprehend the mystery. To appropriate the words of L. A. Cormican, Shakespeare manages to avail himself 'of the unique quality of Christianity – its unique combination of belief in profound mystery with the rigorous probing of exact reason found in, e.g., Augustine and Aquinas'.[13] Shakespeare, with characteristic boldness, invokes the unique combination as the basis of the most extravagant Petrarchan hyperbole.

'The Phoenix and Turtle', then, is not merely the last word in the golden style, but, simultaneously, the last word in the plain style. It exhibits Petrarchan wit and audacity as well as moral seriousness and earnestness, and neither of these dissolves into, or is completely subservient to, the other. It is precisely this sort of surprising conjunction of two styles (we might say of two distinct, and often antithetical, ways of looking at the world, of discovering or creating reality) brought to bear on a metaphysical puzzle that I wish to designate as the 'metaphysical style'. (We might also say, instead of two distinct styles, two distinct language games, recalling Wittgenstein's remark in *Lectures and Conversations*, 'What belongs to a language game is a whole culture.'[14] This is the reason why the two styles must sometimes be differentiated as native and Petrarchan, pointing out the presence of two distinct cultures.) To return to James Smith's description, he suggests that if his definition is 'at all adequate, there should be deducible from it *some of the characters* of metaphysical poetry in general' (my italics). But he goes on to describe only one character, the metaphysical conceit, and it seems unlikely that any other characters are readily forthcoming. And, while we might be willing to allow that the sort of metaphor that Smith quotes as examples and the sort of pun that Greville makes on his own name give a compact expression of the collision of two ways of seeing into the reality of things, the description of a style should be more comprehensive, should take account of more elements of language. The Petrarchan hyperbole and its technical exposition in 'The Phoenix and Turtle' is surely at least as extravagant a device as Donne's figure of the compass in 'Valediction: Forbidding Mourning' and is probably more effective for exploring the problem of unity in the relationship of the two lovers. It appears to me indubitable that it exhibits the metaphysical note of tension or strain. The 'metaphysical note' obtains when disparate styles are yoked by violence together for the purpose of exploring metaphysical problems, 'problems either deriving from, or closely resembling in the nature of their difficulty, the problem of the Many and the One'.

The advantages of our thinking about metaphysical poetry in this way are several. We retain the clarity and precision of Smith's definition while allowing for a wider range of description. Smith claims the metaphysical conceit as central because metaphysicians themselves, he argues, despite their distaste for metaphor, despite their aim 'to make reality as transparent to the intellect as possible', are ultimately driven to metaphor.[15] But this same argument will also serve to support the claim that metaphysical poetry will exhibit stretches of plain or literal statement that culminate in or start from figurative language. Such a claim may suggest why Donne has been alternately described as a 'Petrarchist' and as a master of colloquial speech.[16] It may also suggest why the metaphysical style is a logical development of Elizabethan poetry, since the metaphysical style presupposes the existence of at least two clearly defined styles. And finally, it may suggest why two poets as dissimilar as Jonson and Donne may both be said to have effected a marriage of the two styles in lyric poetry and why 'the relationship of Jonson and Donne is that of . . . perfector to inventor'.[17] In Donne we often see the process of thought, that is, the mind in the act of discovering or inventing various apprehensions of reality: hence the often turbulent alternation of styles. In Jonson, though fewer readers have noticed it, the same effort of thought is often antecedent to the poetry and its product incorporated into the ethical questions Jonson investigates: hence the calm deliberation that characterizes much of Jonson's style. His poem on the death of his first son, for example, calmly accepts, as a reality, the fact that his son's being is something that is 'made' by Jonson and simultaneously only something 'lent' to him. Similarly, in 'An Epistle to Master Arthur Squib' (ll. 18–24) he desiderates that a friend must first be his own man, 'But he that's too much that, is friend of none.'[18] Jonson's understanding of metaphysical issues here is as good as anything in his contemporaries, but he presents his understanding largely in moral terms. It is best, then, to reserve the term 'metaphysical style' for the more experimental and processive work that is characterized by the restless alternation of styles.

By 'alternation' I do not mean that the violent yoking or

marriage of the two styles might not be perceived in one figure, such as the metaphysical conceit, or even in one word, such as the metaphysical pun. Indeed, the conceit remains a distingushing feature, just as Smith claims, of the metaphysical style. If, however, we regard the conceit not primarily as an image but as 'the discovery of a proposition referring to one field of experience in terms of an intellectual structure derived from another field . . .',[19] the relation of the conceit to the violent yoking of two styles on a metaphysical issue is clarified. The metaphysical conceit, and the pun as well, are only compact illustrations of the general development of the metaphysical style. Such a development, at any rate, characterizes the first exchange between Gaunt and Richard in Act II.

> *York.* The King is come, deal mildly with his youth,
> 70   For young hot colts being rein'd do rage the more.
> *Queen.* How fares our noble uncle, Lancaster?
> *Rich.* What comfort, man? how is't with aged Gaunt?
> *Gaunt.* O, how that name befits my composition!
>   Old Gaunt indeed, and gaunt in being old.
> 75   Within me grief hath kept a tedious fast,
>   And who abstains from meat that is not gaunt?
>   For sleeping England long time have I watch'd,
>   Watching breeds leanness, leanness is all gaunt.
>   The pleasures that some fathers feed upon
> 80   Is my strict fast – I mean my children's looks,
>   And therein fasting hast thou made me gaunt.
>   Gaunt am I for the grave, gaunt as a grave,
>   Whose hollow womb inherits nought but bones.
> *Rich.* Can sick men play so nicely with their names?
> 85 *Gaunt.* No, misery makes sport to mock itself:
>   Since thou dost seek to kill my name in me,
>   I mock my name, great king, to flatter thee.
>   (II, i, 69–87)

Whatever is to be said about the style of this passage, it is unquestionably turbulent. Coleridge's well-known defence of Gaunt's puns is based primarily on an appeal to psychological realism; but psychology here is not without moral point, and both morality and psychology are referred emphatically to a metaphysical puzzle. The note of tension or strain in Gaunt's speech is the 'metaphysical note', and his speech is best approached in the terms of the metaphysical style.

Gaunt's speech here, in fact, follows well on his previous analysis of the loss of national integrity because that loss operates as a cause of his own decomposition. To argue so is not to ignore the psychological poignancy of his words; indeed, the preceding few lines by York, the Queen, and Richard sharpen that poignancy. York, after hearing Gaunt's analytical panegyric, responds again in the idiom of the native style, supporting the advice in line 69 with the proverb of line 70. (I follow the Arden editor's reading of 'rein'd' for the 'ragde' of Qq and F – York obviously does mean his proverb to support his advice.) Recognizing that the king must be 'dealt' with in some way, he has modified his original advice slightly, although the homely commonplace is still inadequate to the situation. We may even suppose that Gaunt, at first, attempts to follow his brother's advice. If he is not to tax the king with the state of the nation and his responsibility for it, and if that question is still his major preoccupation, it is natural that he should turn to his own personal condition. If public questions are not to be talked about, one is left with isolated personalities. The first words by the Queen and Richard similarly emphasize Gaunt's personal predicament. The Queen's address, 'How fares our noble uncle, Lancaster?', filling as it does the whole blank verse line and taking the form of adjective-noun and then noun in apposition, recalls the dignity and pomp of the oratorical style. It especially recalls the opening line of the play, 'Old John of Gaunt, time-honoured Lancaster.' But in the next line, Richard's, the style has degenerated to insensitive bluff: 'What comfort, man? how is't with aged Gaunt?' It is one thing to draw attention to a man's age when addressing him in his capacity as a counsellor and quite another thing to do so when visiting his sick-bed. He deprives Gaunt of his titles as he himself is later deprived (III, iii, 5–11 and IV, i, 254–9). As well, the absence of any other modifier but 'aged' for 'Gaunt' and the absence of any modifier for the generic 'man' suggests Richard's imperceptiveness about who or what Gaunt individually is, so that

Gaunt may well feel psychologically threatened.

But granting the psychological nicety of the whole exchange, we may go on to observe its overwhelming metaphysical preoccupations. Coleridge's defence of the puns in this passage, in fact, is remarkably co-ordinate with Smith's description of the kind of strain that characterizes thought about metaphysics.[20]

> He that knows the state of the human mind in deep passion must know that, it approaches to that condition of madness, which is not absolute frenzy or delirium, but which models all things to one reigning idea; still it strays from the main subject of complaint, and still it returns to it, by a sort of irresistible impulse. Abruptness of thought, under such circumstances, is true to nature, and no man was more sensible of it than Shakespeare.

Coleridge remarks that the mind in deep passion is characterized by rapid associations and by a lack of obvious transitions, but he is not talking about mere free association or stream of consciousness, for these associations adhere to 'one reigning idea'. Now if that one reigning idea happens to be metaphysical, and it does in Gaunt's case, Coleridge's analysis is perfectly congruent with Smith's description of the metaphysical conceit; disparate things are yoked by violence, but stay yoked because their association springs from essence. 'It is no association of things on account of a similarity due to an accident, as that a canoe for a moment rested upon a head; but of things that, though hostile, in reality cry out for association with each other.'[21]

The two most prominent meanings of 'Gaunt' and 'gaunt' are hostile, but in the reality of Richard's England they cry out for association with each other. The antitheses in 'Old Gaunt indeed and gaunt in being old' represent a metaphysical puzzle because they simultaneously assert and deny the unity of action and essence. Gaunt in action ('indeed') is gaunt in essence ('in being'), but by means of the pun on the name the line also claims that the actuality of Gaunt is, in fact, privation. The notions of actuality and privation are here brought as violently together as they are in the following lines from 'A Nocturnal upon St. Lucie's Day':[22]

> But I am by her death, (which word wrongs her)
> Of the first nothing, the Elixer grown.

Furthermore, when Gaunt replies to Richard's 'aged Gaunt' with the remark 'O, how that name befits my composition!', there is a kind of pun on the word 'composition' as well because it refers not only to his physical constitution, but to the whole of what he is, including those 'compositions' such as names or epithets by means of which speakers of the language designate what he is. He invokes a puzzle that is central to metaphysics, the relation of language to reality, when he declares, in effect, that his name and his essence are one and the same thing. And again, though these things may seem hostile, there is an important sense in which they cry out for association with each other.

Richard Altick expresses a commonly accepted view of the attitude of the characters towards language: 'That words are mere conventional sounds molded by the tongue, and reality is something else again, is constantly on the minds of all the characters.'[23] But this view suggests that every character holds a conventionalist position as naive as that of Hermogenes in Plato's dialogue *The Cratylus*. The reality in question is human reality, and it is in the nature of human beings to create and use language; language is their unique responsibility. Inga-Stina Ewbank quotes Altick approvingly and goes on to make a particular point about Richard himself: 'most critics agree that *Richard II* is a milestone in Shakespeare's poetic-dramatic development, and that the play – like its poet-hero – is uniquely self conscious about the power *and* limitations of language'.[24] As a character, Richard is unquestionably self-conscious, probably unduly so, but the 'power *and* limitations of language' is just what he does not understand. Consider the end of one of his plainest and most moving speeches.

> Cover your heads, and mock not flesh and blood
> With solemn reverence; throw away respect,
> Tradition, form and ceremonious duty;

For you have but mistook me all this while.
I live with bread like you, feel want,
Taste grief, need friends – subjected thus,
How can you say to me, I am a king? (III, ii, 171-7)

That kings are made of flesh and blood is true, and it is
extraordinarily moving to hear one admit it, but that is
certainly no reason for throwing away respect, tradition,
form and ceremonious duty. These are the very things by
means of which we establish a sense of coherence and continuity in the face of the mutability of particular things.
Despite the plainness of style, Richard's lines still reveal a
tendency to exploit feeling at the expense of matter, for
he intends his rhetorical question (l. 177) primarily as an
invitation to the others to commiserate with him, but the
question really does need an answer. Carlisle, in the lines
immediately following, advises him to take action, but
Richard just as urgently needs to take thought. His failure
to distinguish properly between the particular and the
universal is a metaphysical error with serious implications
for human conduct, that is, for moral and political action.
Action issues out of one's best insight into what is real.
Far from the radical division of language and reality that
Richard (along with some of his critics) asserts, there is
an essential unity of the two. The same world (that is, the
human world) that is responsible for the maintenance of
language is responsible for sustaining kingship. The word
'king' is simultaneously a literal description of the individual
being in which kingship is necessarily embodied and a metaphorical description of the human community, a fact which
we recognize in the simple and profound declaration 'The
king is dead, long live the king!' Richard is too little conscious of the nature of language and of kingship.[25] The 'poet-
hero' of *Richard II* falters through his inability to understand
a metaphor and to make full use of language. That is to say,
despite what numerous critics have said about him, he fails
to be poetic enough to merit the epithet 'poet-hero'.
    When Richard responds to Gaunt's punning on his own
name by asking 'Can sick men play so nicely with their
names?', 'nicely' means primarily 'fancifully', or 'foolishly',

and he supposes that Gaunt has been merely indulging in the verbal ingenuity of the golden style. But Gaunt's reply draws attention to the pressure of his subject matter, to his 'one reigning idea': 'No, misery makes sport to mock itself.' 'Misery' is 'distress caused by privation' (*Oxford English Dictionary*) and thus refers both to Gaunt's feeling and to his subject. (Woe and wonder seem to me alike in this respect in that each refers both to an emotion and its cause: 'wonder' designates an emotion and is also a synonym for 'not-knowing', a state of mind causing the emotion.) His ingenious manner is at once a sign of his emotional state and is justified by his matter. To turn Coleridge's phrase around, what we see represented here in Gaunt is human passion in deep thought.

> Since thou dost seek to kill my name in me,
> I mock my name, great King, to flatter thee.

Editors frequently take the phrase 'kill my name' to refer to the banishment of Bolingbroke, but, considering Gaunt's equation of his name and his essence, this concluding couplet must refer to this and more. No simple answer can be given to the question 'What is Gaunt?', but three of the most prominent answers are: brother to Thomas Woodstock, counsellor to the English throne, and father to Bolingbroke. Richard has 'killed' each of these names in Gaunt and, therefore, in so far as Gaunt's essence subsists in them, it is reduced. There is no small force in the Duchess of Gloucester's first argument in her attempt to stir Gaunt to avenge the death of Thomas (whose murder both clearly believe is Richard's responsibility): 'and though thou livest and breathest,/ Yet art thou slain in him' (I, ii, 24–5). That Gaunt's identity as a counsellor is threatened is sufficiently demonstrated in the exchange with York, where it is clear that Gaunt's opinion on how things should be carries little weight with Richard. The three aspects of his identity are suggested by three items in his punning speech. The 'grief' of line 75 is left unspecified, but the fountainhead of grief in this play, the subject of discussion between Gaunt and the Duchess in I, ii, the occasion of Bolingbroke's challenge and perhaps the chief motive for his banishment, is the murdered Woodstock.

This 'grief' is followed by a reference to his duty as watchman or counsellor to England and one to his pleasure as a father. Pain, duty, and pleasure: this great triad describing the activity of a life is accompanied by another that is crucial to any account of what a character is: past, present, and future. 'Hath kept' and 'have I watch'd' are both in the past tense; 'is my strict fast' is in the present; and 'Gaunt am I for the grave' is future. His vision of the extinction of his being follows inevitably out of his consideration of what he has been in the past. His attempt to think about what he is involves concomitant recognition of what he is not and the painful realization that what he is and what he is not are one and the same thing. If his essence subsists in his name, and if 'Gaunt' is the only title he is left with, then his essence is 'gaunt'. If his being is visible in what he does, and if what he does is scarcely perceptible, then his essence is 'gaunt'.

The organization of this speech is peculiar to the metaphysical style. The golden and the moral styles are brought together in a kind of deadlock that is truly one aspect of marriage, but not harmonious marriage. Each style is stretched to its limit, and each style seems to deal with ostensibly the same theme as the other, but each seems to fight against, rather than support the other. In a sense Shakespeare needs the elaborate static design of the golden style: hence the repeated use of antithesis and paradox and the rapid connotative connections of antithetical pairs such as, 'Gaunt–gaunt', 'fast–feed', 'sleeping–watching', 'grief–pleasure', 'watch'd–looks', 'meat–bones', 'thou–me', 'womb–grave'. At the same time he also needs the moral energy of the plain style, for his character is attempting to live his impossible dilemma. As has been demonstrated, Gaunt's interest transcends mere delight in elaborate design and is focused on understanding what is the case and what he should do. For example, with the exception of the metaphorical 'fasting', the moral indignation in line 81, 'and therein fasting hast thou made me gaunt', could not be plainer. The effort to think things through rationally is evident in the careful analysis of the most important aspects of his being, considered in the past, present, and future. And the attempt to reach sufficient insight to guide conduct is illustrated in Gaunt's use of the figure Thomas Wilson calls 'gradation': 'Gradation is when a sentence is dissevered by degrees, so that the word which endeth the sentence going before doeth begin the next.'[26] Thus: 'For sleeping England long time have I watch'd,/ Watching breeds leanness, leanness is all gaunt.' The momentum generated by this eloquent device is a source of intensified feeling, but the divisions aid the rational investigation of the causes of that feeling. Gaunt is not content merely to indulge his emotions, but endeavours to see what their justification is. He asserts the integrity of his own being in the context of something other and larger than himself – in this case, England – but since England is itself diminishing, he sees his own disintegration. His allegiance to his country ought to increase his being, but with Richard as the chief representative of that country, deflecting such loyalties to less honourable purposes, allegiance to it becomes mere flattery. The metaphysical style, then, brings two opposed ranges of thought and feeling (two opposed perceptions of reality) into violent conjunction in order to exhibit a certain kind of impasse in human affairs.

Actually, the impasse should not be thought of as exactly a *cul-de-sac* because, while it represents the limits of a certain kind of investigation, the resulting clarity in locating the boundaries of human perception invigorates other kinds of endeavour. Beyond a certain point Gaunt's personal predicament is impenetrable, but his realization of that fact and some of its causes lends a kind of potency to his more didactic remarks that they could not achieve any other way. The panegyric by itself might make his moral analysis seem grandiose or even vaporous; the personal predicament, without its social and political context, would be wholly unintelligible.

With the main points established, it is possible to proceed more quickly through the rest of the exchange between Gaunt and Richard until we glimpse the mature Shakespearean style. In the series of one-line exchanges (II, i, 88–92) the hostility between the two becomes more overt, and this leads Gaunt to reprove Richard in strongly moral terms.

> Thy death-bed is no lesser than thy land,
> Wherein thou liest in reputation sick,

> And thou, too careless patient as thou art,
> Commit'st thy anointed body to the cure
> Of those physicians that first wounded thee:
> 100 A thousand flatterers sit within thy crown,
> Whose compass is no bigger than thy head,
> And yet, incaged in so small a verge,
> The waste is no whit lesser than thy land.
> O, had thy grandsire with a prophet's eye
> 105 Seen how his son's son should destroy his sons,
> From forth thy reach he would have laid thy shame,
> Deposing thee before thou wert possess'd,
> Which art possess'd now to depose thyself.
>   (II, i, 95–108)

The style here is essentially plain and certainly didactic, though it incorporates a good bit of the Petrarchan enrichment. Terms of moral approbation and disapprobation predominate: 'in reputation sick', 'careless patient', 'cure', 'anointed body', 'physicians', 'flatterers', 'waste', 'destroy', 'shame', 'possess'd'. The spiritual sanctions underlying Gaunt's use of these terms are never very far to seek. Explicit in 'anointed body', they are also invoked in terms such as 'flatterers' and 'waste'. A flatterer is one who gives false praise to serve his own purposes; Gaunt denounces flattery throughout this passage not merely because it is false, but because it is actively hostile to the service of larger purposes, to the disinterested attachment germane to spiritual life. 'Waste', according to Onions's *A Shakespeare Glossary*, has a specific legal meaning that is relevant here: 'destruction of houses, woods, lands, etc., done by the tenant to the prejudice of the heir'.[27] The implication is that Richard's 'land' is not merely his; he is something like a 'tenant' holding the land in trust for something other and larger than himself. A similar pun on 'verge' (meaning either 'limit' or 'the area extending to a distance of twelve miles round the king's court, and, therefore, under his direct jurisdiction')[28] suggests the paradox of kingship. The land, the verge, the crown are Richard's, but they are not his to waste. The chiasmic ordering of lines 107 and 108 enforces the same point: possession of the throne by an individual does not mean that the throne is subject to the whims of one individual, and to imagine that it is is to fail to be a king.

In other words, the charge 'Landlord of England art thou now, not king' that is properly the climax of Gaunt's diatribe is not simply a remark about the economic state of the nation but a serious moral and spiritual denunciation.

> Why, cousin, wert thou regent of the world,
> 110   It were a shame to let this land by lease;
> But for thy world enjoying but this land,
> Is it not more than shame to shame it so?
> Landlord of England art thou now, not king,
> Thy state of law is bondslave to the law,
> 115   And thou –
> *Rich.*   A lunatic lean-witted fool,
> Presuming on an ague's privilege,
> Darest with thy frozen admonition
> Make pale our cheek, chasing the royal blood
> With fury from his native residence.
> 120   Now by my seat's right royal majesty,
> Wert thou not brother to great Edward's son,
> This tongue that runs so roundly in thy head
> Should run thy head from thy unreverent shoulders.
>
>   (II, i, 109–23)

Peter Ure remarks that in line 115 'Richard breaks into Gaunt's speech and uses his *thou* as if it referred to Gaunt himself', but Shakespeare, by means of the integrity of the line established through observing the convention of blank verse, refers the meaning primarily to Richard himself. In other words, the poetry (that is, the metre) insists on this as the primary meaning, whereas theatrical declamation would force the meaning the other way, limiting and damaging the intention expressed in the line.

And since Richard's whole speech refers in a more important way to himself than to Gaunt, the right reading of the line is critical. Richard's refusal, or his inability, to recognize the legitimate basis of Gaunt's complaint is represented as a failure of intelligence amounting to a kind of madness. He fails to perceive the nature of Gaunt's sickness and of its implications for his own case, and he refuses to understand the distinction between 'landlord' and 'king,' a distinction crucial to Gaunt's view of the nation and a clear statement of the antithesis embedded in 'a paltry farm' versus 'this royal throne of Kings'. When Richard refers to 'thy frozen admonition' (l. 117) he means what Sidney calls a 'winter-starved' figure or what the classical rhetorician, Demetrius, calls 'frigidity', that is, the application of figures and phrases formula-like, without sufficient regard to the matter.[29] But Gaunt's figure, though aggressively stated, has a propriety that Richard would do well to ponder. Instead he is pre-occupied with the effect that the admonition has on his own countenance, and in

> Make pale our cheek, chasing the royal blood
> With fury from his native residence

he is guilty of the very frigidity he alleges in Gaunt. That is, he is absorbed in the emotional effect of his own figure to the exclusion of the intellectual content that should accompany that effect. Ure's note (citing Herford) is once again helpful: 'All this may imply that "high colour, easily yielding to deadly pallor, was part of Shakespeare's conception of Richard." But pallor is also a conventional sign of shock in Shakespeare.' Shock, we remember, is that species of fear, sometimes called amazement or stupefaction, that is an impediment to thought. Richard is simply stunned by Gaunt's speech and is thereby rendered incapable of pondering its significance; he recognizes that it is an admonition without recognizing what the admonition is. And like Soliman in *Mustapha*, he is paralysed by a kind of fear that can find expression only in hostility. Thus the frigid style of lines 115–19 turns naturally into the bombastic style of lines 120–3, including the line-filling oath of line 120, the resounding epithet of line 121, and the wild threat of lines 122 and 123. It is worth noting that line 122, 'This tongue that runs so roundly in thy head' repeats the charge of frigidity and that line 123, 'Should run thy head from thy unreverent shoulders' adds the charge of a lack of wonder or awe. Neither charge is applicable to Gaunt; both are applicable to Richard. The whole of Richard's speech, then, redounds to his discredit, and it is for this reason that the ironic transposition of line 115 introducing the speech must be clearly understood.

Shakespeare's verse, in other words, here approaches that complexity that will come to be characteristic of his style, and which, because it is unprecedented and inimitable, we call simply Shakespearean. Gaunt's final reply to Richard provides the fullest glimpse in *Richard II* of that mature style.

> O, spare me not, my brother Edward's son,
> 125 For that I was his father Edward's son;
> That blood already, like the pelican,
> Hast thou tapp'd out and drunkenly carous'd:
> My brother Gloucester, plain well-meaning soul,
> Whom fair befall in heaven 'mongst happy souls,
> 130 May be a president and witness good
> That thou respect'st not spilling Edward's blood.
> Join with the present sickness that I have,
> And thy unkindness be like crooked age,
> To crop at once a too long withered flower.
> 135 Live in thy shame, but die not shame with thee!
> These words hereafter thy tormentors be!
> Convey me to my bed, then to my grave –
> Love they to live that love and honour have.
> (II, i, 124–38)

J. V. Cunningham, in his unpublished dissertation, speaks of the Shakespearean 'transmutation' that turns 'idea into intuition'. He goes on to define intuition as 'a concentration of consciousness, with a subsequent heightening of the intensity of apprehension and a corollary shortening of the span of attention'.[30] An intuition, as presented in Shakespearean metaphor, offers different orders of experience and understanding possessed simultaneously in synthesis. Though characterized by its opposition to discursive reasoning, intuitive thought is not irrational, nor is it idiosyncratic; at its best it is impersonal.

Consider three lines in the middle of Gaunt's speech:

> Join with the present sickness that I have,
> And thy unkindness be like crooked age,
> To crop at once a too long withered flower.

97

Gaunt himself is very old: he is 'crooked age', he is in an advanced state of decay ('a too long withered flower'), and he is about to die – the flower is about to be cropped. A natural process, the process of aging, leads inevitably to 'present sickness' and culminates in death. But added to this is an unnatural process, referred to most explicitly in the word 'unkindness', which, as Wells reminds us, would have had a stronger sense for the Elizabethans than it has for us.[31] This sense, playing heavily on the multiple meanings of the word 'kind', is particularly appropriate to the quarrel between Gaunt and Richard, having to do with the bonds of nature and kinship, the proper relationship between kin, and between a king and his subjects. The word 'like' indicates a simile, though we are meant to comprehend not only similarity, but difference – in fact, mainly difference. Unkindness is not being likened to old age; the point is that two highly disparate things produce the same result. This is very far from simile as it is ordinarily understood and very close to the inimitable phrase in *Macbeth*: 'And Pity, like a naked newborn babe/ Striding the blast . . .', where, as F. R. Leavis points out, the word 'like' attributes a radically disjunctive sense of power and vulnerability to Pity.[32] The agency of crooked age is a natural process; unkindness is unnatural; yet the two are alike in serving a common end: both bring death. Furthermore, while crooked age represents feebleness, unkindness (particularly the unkindness demonstrated by Richard) is violent and energetic (consider Richard's preceding speech). Gaunt's death is caused by Richard's youth as well as by Gaunt's old age, by Richard's violence as well as by Gaunt's feebleness. And it is caused by Gaunt's own violence as well as by his feebleness. This cause fulfils the prophecy issued by York earlier in the scene that Gaunt will lose his breath in talking to Richard. Even while announcing that he is sick and feeble, Gaunt demonstrates vigour and agitation, seen clearly in the series of imperatives of which 'Join with . . . ' is one. Gaunt's sickness is joined by his agitation in the figure of crooked age, and that agitation is clearly attributable to, but not the same as, Richard's unkindness. Moreover, Richard's unkindness is a sickness to which Gaunt responds properly (that is, healthily) with

98

an admonition. Richard's sickness, for that is what he has despite the outward appearance of youth and health, is in fact the product of youthful irresponsibility and immaturity, which is so susceptible to disease that it might as well be crooked age. Gaunt is old, physically sick and feeble, suffering under a natural process, concerned for the commonwealth, a respecter of the ties of kinship, and is spiritually healthy and vigorous; Richard is young, physically healthy and energetic, perpetrating unnaturalness, oblivious to the commonwealth, a violator of the ties of kinship, and is spiritually diseased and indolent. Thus, despite the use of the word 'like', the dominant impression of the metaphor is the vast difference between Gaunt and Richard.

The maintenance of distinctions, of course, is the hallmark of reason. Shakespearean intuition, far from being irrational, is a triumph of condensed rationality. And, though we may be startled to find how much lengthy and clumsy discursive analysis is necessary even to approach the full significance of Shakespeare's expression, and how insecure such analysis seems to be in comparison to the original expression, the intuition is yet the product of reason and is accessible to rational understanding. An intuition is an expression that is central, brief, and compendious. The Shakespearean metaphor reminds us of what is well-known or obvious – so obvious that we are apt to forget or overlook it (in this case, that both natural and unnatural acts contribute to the coming on of death) – and it does this with a felicity of phrasing that makes it seem indisputably right. It crystallizes and focuses a whole tradition of human thought and experience so that, although necessarily spoken by an individual speaker, it attains to a kind of impersonality or universality. Cunningham comments on this phenomenon:[33]

The spontaneous phrase may sum in a few words and with a compelling accent what the analytic mind has failed to display in many pages. There is, when it is successful, a kind of excess in spontaneous utterance, a kind of going out and beyond the normal personality. We often attempt to explain this by such catchwords as 'inspiration' or 'inevitability'. It is the kind of impersonality which Paul Valery notes in the following sentence, though he notes it to disapprove of it: 'The spontaneous thing,' he says, 'however excellent, however charming, never seems to me to be quite mine'.

But what is involved in such triumphant facility? Perhaps we should ascribe it to the Grace of God or to some daimoniac influence, but it would be indecorous to trouble the supra-terrestrial with such terrestrial concerns. Would it not be better to say that the man who has a perfected mastery of his medium and of his subject and who in addition is moved to exercise these upon a happy occasion may often do his best work most easily? But this is to say that he has attained the habit of art, it is to say that the perfected mastery which we postulate is the stable, habitual, and intimate adjustment of creation and criticism in the act of production.

Cunningham's explanation of spontaneity in poetry is directed towards the poet's technique and is, as it seems to me, unanswerable. We may go on, however, to observe the ramification of this view for the creation of tragic character. John of Gaunt's metaphor is of the same order, though not as great as, 'reason panders will' from *Hamlet* and 'ripeness is all' from *King Lear*. Indeed, the figure of crooked age cropping 'at once a too long withered flower' has an inherent affinity with 'ripeness is all'. As Richard says later, 'The ripest fruit first falls, and so doth he' (l. 153). The death of individual human beings is a fact that is inevitable, universal, and providential; to recognize and accept this fact is the aspiration of the tragic hero. On the other hand, it is an act of presumption on Richard's part to pretend to recognize and accept it on someone else's behalf. Gaunt's metaphor is simultaneously an acquiescence in his own inevitable death and a rebellion against the meddling and officious human will that would 'rough hew' that end. It is a more vigorous account of the simple truth with which Gaunt admonishes Richard in Act I.

> Shorten my days thou canst with sullen sorrow,
> And pluck nights from me, but not lend a morrow.

(I, iii, 227–8)

Samuel Johnson, in the notes to his edition of the play, singles out these lines for special commendation: 'It is a matter of very melancholy consideration, that all human advantages confer more power of doing evil than good.'[34]

In Gaunt's final speech, sadness deepens into serenity. The feeling is more impersonal and universal, and the thought more profound. The verbs in '*Join* with the present sickness that I have/ And thy unkindness *be* like crooked age . . .' are an ironic use of the optative subjunctive mood. A. C. Partridge explains that the optative subjunctive exists for the expression of realizable wishes and resembles the imperative, 'as in *Rule*, Britannia.'[35] In commanding Richard to 'join' and 'be', Gaunt is pointing out the impropriety in Richard's behaviour that allows such wishes to be so nearly realizable. Apprehending fully the human actions contributing to his decline, and subordinating them to the mysterious natural processes that delimit men's lives, Gaunt expresses the emotion appropriate to the imminence of his own death ('let it be'). Tragic impersonality is acquiescence in the deepest understanding of human consciousness. The Shakespearean intuition, then, has a peculiar fitness for the conclusive tragic action, death, for to repeat our definition: intuition is a concentration of consciousness, with a subsequent heightening of the intensity of apprehension and a corollary shortening of the span of attention.

The tone of John of Gaunt's last speech is determined largely by the series of imperatives and subjunctives. The most common error in reading the speech is to get the tone wrong by attributing too much weight to the energy of the imperative and too little to the thought of the subjunctive.[36] A. L. French, for example, offers an extremely interesting surmise about the motivation behind Richard's seizure of the Lancastrian estate and Bolingbroke's return to England. Adopting the view that the drama asks us to 'take Bolingbroke's return to be the *consequence* of Richard's action, though temporally this is impossible', French argues that Bolingbroke has no alternative but to return because Richard's action is making him a nonentity, 'not only lacking an inheritance, not only lacking rights, but also lacking any place in the social-moral order'.[37] Thus, it is not necessary to impute any ulterior motive (beyond survival) to Bolingbroke's return, nor is it necessary to suppose him capable of what he is clearly not capable of – any very deep view of the implications of his return. On the other hand, neither is Richard's action a product of thought. Though he had previously considered using Lancastrian 'coffers' (I, iv, 61), his sudden decision to seize the whole estate is, as French claims, an act of revenge 'for being accused of murder in public by Gaunt. Richard cannot strike at Gaunt, who is now beyond man's reach; so he will strike at Gaunt's son, Bolingbroke – of whom he is in any case violently envious (see I, iv, 23f.) and who painfully embarrassed him over the Woodstock affair. Is not motivation of this kind eminently Shakespearean?'[38] To French's question, we may return a tentative 'yes'. The 'yes' is only tentative because, while Richard's motivation is complex, it is not as eminently Shakespearean as the thought evinced in John of Gaunt's last speech.

French misses this fact because he supposes the tone to be predominantly one of anger. He believes that Gaunt's purpose is accusatory, that 'Gaunt's answering blow is annihilating', and that 'Gaunt has changed his mind' about taxing Richard with the murder.[39] To be sure, there is some anger in the following lines: 'That blood already, like the pelican,/ Hast thou tapp'd out and drunkenly carous'd' (ll. 126–7): especially in line 127, though the allusion to the pelican in the previous line, with its suggestions of sacrifice, qualifies the anger. Gaunt, one remembers, was prepared to contemplate the extremity of self-sacrifice (ll. 67–8), and the accusation here seems to be primarily that Richard does not understand the nature of such sacrifices. There is even some anger in the two lines preceding these: 'O, Spare me not, my brother Edward's son,/ For that I was his father Edward's son' (ll. 124–5); though here the epithets that might look bombastic are repeated to enforce the distinctions that are latent, but unrealized, in Richard's purely bombastic epithet (l. 121). But Gaunt's imperative is not an annihilating blow. It is one last resigned attempt to make Richard perceive the fundamental truth about his reign. We might paraphrase lines 124–31 crudely: 'Do not pretend that ties of blood will prevent you from killing me, for Gloucester's death should be sufficient proof to disabuse you.' The paraphrase brings out the element of argument in Gaunt's imperatives. It leaves out the resonance of thought and feeling in that argument.

> My brother Gloucester, plain well-meaning soul,
> Whom fair befall in heaven 'mongst happy souls,
> May be a president and witness good
> That thou respect'st not spilling Edward's blood.
>
> (ll. 128–31)

These lines are essentially plain. They are the most explicit statement of what a number of Richard's subjects believe to be the literal truth and what none of Richard's associates takes the trouble to deny.[40] The verb in line 130 is in the optative subjunctive mood. It directs attention to a wish so nearly realizable that everyone but Richard admits it to be a fact. That Gaunt should need to wish Richard recognize this truth is perhaps occasion for regret, but, as line 129 suggests, any attempt to redress Gloucester's misfortune lies in 'the will of heaven' (I, ii, 6). Gaunt, in other words, has not in the least 'changed his mind' about avenging the murder of Woodstock. His speech is motivated not by revenge, but by the desire to breathe wholesome counsel to his king.

And even though that desire draws its energy in part from anger, the dominant tone of the speech is resigned. Gaunt's opening phrase 'O, spare me not' is not primarily an angry imperative, but a calm and rueful declaration: 'I do not wish to be spared for the reason you give.' The tone of Shakespeare's plain style, in other words, is harmonious with the tone of the Shakespearean metaphor. The conjunction of the two is not inconsistent. The boldness and resonance of metaphor depends upon a concise and vigorous plain style. Gaunt's speech concludes:

> Live in thy shame, but die not shame with thee!
> These words hereafter thy tormentors be!
> Convey me to my bed, then to my grave –
> Love they to live that love and honour have. (ll. 135–8)

Though these lines might be read as an expression of despair, they are an expression of acquiescence in the existing order of things. That that order perpetuates shame is the simple truth. But acquiescence is possible only for a man on his death-bed; for the living it is torment. To summarize the point of the speech in another way, Gaunt can give advice (imperative) by saying what should or should not be the case (optative or subjunctive or both) and finally by describing what is the case (ironic optative or indicative). The last line of his speech is, in fact, indicative though it feels like the optative subjunctive because of the inverted word order, because of the momentum of the preceding lines, and because his own case is so clearly excluded from the indefinite plural 'they'. It is his last word; and it is tragically impersonal.

In affirming the values (love and honour) that give order to human lives, Gaunt delivers his last two lines in a form that itself exhibits a hierarchical order – the closed couplet. I will have more to say about this form later, but for the moment it will serve to introduce the immediate issue – the way in which Gaunt's character in action and the style by which that is delineated provide a standard for measuring the diction, thought, character, and action of other figures and other stretches in the play. That in Gaunt Shakespeare achieves a depth of perspective consciousness worthy of tragedy, there can be no doubt. But this very depth exposes the shallowness of some other parts of the work. Richard and York, in the final eight lines of the stretch I have been using as a touchstone, continue to employ the form introduced by Gaunt – the closed couplet.

> *Rich.* And let them die that age and sullens have,
>   For both has thou, and both become the grave.
> *York.* I do beseech your Majesty, impute his words
>   To wayward sickliness and age in him;
>   He loves you, on my life, and holds you dear,
>   As Harry Duke of Herford, were he here.
> *Rich.* Right, you say true; as Herford's love, so his;
>   As theirs, so mine; and all be as it is. (II, i, 139–46)

As a form, the closed couplet provides a 'core of connotation' suggesting balance, clarity and detachment. The suggestion may or may not be realized, of course. In York and Richard, the perspectives of polyphonic cosmic coherence are reduced to simple-minded antitheses. In attempting to defend Gaunt, York does little more than corroborate Richard's 'age and sullens' with 'sickliness and age'. On the last two couplets Stanley Wells comments: 'York means that Gaunt loves Richard as much as he loves his son; but Richard embarrasses him by taking him to mean "as much as Bolingbroke loves you".' Richard's last couplet gives the impression of being packed with careful distinctions, but in fact it reduces everything to a conflict of personalities. Ignoring completely the spiritual and moral authority that infuses almost every word by John of Gaunt, ignoring too the power of the optative and the subjunctive to create reality, Richard accedes to a lesser vision of reality: 'and all be as it is'. From the perspective of John of Gaunt and from the perspective of II, i, 1–146, that reality is seen to be less than tragic. Yet it is also true that the larger part of *Richard II* (and almost every effort of critical interpretation) is given over to studying the opposition of Richard and Bolingbroke. To that opposition we now turn.

6 · Reductions: style and the character of Bolingbroke

As he does for the character of John of Gaunt, Shakespeare bestows on Bolingbroke a mastery of style ranging from eloquent to plain speech. Something curious happens, however, in Bolingbroke's speeches, and neither his plainness nor his eloquence has the resonance that characterizes Gaunt. Even in those situations where Bolingbroke's speech and action might appear in a most favourable light, he is presented in language that cannot but reduce his stature.

A high point of sympathy for Bolingbroke in the play comes in Act I, scene iii when, after pressing for justice in the case of Woodstock's murder and after risking his life in order to arraign Thomas Mowbray in that case, he must suffer banishment. The sentence of banishment is not only passed down by his king, who is obscurely implicated in the murder, but also agreed to by his father (I, iii, 233–46). Gaunt's attempt at consolation has a Polonius-like flavour that makes Bolingbroke's refusal to be consoled seem not wholly improper. But at the same time, the refusal is not wholly admirable either.

> *Gaunt.* All places that the eye of heaven visits
> Are to a wise man ports and happy havens.
> Teach thy necessity to reason thus –
> There is no virtue like necessity.
> Think not the king did banish thee,
> 280 But thou the king. Woe doth the heavier sit
> Where it perceives it is but faintly borne.
> Go, say I sent thee forth to purchase honour,
> And not the king exil'd thee; or suppose
> Devouring pestilence hangs in our air,
> 285 And thou art flying to a fresher clime.
> Look what thy soul holds dear, imagine it
> To lie that way thou goest, not whence thou com'st.
> Suppose the singing birds musicians,

The grass whereon thou tread'st the presence strew'd,
290   The flowers fair ladies, and thy steps no more
Than a delightful measure or a dance;
For gnarling sorrow hath less power to bite
The man that mocks at it and sets it light.
Bol.   O, who can hold a fire in his hand
295   By thinking on the frosty Caucasus?
Or cloy the hungry edge of appetite
By bare imagination of a feast?
Or wallow naked in December snow
By thinking on fantastic summer's heat?
300   O no, the apprehension of the good
Gives but greater feeling to the worse.
Fell sorrow's tooth doth never rankle more
Than when he bites, but lanceth not the sore.
(I, iii, 275–303)

The generalizations comprising the first seven lines of Gaunt's consolation are proverbial and therefore, for our purposes, are plain style. But the notions, as applied here, are platitudinous, coming as they do rather too easily and without sufficient reference to any particular case.[1] It is not until line 282, and following, that Gaunt introduces three reasons that are genuinely conciliatory. While it is not satisfactory to deny the king's part in the action (ll. 283–4), it is true that Bolingbroke has been 'sent forth' by his father (here privately and earlier publicly) to purchase honour. 'Devouring pestilence', at least in a figurative sense of depravity and subterfuge, is certainly present in England. And the spiritual hint in 'Look what thy soul holds dear' should be persuasive in view of Bolingbroke's avowed concern with the spiritual welfare of his country and his own persistent interest in pilgrimage.

If this were all, Bolingbroke would have to refute arguments of some substance. But the speech of consolation becomes progressively more eloquent and more purely fantastic. The imagery of lines 288 to 291 is from the standard repertoire of the golden style, so that the stoical generalization coming at the end loses some of its force. 'Mocks at it' (l. 293) appears to mean primarily 'escapes from sorrow' or 'replaces it with imaginary delights' rather than 'diminishes its power by setting it in a proper scale of value'. Bolingbroke's reply, then, seems to be rightly indignant and properly sceptical of 'fantastic' consolations. Using an anti-Petrarchan plain style such as invigorates sonnet 130 'My mistress' eyes are nothing like the sun', Shakespeare has Bolingbroke elaborate a series of antitheses in order to reject the unsatisfactory and solipsistic golden world of consolation. Unfortunately, he rejects the moral and spiritual elements along with the fantastic. His concluding generalization beginning at line 300 mentions 'the good', but the only particular goods he cites are protection from extremes of heat (ll. 294, 295) and cold (ll. 298, 299) and freedom from hunger (ll. 296, 297). 'The good' for Bolingbroke is comprised of shelter, clothing, and food. He is, in other words, a utilitarian and a materialist. Or, to put the point another way, Bolingbroke here rejects the way of looking at the world represented by the golden style, but the turn is not toward the moral style; the turn is toward a plain style devoid, as far as possible, of moral energy.[2] Here, as not infrequently elsewhere, Shakespeare seems to anticipate prevalent attitudes of the modern world.

Bolingbroke's character, however, is not simply a matter of material interests and practical energies. In matters touching his own person he is capable of a fine sense of moral outrage, though since the outrage is not conditioned by perspectives as broad and deep as those of John of Gaunt, the morality gives way to political opportunism and private grievance. Following Richard's intolerable seizure of his 'rights and royalties', Bolingbroke continues to appear in a fairly sympathetic light at the opening of Act III. Nor does his brisk dispatch of Bushy and Greene do him much discredit, though it should be noted that he disclaims responsibility even in the act of assuming power (III, i, 5-7).[3] But after a number of vague and unsubstantiated general accusations, he reveals his essential character in a list of his real personal grievances.

> Myself – a prince by fortune of my birth,
> Near to the king in blood, and near in love,
> Till you did make him misinterpret me –
> Have stoop'd my neck under your injuries,
> 20   And sigh'd my English breath in foreign clouds,

Eating the bitter bread of banishment,
Whilst you have fed upon my signories,
Dispark'd my parks and fell'd my forest woods,
From my own windows torn my household coat,
25 Rac'd out my imprese, leaving me no sign,
Save men's opinions and my living blood,
To show the world I am a gentleman.
This and much more, much more than twice all this,
Condemns you to the death. See them delivered over
To execution and the hands of death. (III, i, 16–30)

As A. L. French claims, the emphasis of line 27 must mean, 'to show the world I am *even* a gentleman – far less a nobleman of the blood-royal'. French goes on to point out that 'this charge is the climax of his indictment, and that his accusations that Bushy and Greene have made free with his wealth are less emphatic. It is the moral insult, the attack on his identity as a person, that really hurts – just as Richard intended it should, when he took his original decision in a moment of folly prompted by uncontrollable rage.'[4] French also remarks on the irony that Richard learns the same existential lesson (IV, i, 255-9) when he becomes 'an un-person, just as Bolingbroke was'. But without denying the validity of this argument, it is possible to observe that Bolingbroke's concept of his own identity is narrowly confined in a way that Gaunt's view of himself is not.

To begin with, despite the legitimacy of his complaint, one must be struck by its narrow focus. The vigorous metaphors involving 'English breath' and 'bitter bread' and the trenchant and energetic verbs, 'stoop'd', 'sigh'd', 'fed', 'dispark'd', 'fell'd', 'torn', and 'rac'd', are all directed toward an intense sense of his own isolated identity, without much regard for its larger implications. The most prominent word throughout the speech is some form of the first person singular, usually the possessive adjective 'my'. Bolingbroke's repeated 'my' may be contrasted with Gaunt's 'this'. The contrast reveals how incapable Bolingbroke is of perceiving his own individual identity in the context of national and spiritual identity. Of course he does make gestures in this direction. It may be the case that his motives in demanding some sort of resolution to the question of responsibility for Gloucester's murder were honourable; it may be true that his intentions were mis-interpreted to the king. But Shakespeare characterizes him as either incapable of saying or reluctant to say what those motives were or how they were misinterpreted. The conclusion of the speech is no more than a rhetorical flourish, and any reasons, beyond the merely personal, for executing Bushy and Greene are excluded by the gesture.

> This and much more, much more than twice all this,
> Condemns you to the death.

As Kenneth Muir notes, 'he does not mention the forced loans and the farming of the land';[5] nor does he mention the death of Woodstock. His earlier concern (if he had it) for larger moral issues has receded, and the elaborate balance of the eloquent style is used merely to hide the absence of matter. He uses eloquence not to enrich moral understanding, but to avoid it.

A similar act of evasion occurs in Act III, scene iii. This scene involves the crucial confrontation of Bolingbroke and Richard at Flint Castle. Sympathy for the two characters is about equally balanced. Richard's increasing vulnerability renders his case more poignant, but his foolishness is still much in evidence. Bolingbroke's grievances are still very real, but his inability to contemplate the full reach of his actions reduces the stature of his character and strictly qualifies our admiration of it. The inability is exhibited in Bolingbroke's long speech before Flint Castle. R. F. Hill, following Coleridge, suggests that the 'personification of the ruined castle insinuates the ruin of Richard himself' and that 'Bolingbroke's rhetoric is an instrument for the execution of power'.[6] This may be so, but it is also an instrument for thwarting the sources of human responsibility.

> *Bol.* Noble lord,
> Go to the rude ribs of that ancient castle,
> Through brazen trumpet send the breath of parle
> Into his ruin'd ears, and thus deliver:
> 35 Henry Bolingbroke
> On both his knees doth kiss King Richard's hand,

And sends allegiance and true faith of heart
To his most royal person; hither come
Even at his feet to lay my arms and power,
40   Provided that my banishment repeal'd
And lands restor'd again be freely granted;
If not, I'll use the advantage of my power
And lay the summer's dust with showers of blood
Rain'd from the wounds of slaughtered Englishmen –
45   The which, how far off from the mind of Bolingbroke
It is such crimson tempest should bedrench
The fresh green lap of fair King Richard's land,
My stooping duty tenderly shall show.
Go, signify as much, while here we march
50   Upon the grassy carpet of this plain.
Let's march without the noise of threat'ning drum,
That from this castle's tottered battlements
Our fair appointments may be well perus'd.
Methinks King Richard and myself should meet
55   With no less terror than the elements
Of fire and water, when their thund'ring shock
At meeting tears the cloudy cheeks of heaven.
Be he the fire, I'll be the yielding water;
The rage be his, whilst on the earth I rain
60   My waters – on the earth, and not on him.
March on, and mark King Richard how he looks.

                                   (III, iii, 31–61)

This speech presents a shifting tone that betrays Bolingbroke's equivocal position. Plain language evades moral questions by tailing off into metaphoric language that is unreal and basically unserious. Following the oblique threat of the opening personification and the self-aggrandizement of line 35, Bolingbroke offers a reasonably plain declaration of intention – an intention, however, which founders on the word 'freely'. To quote Deighton's slight rephrasing of the lines, Bolingbroke will give up his arms and power 'provided that the repeal of my banishment and the restoration of my lands be *unconditionally* granted' (my emphasis).[7] The plain style is on the verge of exposing deep problems. If he does give up his power, how will he enforce his provisos? And what is to prevent Richard from imposing provisos and conditions of his own, as indeed he must if he really is to be king? Line 42 purports to address itself to these questions, but, in fact, it evades them. The answer in each case, indeed, is civil war, but by reverting to the golden style Bolingbroke finds a way of not taking the answer seriously. The imagery of blood as showers laying the summer's dust and the contrast of colours in 'crimson tempest' and 'fresh green lap' are intrusions from the pleasant style. Bolingbroke is regarded by a number of characters as a master of this style (for instance, Northumberland: 'your fair discourse hath been as sugar,/ making the hard way sweet and delectable'), and there are enough examples to support this claim. But the golden style here is not an enrichment or further exploration of moral understanding by means of the sensory particulars of experience, but an escape from the demands of such understanding by means of delight in figures and sensory details valued for their own sake. Instead of an accurate description or analysis, Bolingbroke offers a kind of cartoon sketch of war; instead of serious contemplation, a kind of escapist fantasy.

His vacillation in tone is sometimes attributed to hypocrisy.[8] Already resolved on seizing the throne, he is said to resort to expressions of deference or hesitation simply as a way of disguising his fixed motive. Coleridge, on the other hand, interprets the disclaimers introduced in lines 45 and 58 as responses to silent reproof from York, checking the natural bent of Bolingbroke's mind and the flow of the subject.[9] But both of these interpretations depend on ideas imported into the text. It is simpler, and more to the point, to observe that, whatever his motives and whatever York's influence, Bolingbroke just does not attempt to think through his position clearly or persistently. Enjoying the pomp and glamour of his position (ll. 49–53), he professes to consider the real meaning of the confrontation in line 54, a line beginning significantly with the word 'methinks.' The thought, however, is less than serious. 'Fire and water', 'thund'ring shock', and 'cloudy cheeks of heaven' are images that (as is typical of the golden style at its purest) take on a kind of autonomous existence cut loose from ethical moorings. The analogy between human action and the motion of the elements simultaneously claims that such confrontations are inevitable and (therefore) disclaims any human responsibility for them. The analogy, in its misleading simplification, forfeits the very notion of men acting in a causative character. The equivocations, then, of lines 58–60 are the result not of hypocrisy or reproof, but of the fundamental incongruity of the analogy: human agents are impelled by human intentions; the natural elements are not. Bolingbroke falters whenever his speech borders on the explicit recognition of intentions. At least two of Shakespeare's editors (Wells and Muir) believe that line 59 offers a pun on 'rain' (equals also 'reign'), but besides being discordant with the syntax of line 60, such a meaning demands a more explicit declaration of motive than the rest of Bolingbroke's speech warrants. His thought simply does not go so far. The instability of tone throughout is owing to the fact that while the whole speech consistently borders on questions of cause and consequence, Bolingbroke just as consistently avoids pondering such questions. The play, *Richard II*, 'connects events by reference to the workers', but Bolingbroke, as a particular character within that play, by continually refusing to contemplate his own intentions, by consistently disclaiming responsibility, and by repeatedly excluding the larger moral and spiritual concomitants of his actions, undermines the possibility of giving 'a reason for them in the motives'. A master of the blunt style, a master of the pleasant style, he is no master of the enriched moral style. He is, therefore, radically untragic.[10]

7 · Deflections: style and the character of Richard

Although Bolingbroke is untragic, Shakespeare clearly does aim to invoke, in the confrontation of Bolingbroke and Richard at Flint Castle, some of the most important conventions and purposes of tragedy. Richard appears on the walls of Flint Castle. His height with respect to Bolingbroke represents in tableau-form their contrasting positions. It also sets up the dramatic reversal of those positions effected most explicitly in Richard's famous lines beginning: 'Down, down I come, like glist'ring Phaeton,/ Wanting the manage of unruly jades' (III, iii, 178–9). Among other things, the scene presents a vivid example of the medieval tragic convention of 'the fall of princes.' An associated convention is 'the wheel of fortune', and if Brereton is right in claiming that the emphasis on coming down into the 'base court' is meant to remind us that, in Holinshed's account, the Duke of Gloucester is arrested by Richard 'in a precisely similar situation', then it may be that Shakespeare intends to suggest that 'the wheel has come full circle.'[1] More important than either of these conventions, however, is the tradition, invoked with renewed vigour in English Renaissance drama, that stipulates the emotional effects of tragedy as woe and wonder. Having designated 'terror' (III, iii, 55) and 'shock' (l. 56) as possible emotional effects and having directed his followers to 'mark King Richard how he looks' (l. 61), Bolingbroke, when Richard appears on the walls, utters two words that are an expression of wonder: 'See, see, King Richard doth himself appear' (l. 65). They remain so, whatever the inflated imagery that follows is meant to insinuate about Richard's future. York is more explicit about the appropriate emotional responses to Richard's predicament, and Richard himself more explicit yet.

> *York.* Yet looks he like a king. Behold, his eye,
> As bright as is the eagle's, lightens forth

70   Controlling majesty; alack, alack for woe
          That any harm should stain so fair a show!
      Rich. [to North.] We are amaz'd, and thus long have
          we stood
          To watch the fearful bending of thy knee,
          Because we thought ourself thy lawful king;
75   And if we be, how dare thy joints forget
          To pay their awful duty to our presence?
                         (III, iii, 68–76)

York's 'behold' (l. 68) advances even closer than Boling-broke's 'see, see' (l. 62) to the meaning 'wonder at'. And his apprehension of woe (l. 70) is stated directly. Richard expresses amazement (l. 72), that is, paralysed surprise, at the absence of fear (l. 73) and awe (l. 76), that is, at the absence of wonder, in Bolingbroke's emissary. These emotional effects and the tradition out of which they grow are more important than the medieval conventions because it is precisely here that Shakespearean tragedy germinates.[2] It is often said that Shakespeare in *Richard II* and Marlowe before him in *Edward II* perfect the language of suffering and thus prepare the way for the great tragedies. But woe or suffering, even acute personal suffering, is no guarantee of profundity or even of lively interest. Chaucer's Monk tells a number of tales that are deadly in more ways than one. Woe, inherently present in the notion of 'the fall of princes' or 'the wheel of fortune' and intensified in the personal portraits of Marlowe and Shakespeare, is not enough, by itself, to sustain great tragedy. What is needed is the kind of wonder that is at once an emotional response and a stimulus to thought – a kind of wonder capable of investing woe with significance and of exploring the universal implications of the demise of great human characters. What is also needed is a style capable of carrying such a weight of thought and of indicating the emotional response appropriate to it. The major question, then, to ask of the character of Richard in *Richard II* is, 'to what extent does his language justify or satisfy the claims made for the emotional effects proper to his predicament?'

The answer may be sketched first in its simplest and crudest

terms. Richard displays a mastery of style (and hence of understanding) greater than Bolingbroke's (in this play) and less
than Gaunt's. He is represented, clearly but infrequently, using
a plain style that embodies moral understanding and that sometimes achieves a flexibility approaching the classical plain style.
His more frequent mode is the eloquent style devoted to the
elaborate rendering of exquisite feeling. The feeling is much
more intense than anything in Bolingbroke and the moral
understanding more candid. But although these two basic
styles undergo certain adaptations in Richard, they fall short
of the Shakespearean perspectives available in Gaunt. These
adaptations produce a golden style that uses some of the devices of the libertine style of some Renaissance prose and a
moral style that is deflected from moral purposes at certain
crucial moments. Neither achieves the reality of tragic vision.

Some of Richard's plainest language and some of his most
Petrarchan language appear in Act V. Two passages from this
act show the most clearly definable strains in his character.
Richard seems to resort to the plain style in moments of
resignation hovering on the edge of despair. Since he usually
capitulates to his feelings and since the illuminations are
usually focused on the actions of others, they are seldom sustained for long. But limited as they are, they are real and
they are true. His response to Northumberland's demand that
he read out a list of his crimes in Act IV we have already
examined. A similar sharp focus is directed at Bolingbroke
at the end of the Flint Castle scene in what is effectively
Richard's arrest: 'Well you deserve. They well deserve to
have/ That know the strong'st and surest way to get' (III,
iii, 200–1). This flat-footed analysis of power is followed by
an aphoristic analysis of the limitations of love (ll. 202–3)
and a less than fully explicit recognition of Bolingbroke's
intentions. In giving voice to those intentions before Bolingbroke does so himself, Richard reveals his tendency to move
rapidly from resignation to despair.

In Act V, however, his analysis embracing both Northumberland and Bolingbroke is sustained at some length.

> . . . thou shalt think,
> 60   Though he divide the realm and give thee half,

It is too little, helping him to all;
He shall think that thou which knowest the way
To plant unrightful kings, wilt know again,
Being ne'er so little urg'd, another way
65   To pluck him headlong from the usurped throne.
The love of wicked men converts to fear,
That fear to hate, and hate turns one or both
To worthy danger and deserved death. (V, i, 59–68)

Despite the monosyllabic diction, the regular iambic metre, and the repeated placing of the caesura after the third foot, these lines exhibit a flexibility of syntax and a weight of thought that surpass the native plain style. For example, the controlling parallelism 'thou shalt think – he shall think' is supported by numerous other parallels skilfully woven into the text: 'little-all', 'knowest-know again', 'the way-another way', 'plant–pluck', and culminating in 'danger–death'. Only the first and last of these are line-defined; the others are managed within the flexible syntax that typifies the classical plain style. Similarly, the classical plain style incorporates, but subdues, the perceptions of figurative expression. The imagery of planting is here no more than the merest hint, but it resonates with the more elaborate allegory of the garden (III, iv).[3] In addition, the extremity of having the king himself planted and plucked reflects ironically on Bolingbroke's avowed intention of simply weeding the commonwealth and plucking the caterpillars (II, iii, 165–6; III, iv, 50–3). The word 'headlong' in line 65 is not, in itself, highly visual, but it probably alludes to the tradition of kings falling from fortune's wheel. And finally, the last three lines, the most abstract and general analysis of the whole situation, are the most clearly influenced by the classical plain style. The technique of 'gradation' – the same technique used by John of Gaunt (II, i, 77-8) – offers a progression, 'love of wicked men to fear to hate to danger and death', that is not only psychologically accurate, but also morally accurate. It approaches the universality of tragedy. The love of wicked men manifests itself in one very important sense as flattery, praise offered in the service of pure self-interest, and therefore inimical to larger interests. Richard's diagnosis, then, sharply delineates a deep disease in human affairs. It is proven true by the subsequent falling out of Bolingbroke and Northumberland in *1 Henry IV*, and its centrality is reinforced by Henry's allusion to it in *2 Henry IV*, III, i, 66–79. But despite its general potency, and despite his clarity about the relationship of Bolingbroke and Northumberland, there is little evidence that Richard himself sees its application to his own particular case, even though he has heard Gaunt's warnings against flattery and even though one of his own followers brings a very similar observation to bear on Richard.

> Sweet love, I see, changing his property,
> Turns to the sourest and most deadly hate.
> (III, ii, 135–6)

Despite the urbanity of Richard's plain style and despite its general accuracy, it is never used for the purpose of introspection and it is not sufficiently supported with the details of his own particular experience.

In addition, he never sticks to the plain style for long. Immediately following this exchange with Northumberland comes Richard's parting from his Queen, rendered in sugared language reminiscent of the Elizabethan love sonnets (or of *Romeo and Juliet*)

> *Queen.* And must we be divided? must we part?
> *Rich.* Ay, hand from hand, my love, and heart from
>   heart.
> *Queen.* Banish us both, and send the king with me.
> *North.* That were some love, but little policy.
> 85 *Queen.* Then whither he goes, thither let me go.
> *Rich.* So two, together weeping, make one woe.
>   Weep thou for me in France, I for thee here;
>   Better far off than, near, be ne'er the near.
>   Go count thy way with sighs; I mine with groans.
> 90 *Queen.* So longest way shall have the longest moans.
> *Rich.* Twice for one step I'll groan, the way being
>   short.
>   And piece the way out with a heavy heart.
>   Come, come, in wooing sorrow let's be brief,
>   Since, wedding it, there is such length in grief:

95   One kiss shall stop our mouths, and dumbly part;
    Thus give I mine, and thus take I thy heart.
   Queen. Give me my mine own again;'twere no good part
    To take on me to keep and kill thy heart.
    So, now I have mine own again, be gone,
100   That I may strive to kill it with a groan.
   Rich. We make woe wanton with this fond delay.
    Once more, adieu; the rest let sorrow say.
        (V, i, 81–102)

Actually, these lines are more eloquent than many Petrarchan love sonnets. The standard 'speaking silence' of the Petrarchan lover – 'dumbly part' (l. 95) – is spoken of at some length. The standard notion that lovers are united in love is inverted to say that they are one in woe (l. 86). The convention of religious analogy, never very far distant from Petrarchan attitudes, is alluded to in line 85 and perhaps in line 88, with a suggestion of platonic austerity, since neither line is erotic in content; the echo of Ruth, i, 16 in line 85 evokes the concept of pure loyalty, and the one goal for which degrees of nearness are without meaning (l. 88) is the eternal or the ideal. The convention of the Petrarchan lover measuring quantity by means of the quality of his feelings (or vice versa) is elaborated in lines 89 through 92. In lines 96 through 100, as Peter Ure explains,[4]

> a conceit such as is often found in Elizabethan sonnets is here developed. Richard introduces the well-worn idea of the lovers exchanging hearts in a kiss; after the kiss (at l. 96), Isabel insists on having her own heart back, because she does not want to keep her lord's heart and kill it with the grief that she will suffer for his absence; so they kiss again (at l. 98), and Isabel bids Richard be gone so that the pain of his departure may quickly kill the heart, her own, of which she has re-possessed herself in the second kiss.

As Ure's admirably clear commentary suggests, Shakespeare pushes the conventional conceit far beyond its normal development.

To this standard repertoire is added an elaborate play with

balance, antithesis, and figures of sound. The device of stichomythia tied together in couplets is particularly useful for intensifying feeling. The poignancy of the imminent parting is highlighted by the closely knit couplet form. Yet the form here (ll. 81–6) is not the perfectly unified form of the closed couplet because the pause at the end of the first line in each case is as strong as the pause at the end of the second line. The Queen, who in each case speaks the first line, resists the parting; Richard, who has the emphasis of couplet closure, acquiesces. The interpolation of Northumberland in the middle couplet is a melodramatic stroke that is almost operatic. And, of course, the repeated rhyme words 'heart' and 'part' drive home the one dominant feeling. The feeling is no doubt very real and very ardent, but from any other perspective than that of the lovers, which even with them is only momentary, it appears excessive in its narrowness. Richard, at least, in 'wooing sorrow' and 'wedding it' with such intensity has scarcely any energy left for directing events or for inquiring after 'reasons for them in the motives'.

Much of Richard's language throughout the play, while not so obviously Petrarchan, is similarly and predominantly ornate. Committed to exploiting his feelings, his habitual mode may be called the libertine golden style. If the Petrarchans succeeded in enriching 'the sensuous texture of the language',[5] that sensuousness might fairly be called libertine when it is employed free from (as far as possible) the demands of human action and moral understanding and correspondingly free from the demands of rational form. I call the golden style 'libertine' by analogy with what Morris Croll calls the 'libertine' or 'loose' period in the new plain style created by such prose writers as Bacon, Browne, and Montaigne. In prose, libertine periods exhibit 'what Bacon calls "the method of induced knowledge"; either they have no predetermined plan or they violate it at will; their progression adapts itself to the movements of a mind discovering truth as it goes, thinking while it writes.'[6] By analogy: the libertine golden style exhibits the 'method of induced imagination'; its members have no predetermined plan or they violate it at will; their progression adapts itself to the movements of a mind discovering images as it goes, fantasizing while it speaks.

In his 1939 essay, speaking mainly of the sonnets, Yvor Winters argues that 'Shakespeare is minutely aware – almost sensuously aware – of the invading chaos, the unmanageable and absorptive continuum, amid which the ethical man, the man of free choice and of usable distinctions, exists.' He continues, contrasting Shakespeare with Jonson and Donne:[7]

> Still speaking as cautiously and as relatively as possible, I should say that Shakespeare tends to approach the metaphysical in a more direct and immediate fashion, as regards the experience, an approach which, paradoxically, leads to a more evasive, or at least elusive expression. That is, he constantly sees the matter that haunts him as a quality, and frequently as an almost sensuous quality, of something else, and so treats it indirectly.

Richard, as a character, is minutely, almost sensuously aware of invading chaos, but not concomitantly aware of free choice and usable distinctions. It is also characteristic of him to see the matter that haunts him as a quality of something else. Winters's remarks are worth pondering for another reason. In the revision of his essay appearing as the first chapter of *Forms of Discovery* in 1967, the preceding remarks are either excluded or substantially altered, presumably because he is more deeply distrustful of Shakespeare's method, which even in 1939 he regarded as 'the first step in the dislocation of feeling from motive which has been carried to its logical conclusions in the 19th and 20th centuries.'[8] For Winters, in other words, the method is suspect because it precipitates the disintegration of rational form. We may also observe that, pursued single-mindedly, the method is antagonistic to tragedy. The golden style is irresponsible when it is not responsive to the real world. The libertine golden style frequently makes no attempt to find out reality and presents a character content with his own imaginings – a character who is, therefore, a solipsist. Solipsism in a king is fatal; the solipsist and the tragic hero are mutually exclusive.[9]

Yet there is little doubt that the libertine golden style can be used creatively. The persistence, the survival, of the ethical man amid the invading chaos, amid the unmanageable and absorptive continuum is, in truth, the subject of tragedy. In the way that the 'method of induced knowledge' proved enormously fruitful for Bacon and his successors in making the non-human world subservient to the will of human beings, the 'method of induced imagination' (or free association) proved enormously potent for Shakespeare in evoking the unmanageable continuum that eludes forever the will of human beings. In their various ways, the great tragic figures, Hamlet, Macbeth, Lear, are powerfully, and sometimes almost solipsistically, imaginative even when straining hardest to understand their respective situations. Shakespeare, not too surprisingly, is capable of resorting to either method: the most profound and moving recognition scene in *King Lear* (IV, vii, 59-75), for example, is clearly influenced by the libertine or loose plain style that Shakespeare probably learned from Montaigne.[10] Lear's plain recognition of Cordelia is the more effective for being contrasted with his previous ornate misapprehensions of her. The achievement of ethical distinctions is the more impressive for being located in the context of invading chaos. The libertine golden style is valuable primarily for depicting a character in the act of wondering; but wondering without, at least, the possibility of learning or knowing is mere self-indulgence.

In this respect, *Richard II* relies too heavily on what now seems to be a peculiarly modern notion of wonder, wonder as purely escapist or fantastic. Richard's golden style, successful for depicting his own intense feeling, is too free, too private, and too idiosyncratic to enrich his moral understanding. Upon landing on the coast of Wales, Richard apostrophizes the earth.

> *Rich.* Barkloughly castle call they this at hand?
> *Aum.* Yea, my lord. How brooks your grace the air,
> After your late tossing on the breaking seas?
> *Rich.* Needs must I like it well. I weep for joy
> 5   To stand upon my kingdom once again.
> Dear earth, I do salute thee with my hand,
> Though rebels wound thee with their horses' hoofs.
> As a long-parted mother with her child
> Plays fondly with her tears and smiles in meeting,
> 10   So weeping, smiling, greet I thee, my earth,

> And do thee favours with my royal hands;
> Feed not thy sovereign's foe, my gentle earth,
> Nor with thy sweets comfort his ravenous sense,
> But let thy spiders that suck up thy venom
> And heavy-gaited toads lie in their way,
> Doing annoyance to the treacherous feet,
> With which usurping steps do trample thee;
> Yield stinging nettles to mine enemies;
> And when they from thy bosom pluck a flower,
> Guard it, I pray thee, with a lurking adder,
> Whose double tongue may with a mortal touch
> Throw death upon thy sovereign's enemies.
> Mock not my senseless conjuration, lords:
> This earth shall have a feeling, and these stones
> Prove armed soldiers ere her native king
> Shall falter under foul rebellion's arms. (III, ii, 1–26)

(lines 15, 20, 25 are numbered in the margin)

C. H. Herford's remark on the last half of this speech is apt: 'Richard, in the crisis of action, creates about him a fairyland full of wise and faithful beasts.'[11] The matter that haunts Richard is the allegiance of his subjects, which he sees here under the guise of the allegiance of the earth, spiders, toads, nettles, flowers, and adders. The change of address in line 23 introduces a slightly embarrassed and self-conscious apology to the reasonable men whose allegiance he might more profitably have invoked. But despite the apology, he does not really overcome a basic satisfaction with the libertine world of his own conjuring.

The word 'senseless' in line 23, though it carries, perhaps, a hint that his conjuration is ultimately pointless, and though it certainly admits that he has been addressing things lacking sense, is primarily a defiant admission that he has been making claims for which there is no sensible evidence. In this admission the essential difference between the libertine golden style and the new prose plain style can be seen clearly. The 'method of induced knowledge' is concerned above all with the evidence of the senses; the method of induced imagination with conjuration. Yet allowing for this difference, we can also see clearly the propriety of the analogy between the two styles. Richard's imagery proceeds mainly by way of association. For example, 'sweets' (l. 13) suggests its opposite 'venom' (l. 14) which in turn evokes the 'stinging nettles' (l. 18) and 'lurking adder' (l. 20).

The punctuation of the speech reveals an even more important basis for the analogy between the two styles. Peter Ure, along with almost every other modern editor, obscures the tone of the speech by including too many full stops. Pollard remarks that: 'In . . . [this] passage we find . . . [the colon] used, together with the unusual semi-colon, [with special dramatic significance, which in a modern play would be expressed by a stage direction] . . . Richard is returned from Ireland and Aumerle asks him "How . . . seas?" The King answers: "Needes . . . hands." Clearly he has sat down on a bank, and between these unrhymed couplets is caressing the earth.'[12] Now Pollard seems to think the punctuation important as a means to indicate certain gestures, but it is chiefly important for indicating a movement of mind – free-flowing and somewhat languorous. For example, the editor of the Variorum edition puts a colon at the end of line 7, 'Though rebels wound thee with their horses' hoofs:', where most modern editors put a period. There is a temptation to read a full stop at this point because the next line appears to take up a wholly new idea in the 'long parted mother' simile, but even this extravagant simile finds its way back to the original idea of saluting with the hands (line 11). And, in fact, the simile itself merely elaborates on the notion present in 'I weep for joy' (l. 4). The whole passage, in other words, is connected even though only very loosely. Modern editors introduce anywhere from six (Muir) to eight (Black and Wells) full stops in a passage for which the Quarto of 1597 authorizes only one period at the end of the speech.[13] Elizabethan texts are not very reliable in the matter of punctuation, and clearly some emendation is necessary, but Pollard argues that this particular Quarto (Q1) 'is likely to be fairly close to Shakespeare's autograph' and that 'in some of the set speeches' Q1 'preserves what looks like authorial dramatic pointing'.[14] The colon, the semi-colon, and the comma perform a function here analogous to the function of the 'loose' conjunctions that Croll identifies as characteristic of the libertine style:[15]

the conjunctions . . . that allow the mind to move straight on from the point it has reached. They do not necessarily refer back to any particular point in the preceding member; nor do they commit the following member to a predetermined form. In other words, they are the loose conjunctions, and disjoin the members they join as widely as possible. *And, but,* and *for* are the ones employed in the two sentences [From Bacon and Pascal] ; and these are of course the necessary and universal ones. Other favorites of the loose style are *whereas, nor* (= *and not*), and the correlatives *though . . yet, as . . . so.*

Croll's analysis of the style receives corroboration from Erich Auerbach, who points out in Montaigne the habit of suppressing or minimizing syntactic vincula.[16]

A look at Montaigne, in fact, and at Auerbach's discussion of him may help to clarify Shakespeare's use of the libertine golden style in *Richard II*. I do not suppose that Shakespeare read Montaigne prior to Florio's translation in 1603, but, on the other hand, I see no reason for not supposing Shakespeare capable of creating, on his own, effects similar to Montaigne's. Montaigne, unlike Bacon, is not particularly interested in investigating the external world; he investigates himself. His justification for doing so rests on the premise stated in the famous sentence declaring that the human condition is realized in any and every human being. As Auerbach explains:[17]

With this sentence he has evidently answered the question of the significance and use of his undertaking. If every man affords material and occasion enough for the development of the complete moral philosophy, then a precise and sincere self-analysis of any random individual is directly justified. Indeed, one may go a step further: it is necessary, because it is the only way – according to Montaigne – which the science of man as a moral being can take. The method of listening (escoutons y) can be applied with any degree of accuracy only to the experimenter's own person; it is in the last analysis a method of self-auscultation, of the observation of one's own inner movements. One cannot observe others with the same exactness: *Il n'y a que vous scache si vous estes lasches et cruel ou loyal et devotieux; les autres ne vous voyent point, ils vous devinent par conjectures incertaines* ... (3, 2, pp. 45–46). And one's own life, the life to whose movements one must listen, is always a random life, for it is simply one of the millions of variants of the possibilities of human existence in general. The obligatory basis of Montaigne's method is the random life one happens to have.

Auerbach's analysis of the method is brilliant, and his claim that Montaigne is an important innovator for the representation of reality in Western literature is undeniable; but in an age compelled to overhear legions of self-auscultating individuals pour out their random musings, we may want to consider why the method by itself invariably falls short of the reality of tragic vision. If it is the 'self' one is listening to, and if it is also the 'self' that is doing the listening, the method could be schizophrenic, since it provides for no clear contact with an external reality. Or, to put the point in terms that avoid psychologizing pretensions, the method of self-analysis is possible only by imitating or imagining the conversation of two or more human beings. Or, to shift ground slightly, if what one hears in self-auscultation is language, then the words in themselves are sufficient evidence that the method is based on something larger and something beyond the pseudo-empirical observations of one's own inner movements, for no human being ever invented a language all on his own. (Even the notion that it might be possible to invent a language – mathematical, scientific, or otherwise – is a notion only made possible by the language we already have.) If others divine the individual self by means of uncertain conjectures, the individual's own divination of himself is also, in some important sense, largely conjectural. The libertine style may be valuable for extending self-awareness, for revealing deep personal preoccupations and hence deep feelings; but pursued single-mindedly it fails by being too oblivious of an essential fact of human reality: that even self-analysis is in some central way a collaborative and communal achievement.

To resort to Coleridge's terms, individuality can be perceived as a universal not by merely observing the random life of random individuals, but by seeing the connections of the individual and the communal.

The libertine golden style of *Richard II* has a clear affinity with Montaigne's libertine style in that both employ a similarly fluid or loose syntax and both delight in the flow of random concrete detail from the imagination. Richard's style, however, comes more perilously close to the traps of solipsism because the licence of something approaching free association and of a relaxed syntax provided for in the libertine style combine with the inherent tendency of the golden style to create, as Sidney puts it, a golden world instead of a brazen, so that there are more elements at work to seal off connection with the real, that is, the moral world. Similarly, it is the conjunction of the libertine and the golden elements that makes it possible for Shakespeare's golden style to absorb a good many details that are unpleasant or ugly in themselves. We have already seen the languorous and unreal imputation of feelings of loyalty to such objects as spiders and toads, nettles and adders. After brief and somewhat obscure reproofs from Carlisle and Aumerle, Richard continues in the same vein.

> Discomfortable cousin! know'st thou not
> That when the searching eye of heaven is hid
> Behind the glove and lights the lower world,
> Then thieves and robbers range abroad unseen
> 40 In murthers and in outrage boldly here;
> But when from under this terrestrial ball
> He fires the proud tops of the eastern pines,
> And darts his light through every guilty hole,
> Then murthers, treasons, and detested sins,
> 45 The cloak of night being pluck'd from off their backs,
> Stand bare and naked, trembling at themselves?
> So when this thief, this traitor, Bolingbroke,
> Who all this while hath revell'd in the night,
> Whilst we were wand'ring with the Antipodes,
> 50 Shall see us rising in our throne the east,
> His treasons will sit blushing in his face,

> Not able to endure the sight of day,
> But self-affrighted tremble at his sin. (III, ii, 36–53)

As in Richard's preceding speech, the style here creates a fairy otherworld, where threats are not quite real; he conjures up a world of imagination over which he has control. It is the libertine style that permits the illusion of control and thus allows the golden style to incorporate a number of disreputable items without seriously disturbing the presiding mood of pleasant feeling and self-satisfaction. The passage is organized around an implicit 'as . . . so' construction, although one does not notice this until the appearance of 'so' in line 47, and if one attempts to locate precisely the position of the implicit 'as', it turns out to be impossible. (If 'so' in line 47 means 'therefore', the passage is not only loose, but a *non-sequitur*.) In other words, the loose correlative 'as . . . so', further loosened by syntactic imprecision, procures for the mind considerable leisure and latitude without ever calling it to strict account. In this way, what purports to be thought about a serious issue turns out to be nothing more than connivance with a predetermined emotion, an emotion, we may note, that has not even the respectability of sincere belief. Aumerle may well admit to 'knowing' that thieves and murderers flourish at night and avoid daylight, but he may still wonder how that fact guarantees Bolingbroke's discomfiture.

A great deal has been written about the correspondence of the sun and the king in *Richard II*, and most of what is written claims that such comparisons contribute to the splendour and majesty of the character of Richard.[18] But once again we must insist that the effect of such imagery is wholly dependent on context and intention and is not subject to statistical tabulation. The 'searching eye of heaven' that 'fires the proud tops of the eastern pines', indeed impressive by itself, is, in context, another example of Richard seeing the matter that haunts him – here questions about his own authority and the loyalty of his subjects – as a quality, almost a sensuous quality, of something else. To borrow once more from C. H. Herford: 'his argument could hardly be more magnificent – or more irrelevant'.[19] For the passage on Night (ll. 39–46), Peter Ure suggests, as an analogue, Prince Arthur's apostrophe to Night, *Fairie Queen*, III, iv, st. 58-9.[20] Whatever the precise similarities of the two, the mention of Spenser has a general propriety in that, like Spenser, Shakespeare here develops a kind of imaginary narrative to provide a framework for the elaboration of exquisite feeling. Spenser's work is proof that the tenuous elaboration of refined feeling can be accomplished in narrative as well as lyric poetry. In Shakespeare, the sequence of 'when–then' clauses (ll. 37, 39, 41, 44, and 47) suggests a movement through time, but instead of measuring time by a series of narrative acts, the passage presents the narrative acts as a natural and inevitable accompaniment of time. In this way Shakespeare outdoes the Spenserian mode by referring absolutely everything to Richard's feeling of self-righteousness and (with the help of the libertine style) by referring that self-righteousness to nothing but itself.

Hence, Richard's famous statement on the Divine Right of Kings, following immediately on the passage quoted above, is highly suspect.

> Not all the water in the rough rude sea
> Can wash the balm off from an anointed king;
> The breath of worldly men cannot depose
> The deputy elected by the Lord; (III, ii, 54-7)

'Here is the doctrine of indefeasible right expressed in the strongest terms', wrote Samuel Johnson in 1765, and these same lines, anthologized in *England's Parnassus* in 1600, have never been without their admirers from very early on.[21] Indeed, as an anthology piece, the passage is very impressive. But coming as the climax of Richard's speech, it expresses a tone of confidence that is the product, not of thought, but of a fantastic analogy. The affirmation of indefeasible right is not made with any clear recognition of what things might challenge such right and, as a result, is more than slightly orotund. 'Rough rude sea', for example, is a wonderful mouth-filling phrase, but it exists principally because of its sound, and even if it glances at Richard's recent sea-passage,[22] it still says nothing at all about the sort of threat Bolingbroke poses for the Lord's deputy. Once more Shakespeare's golden style absorbs blunt diction, or unpleasant intrusions of reality, into the presiding mood of self-righteous confidence. A similar effect can be observed with the phrase 'surly sullen bell' (Sonnet 71) which gets absorbed into the exquisite anguish of love the poet expresses for the person addressed. A plain style poet, such as Ralegh or Gascoigne, would have made words such as 'rough', 'rude', 'surly', or 'sullen' stand out with abrasive effect, but Shakespeare, in his way, subdues even these to a characteristic mellifluousness. In its context, Richard's celebration of Divine Right is little more than a self-protective solipsism elevated to grandiose proportions.

And the solipsism is something that Richard never really escapes. By contrast with John of Gaunt, who acquiesces in the existing order only after strenuously trying to improve it and understand it from several different perspectives, Richard is habituated to this one mode of perception – the libertine golden style. His attitude of resignation and his vision of religious truth are both a kind of mummification of his own very private feelings. ''Tis very true, my grief lies all within,/ And these external manners of lament/ Are merely shadows to the unseen grief/ That swells with silence in the tortur'd soul./ There lies the substance: (IV, i, 295–9). Richard's answer here near the end of Act IV is a witty rebuttal of Bolingbroke's, 'The shadow of your sorrow hath destroy'd/ The shadow of your face', but it also reveals how essentially self-enclosed he regards his own being. The nostalgia for a secluded pious life indicates a similar vision in more ornate language.

> I'll give my jewels for a set of beads;
> My gorgeous palace for a hermitage;
> My gay apparel for an almsman's gown;
> My figur'd goblets for a dish of wood;
> My sceptre for a palmer's walking staff;
> My subjects for a pair of carved saints,
> And my large kingdom for a little grave,
> A little little grave, an obscure grave. (III, iii, 147–54)

Religion is viewed here not as that which binds all men together, but as that which offers a retreat from the world; nor is it viewed as arduous or demanding: the details of the religious life are all seen to be essentially picturesque. The

130

leisurely development of balanced clauses shows that Petrarchan technique turned to the subject of religious seclusion
can be no less elaborate and no less otherworldly than the
sensual enchantments of courtly love. Even the obscurity of
the grave holds sensual, almost tactile, delights for Richard.

Shakespeare was well aware that a consistent preoccupation with a highly tractable and imaginary 'something else' –
with a golden otherworld – is by no means inconsistent with
attitudes of cynicism, despair, or even quietism.

> Beshrew thee, cousin, which didst lead me forth
> Of that sweet way I was in to despair!
> What say you now? What comfort have we now?
> By heaven, I'll hate him everlastingly
> That bids me be of comfort any more.
> Go to Flint Castle, there I'll pine away –
> A king, woe's slave, shall kingly woe obey. (III, ii, 204–10)

Line 205 is a clear admission that the sweet style is fully
appropriate to the mood of despair, and it raises some interesting questions about the interpenetration of lyric style and
dramatic action. Drama, if it is to engage the deepest human
questions, would appear to find some sort of marriage of the
golden and the moral styles compulsory. Petrarchan techniques were invented for the elaborate and subtle registering
of emotional states. Thus, when a character, who is developed
with some subtlety, is denied (or denies himself) the possibility of action, when such a character despairs, or believes all
acts to be futile, he is reduced to the prolonged and tenuous
elaboration of feeling – but feeling divorced from its motive,
that is, from human action. It is just possible that Shakespeare's point is that the whole process is reciprocal: that is,
not only that technique is sprung loose from motive, but that
habitual adherence to such technique may disqualify one
from action. In any case, what we see in Richard is a parody
of tragic resignation. His attitude of resignation comes
not, as Gaunt's does, as the culmination of understanding
and effort. Instead it comes prior to, and thereby forfeits,
these. Richard exhibits 'kingly woe' without kingly wonder.

It may be that it is Shakespeare's intention so to exhibit
him, but I think not. The golden style of the sixteenth-

century lyric appears to have been Shakespeare's natural medium, the one that he mastered earliest and 'with that facility' that earned him the reputation of never having blotted a line. 'He was (indeed) honest, and of an open, and free nature: had an excellent fancy; brave notions, and gentle expressions'.[23] 'Brave notions' are notions that are finely-dressed, splendid, showy, or handsome. The moral style, by contrast, is not one that Shakespeare cultivated so assiduously in the short poem. Yet the moral style, or some variant of it, is absolutely essential to the creation of thought, character, and action, for it displays human choice – the stuff of drama. As a result, Shakespeare seems to have found his way to the moral style through the pressure of his experience as a dramatist and by virtue of his power of intellect and not always 'with that facility'. The two most memorable passages spoken by Richard in *Richard II* exhibit a genuine effort of thought; they represent a clear intention to explore the nature of kingly wonder. But because the thought is insufficiently profound and is sustained at insufficient length, and because, as compared with Gaunt, the notion of individuality is not so deep nor the vision of national implications so broad, the wonder falls short of being kingly. The moral style is deflected from moral purposes.

In the first, Richard begins by replying to a question concerning the whereabouts of the Duke of York, Lord Governor of England during Richard's absence.

No matter where – of comfort no man speak.
145 Let's talk of graves, of worms, and epitaphs,
Make dust our paper, and with rainy eyes
Write sorrow on the bosom of the earth.
Let's choose executors and talk of wills.
And yet not so – for what can we bequeath
Save our deposed bodies to the ground?
Our lands, our lives, and all, are Bolingbroke's,
And nothing can we call our own but death;
And that small model of the barren earth
Which serves as paste and cover to our bones.
155 For God's sake let us sit upon the ground
And tell sad stories of the death of kings:

How some have been depos'd, some slain in war,
Some haunted by the ghosts they have deposed,
Some poisoned by their wives, some sleeping kill'd,
160   All murthered – for within the hollow crown
That rounds the mortal temples of a king
Keeps Death his court, and there the antic sits,
Scoffing his state and grinning at his pomp,
Allowing him a breath, a little scene,
165   To monarchize, be fear'd, and kill with looks;
Infusing him with self and vain conceit,
As if this flesh which walls about our life
Were brass impregnable; and, humour'd thus,
Comes at the last, and with a little pin
170   Bores thorough his castle wall, and farewell king!
Cover your heads, and mock not flesh and blood
With solemn reverence; throw away respect,
Tradition, form, and ceremonious duty;
For you have but mistook me all this while.
175   I live with bread like you, feel want,
Taste grief, need friends – subjected thus,
How can you say to me, I am a king? (III, ii, 144–77)

The movement of thought in this speech and its general structure can be observed in the shifts in pronoun usage. The first section (ll. 144–54) is dominated by the first person plural: the royal 'we'. In the second section (ll. 155–70), while the presence of the royal 'we' is still felt in the pronoun 'us' (l. 155) and in the imperative 'let us sit upon the ground' (l. 155), there is some attempt to achieve the sense of distance or objectivity provided by the use of the third person. This section in turn is divided into two parts: the first, the series of exempla (ll. 155–60) using the third person plural; the second, a more particular, and for Richard more personal example (ll. 160–70), the third person singular. In the third section (ll. 171–7), only the first person singular and second person plural appear: 'How can *you* say to *me*, *I* am a king?' The royal 'we' is made possible because the king as a figurehead represents the whole community. But in this play the community disintegrates into component parts that can be owned by an individual as property is owned. Bolingbroke assumes the throne by means of the same manoeuvre that recovers for him the Lancastrian estate, which *is* his *own* property. Richard's attitude towards the throne is similarly short-sighted: 'Landlord of England art thou now, not king'. The next logical step is the division of the royal 'we' into its isolated elements: 'yours' and 'mine', 'you' and 'me'.

The problem is clearly metaphysical, 'resembling in the nature of its difficulty the problem of the Many and the One'. Shakespeare has need of the metaphysical style, and there are certain signs that he is looking for it. 'Make dust our paper, and with rainy eyes/ Write sorrow on the bosom of the earth' (ll. 146, 147) approaches the sort of extravagant conceit that has been regarded as characteristic of the metaphysical style. But this conceit is only an anticipation of what later became known in the seventeenth century as Cleveland-izing. The metaphysical style requires something more than mere catachresis. In 'what can we bequeath/ Save our deposed bodies to the ground' and in 'that small model of the barren earth/ Which serves as paste and cover to our bones', Shakespeare attempts that something more. In these lines Richard broods on his own mortality with admirable penetration. The metaphysical puzzle is the puzzle of thought and extension. Kingship is created and sustained by thought; the deposition of a king is, therefore, primarily an act of thought, though it carries with it, as a necessary corollary, the displacement of the king's own person, an extended substance. In 'deposed bodies' Shakespeare gives emphatic recognition to the corollary, even to the point of forcing the word 'depose' back into its root, meaning 'displace' or 'deposit'. When he lists 'sad stories of the death of kings', Richard's first example, 'how some have been depos'd', recognizes at once that, for a king, deposition means death. The same recognition reappears in the figure of 'a mockery king of snow' (IV, i, 260). And similarly, 'that small model of the barren earth' carries simultaneously a perception of the king's mortality and a perception of his representative quality as a 'model'.

Yet despite the flicker of metaphysical illuminations in these lines, they are not finally handled with that facility that would render revision superfluous. The metaphysical style requires two views of reality held in a peculiar balance: two views that 'support and complete, and at the same time deny, each other'.[24] Richard presents two views, but one view keeps slipping from sight or slipping to a position of subordination to the other. He sees that a king, like any other mortal, is subject to death; he sees that a king, unlike any other mortal, has no being apart from his office; but his sense of a king's being withers in the face of his sense of the nothingness. In the much-discussed phrase 'small model of the barren earth,' for example, 'model', as a number of commentators have suggested, 'refers to the flesh, the feature which represents in man the "earth" . . . of the macrocosm'. 'Model', in this interpretation, is superior to 'portion,' Warburton's suggested emendation, because it insists on the king's individuality (the microcosm) and universality (the macrocosm) simultaneously. Yet the next line, 'which serves as paste and cover to our bones', a metaphor 'not of the most sublime kind, taken from a pie', with its possible quibble on 'pie-crust' and 'coffin,' emphasizes the king's mortality at the expense of his universality.[25] Shakespeare's commentators have been quick to construct images of coffins or grave-mounds, and their contents. In a similar way, Richard's grasp of the nature of his own being falters in the phrase 'deposed bodies' where the plural 'bodies' suggests that the 'we' of 'what can we bequeath' is not the royal 'we' after all, but only the first person plural. And again, Richard's response to the question of York's whereabouts – 'no matter where' – is a more crucial evasion of reality than it might seem because, as Lord Governor of England, it is York who has been carrying out the duties of the royal 'we' in Richard's absence. Finally, the tendency of the royal 'we' to slip into a more simple plural is complete in the second section of the speech (especially ll. 155–60), where the sense of community depends merely on the addition of numbers.

Nevertheless, that Richard's attempt to ponder the question of death and the nature of his own being is genuine is confirmed by his attempt to generate moral understanding from his view of reality. In this, though he falls short of Gaunt, he may be contrasted favourably with Bolingbroke. The second section of his speech is not wholly plain in style,

but the 'sad stories of the death of kings' recall such traditional works as the *Fall of Princes*, the *Mirror for Magistrates*,
and the *Monk's Tale* and allude to subject matter that was to
preoccupy Shakespeare in a number of his own plays.[26] The
'moral' is fully traditional, regarding the mutability of fortune. In the second part of the second section (ll. 160–70),
Richard's analysis becomes more personal, more pointed, and
more indulgent. Using imagery that is proverbial (l. 162) and
even biblical (ll. 167, 168), he highlights the vulnerability of
his own position. In the word 'monarchize' (l. 165), he
touches pointedly on a prominent element in his own character; but it is also here that the insufficiency of his view of
reality begins to tell. 'To monarchize' means, at least in part,
to posture as a monarch, to attitudinize. To attitudinize is to
adopt an attitude (usually in the interest of exciting admiration for one's own person) in order to escape the importunity
of the real sort of wonder that is germane to the determination and development of genuine moral attitudes. Richard's
whole speech is a series of imperatives that clamour increasingly for attention as pieces of advice. He opens the third
section of his speech with the following words:

> Cover your heads, and mock not flesh and blood
> With solemn reverence.

The last two words call attention to themselves because,
while Richard succeeds in dismissing reverence, he does not
succeed in banishing solemnity. What could be more solemn
than his whole speech, and particularly the last part? Though
his attempt to ponder seriously the nature of his predicament
is commendable, his embrace of his own vulnerable mortality
as the absolute truth is, finally, only one more way of succumbing to the vice of attitudinizing. In the absence of wonder, the moral style is deflected from its deep purposes; it
degenerates to attitudinizing. The upshot is woe without
wonder and is radically untragic.

Richard's soliloquy at Pomfret Castle (V, v) is the only passage in the play that rivals this speech in Act III for sustained
thought about the nature of kingship and its national and
personal implications. But here again, the moral style is

similarly deflected. The soliloquy opens with some self-conscious remarks about the process of soliloquizing.

> I have been studying how I may compare
> This prison where I live unto the world;
> And, for because the world is populous
> And here is not a creature but myself,
> 5   I cannot do it. Yet I'll hammer it out.
> My brain I'll prove the female to my soul,
> My soul the father, and these two beget
> A generation of still-breeding thoughts,
> And these same thoughts people this little world,
> 10   In humours like the people of this world;
> For no thought is contented. (V, v, 1–11)

Though such an overt preoccupation with the manner of doing a thing is perhaps a characteristic sign of apprenticeship, the apprentice work here is sufficiently ambitious that it rewards close attention. G. Wilson Knight, a fervent admirer of Richard's soliloquy, claims that these lines 'outline a Shakespearian aesthetic psychology', and further, that 'Shakespeare has here temporarily endued his dramatic protagonist with a psychic state closely analogous, if not exactly equivalent, to the process of poetic creation.'[27] Of Richard he says:[28]

> In his final despair and failure, his mind is thrown back on pure contemplation and he sinks on to the restful sweetness of impersonal and wandering thought. In so doing, he finds that he has made a small world of his own: which state is now exactly analogous to the creative consciousness which gives birth to poetry.

This state Knight finds prophetically congruent with remarks by Keats, Wordsworth, Keyserling, and Bergson as well as prophetic of much in Shakespeare's later plays, including *Measure for Measure, Hamlet, King Lear, Timon of Athens, Antony and Cleopatra,* and *Coriolanus.* While Shakespeare's intention in *Richard II* has far-reaching implications, it is not quite so successfully embodied, or so modern, as Wilson Knight imagines. In aiming, by means of a traditional rhetoric, to discover the emotional effects and moral attitudes appropriate to tragedy, Shakespeare creates in *Richard II* a drama of abiding interest even though, finally, it falls short of being the 'tragedy' of King Richard the Second.

To begin with, the 'Shakespearian aesthetic psychology' is firmly grounded on the Ciceronian rhetoric, with its special emphasis on invention, that, as W. S. Howell demonstrates, became the predominant part of traditional rhetoric in sixteenth-century England.[29] 'My brain I'll prove the female to my soul' refers to invention; 'My soul the father' refers to what the Elizabethans would have called 'cause'; 'cause' and invention together produce Shakespeare's art. 'Cause' in this special sense is explained most lucidly by Rosemond Tuve:[30]

> I shall occasionally use this untranslatable Elizabethan term because it combines the meanings of 'poetic subject' and 'poet's intention' so economically. Although close to the Aristotelian 'final cause,' it has, as used by the Elizabethans, less of self-conscious calculation than our words *aim* or *purpose*. *Subject* is open to confusion with 'subject matter,' and in both Latin and English critical treatises *subject* and related words (*object, subjective* reality) are troublesome to translate, retaining implications taken on through scholastic usage even, evidently as late as Descartes.

Richard's 'cause' is 'how I may compare/ This prison where I live unto the world'. Shakespeare's 'cause' is more complex. Preparing his protagonist to meet death, Shakespeare attempts to endue him with the spirit of tragic resignation. Richard's comparison is to be the basis of a final understanding of the relationship of the individual and society, resulting in a *catharsis* of woe and wonder.

To undertake this intention, Shakespeare relies on two of the traditional kinds of oratory. W. S. Howell claims that each of the three kinds of oratory in use in ancient Greece and Rome had its own set of customary moral issues: 'demonstrative oratory was addressed to questions of honor or dishonor; deliberative oratory, to questions of expediency or inexpediency; judicial oratory, to questions of justice or injustice'.[31] Since expediency or inexpediency is now irrelevant to Richard's predicament, Shakespeare turns to the first and last of these. The first part of the soliloquy (ll. 1–41) is demonstrative oratory. The second part (ll. 41–66) is judicial oratory.

Richard opens up the subject of what is in honour due to him by inventing or discovering his matter in the Ciceronian topics. And first, definition. Because 'no thought is contented', thoughts are equivalent to humours; they are, therefore, analogous to 'the people of this world'. Next is division, and for Richard there are three kinds of thought: 'The better sort/ As thoughts of things divine' (ll. 11, 12), 'Thoughts tending to ambition' (l. 18), and 'Thoughts tending to content' (l. 23). Despite the attempt to consider the nature of thought itself, Richard's contemplation is not 'pure', as Wilson Knight claims, nor is it 'impersonal and wandering'. The divisions are clearly arranged in hierarchical order, and each is devoted to preserving Richard's sense of his own limited and enclosed self, intact and immune.[32] Regarding divine thoughts, Terence Hawkes in *Shakespeare's Talking Animals* argues provocatively and ingeniously for great complexity in the phrase 'do set the word itself/ Against the word',[33] but Richard's illustration of this conflict is, in itself, comparatively simple. He finds one biblical quotation, 'Come, little ones', that encourages his personal hope of heaven and one biblical quotation, 'It is as hard to come as for a camel/ To thread the postern of a small needle's eye', that discourages it. But apparent contradiction should be the beginning, not the end, of thought. How a king might be simultaneously a great one in the world and a little one in the sight of God eludes Richard's contemplation. Similarly, ambitious thoughts, for Richard, focus entirely on how he might escape the exigencies of his own fleshly imprisonment and mortality – 'how these vain weak nails/ May tear a passage thorough the flinty ribs/ Of this hard world, my ragged prison walls' (ll. 19–21). Because this particular ambition is impossible, because thought, for Richard, is insufficiently impersonal, he dismisses 'thoughts tending to ambition' as 'unlikely wonders' (l. 19). In fact, the upshot of his consideration of the first two divisions of thought is to banish the emotional effect of wonder, to procure immunity to its promptings.

His third division of thought banishes commiseration.

> Thoughts tending to content flatter themselves
> That they are not the first of fortune's slaves,
> 25 Nor shall not be the last – like silly beggars
> Who, sitting in the stocks, refuge their shame,
> That many have and others must sit there;
> And in this thought they find a kind of ease,
> Bearing their own misfortunes on the back
> 30 Of such as have before indur'd the like.
> Thus play I in one person many people,
> And none contented. (V, v, 23–32)

The mistake (Shakespeare's as well as Richard's) lies in the irony directed at the notion of refuge in the phrase 'refuge their shame.' Commiseration is valuable not because it provides shelter or protection from shamefulness, misfortune or suffering, but because it is the antidote to an 'indulgence in the dramatization of one's nobly suffering self'. The recognition that many have suffered and that others will suffer is a recognition that experience does not begin and end with one's own person. It is the profound recognition that 'experience matters, not because it is mine – because it is to me it belongs or happens, or because it subserves, or issues in purpose or will, but because it is what it is, the "mine" mattering only in so far as the individual sentience is the indispensable focus of experience'. Commiseration or tragic woe is valuable not because it affords the individual any protection from a sense of the suffering of others or because it alleviates, in any way, his experience of his own suffering. Rather, it heightens and intensifies his sense of *both* of these, and, in so doing, establishes tragic impersonality.

Richard, by contrast, is left with nothing but his own personality.

> Thus play I in one person many people,
> And none contented.

In a sense, Richard's invention fails his 'cause', for by defining thoughts as humours he effectively seals himself off from what George Whalley refers to as 'that fertile indirection of the mind that . . . we sometimes call "imagination," and sometimes "thought," and sometimes "intention".'[34] Given his initial premise, Richard has no alternative but to replace thinking with attitudinizing, and in the absence of thought, he has no opportunity to achieve character or tragic action. This is so despite the fact that Shakespeare obviously does wish to represent him as arriving at a position of tragic resignation at the end of the first part of his soliloquy. Richard invokes the 'many' he mentions at line 31 by posturing its extremes, king and beggar, alternately faced with treason and penury and alternately attracted and repelled by both. He moves with such rapidity through such Ciceronian topics as things incompatible with one another, causes, effects, and comparison with things greater or less or equal, that he finally loses sight of his comparison, his initial 'cause': 'And straight am nothing' (l. 38). The conclusion appears inevitable.

> But whate'er I be,
> Nor I, nor any man that but man is,
> With nothing shall be pleas'd, till he be eas'd
> With being nothing.   (V, v, 38–41)

The play of sound in this utterance helps give the impression of finality, of a secure understanding of human affairs. The impression is of the enriched moral style, of aphoristic wisdom polished to urbane eloquence. The balance of 'Nor I, nor any man' makes it appear that the initial comparison of the soliloquy is being summed up. What's more, the play on 'nothing,' which some editors regard as a tangle, could be a characteristically Shakespearean quibble. Stanley Wells gives the alternative readings: 'The first *nothing* may be part of a double negative: "shall be pleased by anything till he has been granted the 'ease' of death"; or it may mean the opposite: "shall be pleased by having nothing (or losing everything) till . . . ".'[35] If the quibble is intended, it lends the utterance the finality of all-inclusiveness. In any case, the utterance has every appearance of complete resignation.[36]

But it is not tragic resignation. In the first place, the attitude announces itself as something achieved after death (and, therefore, pretends to know what it cannot know), whereas tragic resignation is something achieved in this life.

Second, though the two meanings of 'nothing' are, in one sense, opposite, they are alike in another sense. Richard concludes his investigation of what is in honour due to him by considering the question of what has or has not been given to him, what has or has not happened to him, rather than by considering what he is. He supposes the latter question irrelevant ('But whate'er I be') partly because he supposes that man is a fixed and known item ('nor any man that but man is'): hence his incuriosity and his lack of feeling. To be pleased with nothing is no emotion. Tragic resignation or *catharsis* is not the abandonment or the negation of thought and feeling. It is the recognition of having reached the limits of thought and feeling and of understanding that they are the limits. In a sense, Shakespeare's invention, too, fails his 'cause', for instead of a *catharsis* of wonder he substitutes blank incuriosity, and instead of a *catharsis* of woe, nihilism. And so, in the absence of both wonder and woe, the moral style is deflected finally from the line of truth and reason.

As a result, the last part of the soliloquy offers sentimentality in place of serenity, or tragic calm. The introduction of music at line 41 invokes the question of sensibility that is an essential element of justice. While the first part of the soliloquy investigates the matter of honour (that is, the matter of one's standing in the order of the universe), the second part investigates the matter of justice (that is, the matter of the fitness or rightness of that standing). The introduction of music also provides Richard with a new principle of invention and with some impressive lines.

> Music do I hear?
> Ha, ha! keep time – how sour sweet music is
> When time is broke and no proportion kept!
> So is it in the music of men's lives.
> And here have I the daintiness of ear
> To check time broke in a disordered string;
> But for the concord of my state and time,
> Had not an ear to hear my true time broke:
> I wasted time, and now doth time waste me. (V, v, 41–9)

The main principle of invention here, argument based on

similarity or analogy, is augmented and sharpened by topics based on etymology and on conjugates in the multiple meanings of such words as 'proportion', 'disordered', and 'time'. Besides being quite lovely, these lines are moving towards a perception of tragic waste. But here Shakespeare's style fails, and the enormous potential of 'I wasted time, and now doth time waste me' is dissipated in the fantastic comparison of Richard to a clock (ll. 50–60), which does nothing to show what the waste is, how it happened, or what its implications are. The elaborate development of this figure and the concentrated disgust of its conclusion:

> But my time
> Runs posting on in Bolingbroke's proud joy,
> While I stand fooling here, his Jack of the clock,
>   (ll. 58–60)

suggest that Shakespeare is searching for the style that I have called Shakespearean intuition. But the language of most of the latter part of this soliloquy, instead of being central, brief, and compendious, is eccentric, wordy, and diffuse. And even in the energetic lines above, instead of the perspective consciousness of

> Join with the present sickness that I have,
> And thy unkindness be like crooked age,
> To crop at once a too long withered flower,

Richard is left with a simple contrast between Bolingbroke's personality and his sense of his own mechanical nullity. Given this expression of his character, Richard's interpretation of the music as 'a sign of love' (l. 65) cannot but be sentimental, the mere projection of personal longing. He abandons the question of justice, the problem of aligning sympathy and judgment, for self-centred sentimentality: 'love to Richard/ Is a strange brooch in this all-hating world'. And for an understanding of the values that give order to human existence – love, truth, justice, and honour – we turn in this play not to Richard but to Gaunt: 'Love they to live that love and honour have.' The moral style Shakespeare uses to characterize Richard is finally deflected because it is not Shakespearean enough.

8 · Tragic doings, political order and the closed couplet

But whatever our appraisal of Richard's character is, Shakespeare's intention is clearly to dramatize tragic doings. *The Tragedy of King Richard the Second*, as it is titled in the Quarto editions, is called, in the First Folio, *The Life and Death of King Richard the Second*. To understand some of the reasons why Shakespeare's early editors exhibit this difference of opinion and to demonstrate that the Quarto editors offer a title more nearly appropriate for designating Shakespeare's intention, we must examine an element of style that assumes a peculiar importance in this particular play – the heroic couplet. J. W. H. Atkins, commenting on 'Dramatic Criticism' in *English Literary Criticism: The Renascence*, makes the following pronouncement:[1]

> The truth was that Elizabethan dramatists were empiricists first and last, with experiment and practice engaging all attention; and their art was no haphazard growth but an independent creation, developed along definite lines dictated by the native genius and traditions, by popular taste and stage conditions of the time. Irrespective of orthodox doctrine, they shaped their practice, and also their unwritten theory, in accordance with what they deemed to be psychologically necessary for rendering their stories attractive to popular audiences on the Elizabethan stage; and here, if anywhere, lies the key to the understanding of Elizabethan dramatic art.

Atkins, no doubt, overstates the case somewhat. Psychological nicety and popular appeal in tragic drama were considerably sharpened and deepened by the rediscovery, in the Renaissance, of certain ancient principles of tragedy. The medieval notion of *De casibus* tragedy, perfectly consonant with the Donatan tradition involving the fall and death of illustrious personages, was invigorated by a conscious application of the notion of wonder as outlined in Aristotle, Cicero,

Quintilian, St Albert the Great, and St Thomas Aquinas. And some of this work, as Cunningham demonstrates, was done in explicit statements of theory: by Pontanus, Fracastoro, and Minturno, as well as by Sidney and Shakespeare among others. Yet Atkins's claim, in an important sense, *is* true. To appreciate how new *Richard II* in itself is, it is necessary to observe the way in which Shakespeare experiments with existing forms. The closest thing we have to a manifesto of Elizabethan tragedy is to be found in Marlowe's prologue to *Tamburlaine*, Part I:[2]

> From jygging vaines of riming mother wits,
> And such conceits as clownage keepes in pay,
> Weele leade you to the stately tent of War:
> Where you shall heare the Scythian *Tamburlaine*,
> Threatning the world with high astounding tearmes
> And scourging kingdoms with his conquering sword.
> View but his picture in this tragicke glasse,
> And then applaud his fortunes if you please.

Cunningham's comment on this passage is admirably to the point:

> Though these lines have often been quoted, they are worth noticing again, for they are packed with critical doctrine. They are a manifesto. The first two lines constitute an explicit rejection of the old theatrical tradition of the fourteener with its rhyme and its marked regularity of metre ('jigging veins'); of the uneducated, unartful writer ('mother wits'); and of the tradition of the irresponsible clown. In its stead is proposed the modulated and rhymeless line, and the wholly serious play. This play involves a high subject, *war*, and by implication and the enjoinment of decorum a *stately* style, a high and royal style. The effect will be largely one of language and of rhetoric, for there 'you shall hear,' and you shall hear what is grand, or even grandiose, a 'threatening the world,' expressed in 'high astounding terms.' (*CE*, p. 85)

For Shakespeare's fascination with the bombastic rhetoric of blank verse we have the evidence of the first tetralogy, *Titus*

Andronicus, and *King John*, as well as the testimony of Robert Greene. Shakespeare clearly tried his hand at Marlovian tragedy, and in the similarity of *Richard II* to *Edward II* we see a kindred attempt to co-ordinate the multifarious demands of chronicle history with the single-minded insistence of *De casibus* tragedy. But Shakespeare's play introduces a verse technique that is quite at odds with Marlowe's manifesto. In *Richard II*, 'astounding terms' are frequently marshalled within the confines of rhyming decasyllabic couplets. In *Richard II*, the heroic couplet is one of Shakespeare's main instruments for reconciling the claims of history and tragedy and, as a result, for opening into that heightened and deepened perspective on human action in which history is ultimately subsumed by tragedy.

Explicit references to tragedy in the first tetralogy are nearly all comparatively simple, but it is possible to see Shakespeare's idea of tragedy maturing even in those plays whose date of composition likely precedes that of *Richard II*. Cunningham, in an austere conclusion, cites only three plays – *Hamlet*, *Antony and Cleopatra*, *Coriolanus* – as firm examples of an explicit intention to evoke the emotional effect of woe and wonder (*CE*, p. 96). Yet when surveying the early plays, he finds them almost wholly congruent with the Donatan tradition.

> In brief, the tragic atmosphere and the anticipation of the tragic catastrophe is fearful; the catastrophe woeful. The process by which the catastrophe comes about involves intrigue, hypocrisy, political conspiracy and treason, acts of sin, and is conducted by responsible agents. These are the connotations of *tragedy*. The denotation is violent, unexpected death – murder, death in battle, suicide. To these is added rape. (*CE*, p. 50)

To be sure, references to 'tragedy' throughout the three parts of *Henry VI* and even in *Richard III* correspond to this description. Tragedy is a 'scene of death' (*3 Henry VI*, V, vi, 10) or 'untimely death' (*2 Henry VI*, III, ii, 186 and *3 Henry VI*, V, vi, 42), 'contrived' by a 'fatal hand' (*1 Henry VI*, I, iv, 75–6); it is violent death (*Richard III*, II, ii, 39–40) that drives men to distraction, madness, and terror (*Richard III*,

III, v, 4). We may even say that, whatever else they offer, these early plays are scarcely more sophisticated in their idea of tragedy than *Cambises*, for example, written in the 1560s. The killing of Cambises 'by sodain chaunce' exhibits the Stoical moral of the instability of all sublunary affairs, and 'HIS ODIOUS DEATH BY GODS JUSTICE APPOINTED' illustrates Christian retribution for sin.[3] As Madeleine Doran claims, 'these two ways of regarding tragic catastrophe, The Stoic and the Christian, are both to be looked for in Elizabethan tragedy'.[4]

But in at least two plays, *Titus Andronicus* and *King John*, Shakespeare seems to be striving after a more satisfactory evocation of wonder and, hence, a more profound conception of tragedy. Each play is called a 'tragedy' in its first appearance in print. The first Quarto of *Titus Andronicus* concludes with the words '*Finis the Tragedy of Titus Andronicus*', and *King John*, like *Richard II* and *Richard III*, was first called 'The Tragedy of . . .' and then renamed by the First Folio 'The Life and Death of . . .'.[5]

Titus Andronicus makes the more concerted effort of the two to embody the 'affects' that Sidney describes as 'admiration and commiseration'. When the plot laid by Aaron and Tamora begins to take effect, the response of Titus's sons, Martius and Quintus, to the dead body of Bassianus might appear to represent small advance on the fear and trembling that marks the 'deep tragedian' in *Richard III* (III, v, 1–11). Martius is in a 'blood stained hole' with the body; Quintus remains above.

> *Quint.* I am surprised with an uncouth fear;
> A chilling sweat o'er-runs my trembling joints:
> My heart suspects more than mine eye can see.
> *Mart.* To prove thou has a true-divining heart,
> 215 Aaron and thou look down into this den,
> And see a fearful sight of blood and death.
> *Quint.* Aaron is gone, and my compassionate heart
> Will not permit mine eyes once to behold
> The thing whereat it trembles by surmise.
> 220 O, tell me who it is; for ne'er till now
> Was I a child to fear I know not what. (III, iii, 211–21)

147

But notice that Quintus's heart is at once 'compassionate' and 'true-divining'; that it trembles 'by surmise'; and that he fears 'I know not what'. Somewhat later, both Tamora and Titus are more explicit yet in declaring that the emotional effect of tragic events is not only fearful, but also an incentive to thought. Tamora pretends to the appropriate emotion.

> Then all too late I bring this fatal writ,
> The complot of this timeless tragedy;
> And wonder greatly that man's face can fold
> In pleasing smiles such murderous tyranny.
> (II, iii, 264–7)

Titus's feeling is real.

> What shall we do? let us that have our tongues
> Plot some device of further misery,
> To make us wonder'd at in time to come. (III, i, 133–5)

In a sense Lavinia, who has been raped and then deprived of her arms and tongue, represents a type of woe, incommunicable and inscrutable, that frustrates wonder, and, in so far as its cause is imperfectly understood, frustrates sympathy as well. 'Thou map of woe' Titus calls her, attempting to decipher her suffering.

> Speechless complainer, I will learn thy thought;
> In thy dumb action will I be as perfect
> As begging hermits in their holy prayers:
> Thou shalt not sigh, nor hold thy stumps to heaven,
> Nor wink, nor nod, nor kneel, nor make a sign,
> But of these I will wrest an alphabet,
> And by still practice learn to know thy meaning.
> (III, ii, 39–45)

But as Marcus comments, woe threatens to overpower Titus's ability to think.

> Alas, poor man! grief has so wrought on him,
> He takes false shadows for true substances.
> (III, ii, 79–80)

And Titus corroborates the suggestion that his wonder is subverted.

Come, boy, and go with me: thy sight is young,
And thou shalt read when mine begin to dazzle.
(III, ii, 84–5)

Titus means that his sight will be confounded when he reads
to Lavinia 'Sad stories chanced in the times of old.'

Titus Andronicus, in its resolution, anticipates certain
important developments at the end of *Hamlet*. Aaron, a
major cause of confusion in this play, is apprehended by
Lucius, to whom he pleads for the life of his son.

Lucius, save the child;
And bear it from me to the empress.
If thou do this, I'll show thee wondrous things
That highly may advantage thee to hear. (V, i, 53–6)

'I'll show thee wondrous things' means not only 'I will say
things that will cause you to wonder', but also 'I will explain things about which you have already wondered.' In
using the word 'advantage', Aaron himself is being ironic,
but to understand what happened *is* a moral advantage and
proves to be of practical advantage to Lucius before the end
of the play. Aaron then proceeds to give a close general summary of the tragedy that parallels the close general summary
given by Horatio at the end of *Hamlet* (V, ii, 380–7).

'Twill vex thy soul to hear what I shall speak;
For I must talk of murthers, rapes, and massacres,
Acts of black night, abominable deeds,
Complots of mischief, treason, villainies,
Ruthfull to hear, yet piteously perform'd:
And this shall all be buried in my death,
Unless thou swear to me my child shall live. (V, i, 62–8)

When Lucius so swears, Aaron offers a complete explanation
for each of his generalizations, specifying the murder of
Bassianus (l. 91), the rape of Lavinia (l. 92), the massacre of
Quintus and Martius (ll. 104–5), the mischief of the forged
letter and the hidden gold (ll. 106–7), the treasonous alliance of Aaron and Tamora (l. 108), and the villainy of
duping Titus to cut off his own hand (l. 111). And these are
summed up once more as the 'heinous deeds' of a 'black

149

dog' (ll. 122–3). Then, just in case this explanation of the cause of woe in the play does not seem entirely credible, Shakespeare provides Aaron with another speech (ll. 124–44) in which he declares that he has done similar 'dreadful things' in the past, and the list is specified once more: murder, rape, treason, massacres, mischief, and villainies. Clearly, *Titus Andronicus* aims, as *Hamlet* does, at a kind of *catharsis* of wonder.

Actually, the play fails because of over-emphasis. The explanation is insisted upon too much, and most other elements in *Titus Andronicus* are similarly heavy-handed. Yet, it remains invaluable for revealing some of the most important elements accruing to Shakespeare's early concept of tragedy. Stressing its anticipations of *Othello* and *King Lear*, J. C. Maxwell concludes that:[6]

> *Romeo and Juliet* is on almost every count a vastly superior play to *Titus*, but it could be maintained that *Titus* is strictly speaking more *promising*. The author of *Romeo and Juliet* could conceivably have gone in that play as far as he was destined to go in tragedy – and indeed Shakespeare's tragic development does not exactly proceed through *Romeo and Juliet* – but the author of *Titus* was obviously going *somewhere*: though it was not yet certain whether he would steer clear of violent episodic melodrama on the one hand and exaggeratedly Ovidian narrative dialogue on the other.

If Maxwell's argument for a chap-book source for the play is correct, Shakespeare's changes in the material exhibit, especially in the first and in the fifth act, his typical concern 'with civil order and the forces which threaten to overthrow it'.[7] Despite these changes, however, the dominant impression of the play is *not* that individual actions have enormous implications for politics, society, and history, so that one is forced to agree with R. M. Sargent: 'The play deliberately obscures the clear-cut nature of the foreign-native conflict for power . . . the vendetta between the Queen and Andronicus assumes more nearly the status of an inter-family feud.'[8] The passions of rage, grief, and even wonder seem so purely personal as to appear, finally, as only idiosyncratic and extreme. By not invoking securely enough the presence of history, *Titus Andronicus* is also less than fully tragic.⁹

By contrast, *King John* attempts to grapple with a miscellaneous assortment of events from chronicle history and to bind them in tragic unity. Besides the evidence of the title, we have the report (amplified from Holinshed) of Arthur's death as it affects the common people.

> Young Arthur's death is common in their mouths:
> And when they talk of him, they shake their heads
> And whisper one another in the ear;
> 190 And he that speaks doth gripe the hearer's wrist,
> Whilst he that hears makes fearful action,
> With wrinkled brows, with nods, with rolling eyes.
> I saw a smith stand with his hammer, thus,
> The whilst his iron did on the anvil cool,
> 195 With open mouth swallowing a tailor's news;
> Who, with his shears and measure in his hand,
> Standing on his slippers, which his nimble haste
> Had falsely thrust upon contrary feet,
> Told of a many thousand warlike French
> 200 That were embattailed and rank'd in Kent:
> Another lean unwash'd artificer
> Cuts off his tale and talks of Arthur's death.
> (IV, ii, 187–202)

Sudden, unexpected death arouses wonder. There are two additional points to be made about this speech. By dwelling on the reception of Arthur's death among common people, Shakespeare seems to be striving for the verisimilitude that he handles so masterfully in *Henry IV* Parts I and II, and in *Henry V*. The actions of the great affect all levels of society. Second, the details recounted in lines 193 to 200 comprise a kind of dramatic trick. The smith and tailor, neglecting their tasks and distracted – the one with open mouth, the other with slippers on the wrong feet, appear, at first, to be part of the general astonishment at Arthur's death. But, as it turns out, their wonder is focused merely on the news of the French army in Kent. 'Another lean unwash'd artificer' intervenes with news of Arthur's death, and since his news takes precedence over the earlier tale, he heightens the wonder thereat. In this way the claims of tragedy (Arthur's death) subsume the claims of chronicle history (the French wars).

Not all of *King John*, however, is this successful at reconciling tragedy and history. For one thing, the plot is too episodic for any clear focus of attention to emerge. For another, there is no character (or characters) substantial enough to bear the weight of tragedy. The Bastard, easily the most energetic figure in the play, has numerous admirers for his forthright, if somewhat crude, patriotism, but his opportunism and his aggressively blunt, but limited, common sense work rather against than for a sense of tragedy. King John and his adversaries are too small-minded and whimsical to be tragic. Much of the action is organized around the passive Arthur, whose supposed claim to the English throne provides an excuse for the early conflicts between the French and the English, and whose death demoralizes the English nobles and accompanies the general decline of almost everyone's fortunes in the later stages of conflict. There seems to be little of 'causative character' here, and the events of history roll on almost as if without responsible agents of any sort. That Shakespeare is intent upon maintaining something of the emotional effect of tragedy is evident, perhaps, from the number of appearances of thwarted wonder, or amazement, joined with woe late in the play. 'I am amaz'd, methinks, and lose my way/ Among the thorns and dangers of this world' (IV, iii, 140–1) says the Bastard to Hubert. And again to John: 'Your nobles will not hear you, but are gone/ To offer service to your enemy;/ And wild amazement hurries up and down/ The little number of you doubtful friends' (V, i, 33–6). 'Doubtful' in this context means 'apprehensive; full of fear.' And similarly, Lewis to Salisbury, who is weeping: 'This shower, blown up by tempest of the soul,/ Startles mine eyes, and makes me more amaz'd/ Than had I seen the vaulty top of heaven/ Figur'd o'er with burning meteors' (V, ii, 50–3). But the very number of these references and their lack of resolution dissipate the effect; and Shakespeare comes, eventually, to rely on another play and another strategy to attempt a reconciliation of tragedy and history.

In *Richard II*, Shakespeare avoided a number of problems

attendant on *King John* and *Titus Andronicus* and faced many more that were alien to those plays. To begin with, the deposition of Richard represents one unifying act with enormous repercussions for subsequent history, and flowing from this point is the fact that hardly any personal action by either Richard or Bolingbroke is totally devoid of at least the possibility of extra-personal significance. As well, the character of Richard, as he is presented in the source material, Hall, Holinshed, Froissart, perhaps the *Traison*, as well as *The Mirror for Magistrates*, *Woodstock*, and Daniel's *Civil Wars*,[10] provided Shakespeare in a general way with the sort of figure that Aristotle suggests appropriate for tragedy – a mean between extremes – 'a man not pre-eminently virtuous and just, whose misfortune, however, is brought upon him not by vice and depravity'.[11] However, in returning to a period of English history, the later stages of which he had already dealt with at some length, and projecting perhaps already a more extended treatment of the earlier stages, and taking up a subject about which there were conflicting accounts from the past and diverging opinions in the present, a subject which, as numerous references show, could still prove highly inflammatory in contemporary politics, and in dealing more directly than he had ever done before with the problem of personal qualifications and political office, Shakespeare ran the risk of losing his subject in the diverse ramifications of its potentiality. A good part of the reason he did not lose it is to be found in his use of the heroic couplet. *Richard II* is one of the few plays in the whole Shakespearean canon composed entirely in verse; important aspects of the subject are highlighted by an extremely flexible and sophisticated use of verse. The added discipline of the heroic couplet offers simultaneously a way of checking and placing the dynamism of individual thought and feeling and of alluding to the social and political consequences of individual action without digressing or disrupting unity. A. P. Rossiter, for one, thinks that the play 'is seriously flawed by its peculiar dependence on *Woodstock*: peculiar because Shakespeare not only took items from it, but also *left behind* in it explanations badly needed in his play, items taken for granted, or as read, which produce puzzles that cannot be cleared up without reference to the earlier play'.[12] But Rossiter ignores the way in which poetry, and especially the heroic couplet, is capable of filling in, by suggestion, enough of the necessary background to make its meaning or its action self-sufficient and intelligible.[13]

Before proceeding directly to the play, it is perhaps worth considering why the heroic couplet, of its very nature, is the instrument most capable of reconciling diverse and sometimes discordant claims on the attention of the poet. The best explanation is to be found in Yvor Winters's essay, 'The Influence of Meter on Poetic Convention.'[14]

> The heroic couplet, all things considered, appears to be the most flexible of forms: it can suggest by discreet imitation, the effects of nearly any other technique conceivable; it can contain all of these effects, if need be, in a single poem.
>
> What, then, makes the couplet so flexible? The answer can be given briefly: its seeming inflexibility. That is, the identity of the line is stronger in rhymed verse than in unrhymed, because a bell is rung at the end of every second line; the identity of the line will be stronger in the couplet than in any other stanza because the couplet is the simplest and most obvious form of stanza possible. This mathematical and almost mechanical recurrence of line and stanza provides an obvious substructure and core of connotation over which poetic variations may move, from which they derive an exact identity. . . .
>
> In spite of this regularity of basic scheme, there is no confinement of variation. The secondary rhythmic relationships of the couplet are unhampered by the rigidity of the primary, and the resultant set of relationships (the tertiary) between the constant element and the varying element, will be therefore unlimited, at the same time, however, that the constant element is providing a permanent point of reference, or feeling of cohesion, for the whole. The poet may move in any direction whatever, and his movement will be almost automatically graduated by the metronomic undercurrent of regularity. . . .
>
> In the couplet we may have an entirely free play of thought over a rigid metrical substructure.

The heroic couplet, of course, is the characteristic form of such masters as Dryden, Pope, and Churchill; but as W. B. Piper demonstrates in *The Heroic Couplet*, the decasyllabic couplet was by no means a rudimentary form when it came to Shakespeare's hand. Chaucer had used it extensively, and after about 1585,[15]

> The closed couplet evolved by and large from the efforts of many Elizabethan poets (among them Christopher Marlowe, Sir John Harrington, Michael Drayton, Thomas Heywood, Joseph Hall and, of course, Donne and Jonson) to reproduce in English the effects of the Latin elegiac distich, especially as it had been employed by Ovid in his *Amores* and *Heroides* and by Martial in his *Epigrammaton*.

It was Shakespeare's genius to discern something of the potential of the couplet for the drama. The 'core of connotation' to which Winters refers and which is provided by the metrical substructure can be indicated in a general way as the feeling appropriate to such items as clarity, balance, reasonable and definitive judgment, and, above all, order.

Such feeling, of course, has an obvious place in the dramatization of history, and should be enough, in itself, to alert us to the possibility that Shakespeare intended to make the couplet work for a larger design. Many critics, beginning with Pope (1728) and with Samuel Johnson (1765), who said of V, iii, 23–134, 'This whole passage is such as I could well wish away',[16] have found the couplet writing to be generally inferior. E. M. W. Tillyard delivers a blanket condemnation of Shakespeare's couplets in *Richard II* with the tautological remark that, 'to account for the indifferent quality, one may remember that he was never very good at the couplet'.[17] But aside from ignoring the question of what the couplet might be intended to do, this judgment dismisses the possibility that different stretches of couplet writing might be successful in varying degrees. Piper was the first critic to point out the way in which the couplet works in Act I. He speaks of I, i, 152–205:[18]

> We find assembled here the ingredients for an elegant interlude in closed couplets, that is, for an elegant

dramatic tableau: two antagonists and two peace-makers with balanced pleadings and professions. But the ceremonial pattern of utterance, inaugurated by Richard, gives way, with wonderfully expressive effect, before the energy and passion of Bolingbroke. Richard loves kingly show but not kingly exertion, the forms but not the stresses of royalty. The closed couplets with which the passage opens and the closed-couplet situation Richard attempts to prescribe declare his plans: he will calm Mowbray, and Gaunt will calm Bolingbroke in beautifully mirroring attitudes of command and obedience. But the very first application of this inappropriately aesthetic impulse, his and Gaunt's antiphonal commands of peace (ll. 160–165), fails when the two foes, whose motives are deep and complex, resist. Their resistance is, of course, reflected in the breakdown of couplet closure and balance. Mowbray comes, finally, to submit to the king's mode of utterance, that is, to the king's wishes (ll. 178–85), but not Bolingbroke. His powerfully enjambed speech (ll. 187–95) underscores his recalcitrance. Richard's apparent recapturing of this situation, signalized by his reassertion of closed-couplet utterance after a brief lapse into blank verse (ll. 196–205) is hollow; the antagonists, or at least one of them, have not submitted and will not submit to play parts in Richard's royal puppet show. Shakespeare's handling of the couplet throughout this passage, then, underscores the inadequacy of Richard as a king and the fragility of his rule.

Piper's alertness to the flexibility of couplet practice in this passage is enormously helpful to anyone interested in understanding Shakespeare's style, but the conclusions he draws from his analysis are a bit too simple. It is true that Bolingbroke's strongly enjambed couplets at I, i, 187–95 emphasize his individual energy and his antagonism to the king. Bolingbroke is threatening the world in high astounding terms, and by having him run roughshod over the normal places of couplet closure, Shakespeare manages to suggest the modulated and rhymeless line that critical theory deemed the appropriate medium for aspiring minds. But though they fail to observe what Piper calls 'the hierarchy of pauses' of the closed couplet – strong pause at the end of the second line, secondary pause at the end of the first line, and tertiary pauses at mid-line points – Bolingbroke's lines *are* couplets, so that they acknowledge implicitly the very norm they seem to violate. The couplet discreetly imitates the effects of another technique while retaining its own identity; and Bolingbroke's challenge is not simply an opposition to regal authority nor is it only an expression of impatience with a 'royal puppet show'. It is an attempt to make the representative of order and justice live up to his responsibility.

Similarly, Richard's mode of utterance is ceremonial and elegant, and his attempt to impose order is inappropriately aesthetic and facile. But though it is inadequate, it *is* an attempt to impose order.

> This we prescribe, though no physician;
> Deep malice makes too deep incision.
> Forget, forgive, conclude and be agreed:
> Our doctors say this is no month to bleed. (I, i, 154–7)

Richard attempts to avail himself of the couplet's powers of assimilation, to lay claim to both the moral style and the eloquent style, by making a thoroughly traditional analogy of king as physician, proffering moral advice, and by wittily retracting the analogy even while punning on the two meanings that the analogy lends to the verb 'to bleed.' The couplet balance gives the advice epigrammatic point, and it emphasizes the wit of simultaneously assuming and spurning the analogy. However, the two styles are not really assimilated. The eloquence does not support, indeed is irrelevant to, the moral attitude. As a result, the moral style is insufficiently supported by the concrete particulars of experience (What is the malice? What would the incision be? Why would it be too deep?), and degenerates to attitudinizing. Richard's handling of the moral style here is not at all inconsistent, as we have seen, with his character or with his attempts in other passages to achieve moral attitudes. Without claiming undue merit for the couplets in Act I, we may say, at least, that Shakespeare is clearly using the couplet to work out an adjustment

between the temper or tone of individual characters and the
theme of political stability and order.

Furthermore, we may take Piper's method of analysis to
other parts of the play – the end, for example.

> *Bol.* Carlisle, this is your doom:
> 25   Choose out some secret place, some reverend room,
> More than thou hast, and with it joy thy life.
> So as thou liv'st in peace, die free from strife;
> For though mine enemy thou hast ever been,
> High sparks of honour in thee have I seen.
>   *Enter* Exton *with the coffin*.
> 30 *Exton.* Great king, within this coffin I present
> Thy buried fear. Herein all breathless lies
> The mightiest of thy greatest enemies,
> Richard of Burdeaux, by me thither brought.
>   *Bol.* Exton, I thank thee not, for thou has wrought
> 35   A deed of slander with thy fatal hand
> Upon my head and all this famous land.
> *Exton.* From your own mouth, my lord, did I this deed.
> *Bol.* They love not poison that do poison need,
> Nor do I thee. Though I did wish him dead,
> 40   I hate the murtherer, love him murthered.
> The guilt of conscience take thou for thy labour,
> But neither my good word nor princely favour;
> With Cain go wander thorough shades of night,
> And never show thy head by day nor light.
> 45   Lords, I protest my soul is full of woe
> That blood should sprinkle me to make me grow.
> Come mourn with me for what I do lament,
> And put on sullen black incontinent.
> I'll make a voyage to the Holy Land,
> 50   To wash this blood off from my guilty hand.
> March sadly after; grace my mournings here
> In weeping after this untimely bier. (V, vi, 24–52)

Here it is Bolingbroke who tries to prescribe the standard
mode of utterance, again the closed couplet. And again the
materials are at hand for an elegant tableau: majesty at its
most magnanimous, dispensing pardon and commendation,
savouring power for an instant in the sinister implications of

the word 'doom' picked up from the previous line, but essentially relaxed and confident in the exercise of benign intentions. In the balance of the couplet and with respect to Carlisle, Bolingbroke finds judgment, justice, and mercy happily congruent. But with the entrance of Exton and Richard's coffin, the mode of utterance is disrupted. Instead of the closed-couplet hierarchy of pauses, the mid-line pauses are frequently as strong as the end-line pauses and often more emphatic. The syntactic thrusts that overrun couplet closure at line 32 and line 34 create heavy emphasis on 'Richard of Burdeaux' and 'A deed of slander', the very elements that will disturb Bolingbroke's rule to the end. As well, Exton's opening lines carry some of the exultant energy of the bombastic line, even though only the first is unrhymed. Each time Exton speaks, Bolingbroke is forced away from the closed-couplet norm and returns to it only with difficulty; and even after the norm is re-established at line 41 to the end, the influence of Exton's intrusion remains. Bolingbroke's couplets are no longer crisp and confident, but limp and wistful. The feeling created, largely by means of the diction, of course, but partly by means of the rhythm, in the almost total absence of caesuras in the last twelve lines and in the plodding supracouplet movement, is the feeling appropriate to an impotent gesture toward moral rectitude.

Shakespeare seems to regard the closed couplet as holding the promise of moral and political stability, but, with one exception, no character fulfils that promise in *Richard II*. Neither Bolingbroke nor Richard is given couplet lines that express a satisfyingly intelligent moral perspective, though each lays claim to moral feeling, which, in the absence of thought, is but attitudinizing. Nevertheless, the couplets examined so far are moderately successful at indicating something of the momentous and impersonal significance that flows of necessity through the individual beings who are the indispensable focuses of experience. Shakespeare's use of such techniques is part of his attempt to fuse history into tragedy. In a way, the promise of order that the couplet seems to offer and the intrusions that thwart that promise are analogous to the disparity between the intelligence and will demanded of the protagonist by his circumstances and the

limited intelligence and will he can muster – the situation
that Coleridge says produces the deepest effect in drama. Both
Richard and Bolingbroke are pursued by an ineradicable guilt
that is at once their own doing and the legacy of history and
the larger community. Just so much does Shakespeare need
from the chronicle histories and *Woodstock*, and just so
much does the heroic couplet allude to. To refute Rossiter,
the circumstances of Gloucester's death need no further
specification in *Richard II* beyond what they receive in
Bolingbroke's energetic prosecution of the matter as defined
against his father's restraint.

The exception, of course, in realizing the potential of the
heroic couplet in this play is John of Gaunt. Before his son's
banishment will expire, he says:

> My oil-dried lamp and time-bewasted light
> Shall be extinct with age and endless night,
> My inch of taper will be burnt and done,
> And blindfold Death not let me see my son.

225 *Rich.* Why, uncle, thou hast many years to live.
> *Gaunt.* But not a minute, king, that thou canst give:
> Shorten my days thou canst with sullen sorrow,
> And pluck nights from me, but not lend a morrow;
> Thou canst help time to furrow me with age,
230 > But stop no wrinkle in his pilgrimage;
> Thy word is current with him for my death,
> But dead, thy kingdom cannot buy my breath.
> *Rich.* Thy son is banish'd upon good advice,
> Whereto thy tongue a party-verdict gave:
235 > Why at our justice seem'st thou then to lour?
> *Gaunt.* Things sweet to taste prove in digestion sour.
> You urg'd me as a judge, but I had rather
> You would have bid me argue like a father.
> O, had it been a stranger, not my child,
240 > To smooth his fault I should have been more mild.
> A partial slander sought I to avoid,
> And in the sentence my own life destroy'd.
> Alas, I look'd when some of you should say
> I was too strict to make mine own away;
245 > But you gave leave to my unwilling tongue
> Against my will to do myself this wrong. (I, iii, 221–46)

The heroic couplet here is able to suggest by discreet imitation the effect of elegy and lyric, partly through the use of feminine rhymes, partly through flexible placing of the caesura, and partly through lightening of the end-line pauses. Yet the identity of the closed couplet remains intact; indeed, in each interchange, Gaunt holds Richard to the couplet form (Richard tries to turn to blank verse at ll. 233-5 and possibly at l. 225 as well). Gaunt rebukes the king within the form originally prescribed by Richard himself. Despite the elegiac feeling, the hierarchy of pauses is employed throughout to accentuate rational and moral distinctions. In line 228, for example, concluding the couplet that compelled Johnson's admiration, the caesura falls in the middle of the third foot, dividing the line exactly in half and weighing the greater power to destroy against the inability to foster life. The caesura simultaneously marks and mellows the distinction as the intense monosyllables are modulated by the graceful mid-line pause; the ascending degree of accent at the beginning of each half line falls away in the unaccented syllable preceding the caesura and again in the feminine ending. In this way, a clear recognition of the existing order of things becomes tragic resignation.

Lines 239 to 243 have been thought repetitious by a number of readers, including presumably the editors of the First Folio who omitted them, yet Johnson, after glossing 'partial slander' as 'the reproach of partiality', comments: 'This is a just picture of the struggle between principle and affection.'[19] Indeed, the couplet, in which 'partial slander' and 'sentence' are placed in opposition, is wholly necessary because it deepens the simple antithesis of 'judge' versus 'father' by introducing the cost of presuming to correct for an emotional 'bias.' A man ignores his true feeling at his own peril. In realizing the potential of the heroic couplet, John of Gaunt does not discover a radical solution to the questions of crime and punishment that beleaguer *Richard II*, but he attains a fuller recognition than the others of the truth that principles and affections (judgment and sympathy) are both essential elements of justice and that a state which ignores this truth is less than civilized. Gaunt's couplets are, at once, more charged with personal feeling and more fully cognizant of the things that make for civilization than are the couplets of either Bolingbroke or Richard. And in having him abide by the demands of the closed couplet, when both Richard and Bolingbroke fail, Shakespeare brings him closer than either to giving the historical conflict tragic significance.

Samuel Johnson, supported by Winters and Piper, thus provides a way of understanding the superiority of one stretch of couplet writing to others in *Richard II* and a way of linking that stretch to the passage I have already argued for as the standard in the play. We may now turn to a passage that Johnson found to be generally inferior and notice the part it plays in Shakespeare's experiment with the couplet in *Richard II*. The scene (V, iii) is another animated tableau consisting of a series of contrasts. Boliingbroke's difficulty with his wayward son, Prince Hal, is mirrored by York's difficulty with his son, Aumerle. The opposition of York and his wife with respect to their son's transgression represents once more the struggle between principle and affection.

85 *Duch.* O king, believe not this hard-hearted man!
     Love loving not itself none other can.
     York. Thou frantic woman, what dost thou make here?
     Shall thy old dugs once more a traitor rear?
     Duch. Sweet York, be patient. Hear me, gentle liege.
     Bol. Rise up, good aunt.
90   *Duch.*   Not yet, I thee beseech:
     For ever will I walk upon my knees,
     And never see day that the happy sees
     Till thou give joy – until thou bid me joy,
     By pardoning Rutland my transgressing boy.
95   *Aum.* Unto my mother's prayers I bend my knee.
     York. Against them both my true joints bended be.
     Ill may'st thou thrive if thou grant any grace!
     Duch. Pleads he in earnest? Look upon his face.
                                   (V, iii, 85–98)

The style of the couplet in this passage is what Piper has described as the medieval couplet, composed essentially in one-line units and characterized by an irregular stiffness, with heavy stops at the ends of first lines (ll. 85, 87, 89, 95, 97) and incidental mid-line pauses of great weight (ll. 87, 89,

90, 93, 98). It furthermore consists of 'a sequence in serial order of sententiae, maxims, proverbs, or propositions of a similar kind' (ll. 86, 88, 91-4, 95, 96, 97), which constitute 'a cumulative experience of serious insistence'.[20] The metrical stiffness of the couplet here contributes to the stiffness of the scene and gives to each of its several speakers 'the effect of a strictly one-way communication whose truths are perfectly determined; of a speaker, to put its effect another way, who has reached a perfection of wisdom and is no longer responsive to – no longer dependent on – experience, who is not open to new arguments or new impressions'.[21]

In so far as York is concerned, the effect of the medieval couplet is perfectly consistent with the presentation of his character in II, i, 1-146, where, as we remember, he is characterized by the native plain style un-enriched by the sensuous particulars of experience. His steadfastness there and immediately following Gaunt's death (especially II, i, 163-208) has earned him the admiration of many readers. As well, he performs a kind of choric function designating the emotional effects of woe and wonder at II, ii, 98-120 and at III, iii, 68-71 and exhibiting those effects in a bewildered state at II, iii, 83-170 and at III, iii. 7-17, so that the reader has all the more difficulty in viewing him dispassionately. But there can be little doubt that Shakespeare intended to portray in him, to use Coleridge's phrase, 'a man of no strong powers of mind, but of earnest wishes to do right', and to show that earnest wishes are not sufficient to surmount the full complexity of political action.[22] By Act IV, York has almost unwittingly become a kind of tool in Bolingbroke's hands, and there and in Act V he not infrequently drops into a parody of the bombastic style (IV, i, 107-12 and V, ii, 7-40). In his zealous desire to impeach his own son, he is shown still operating according to the habits of allegiance based on tradition when that tradition itself has been dislocated. As Newbolt observed in 1912, 'York's unnatural loyalty reads like a perverted echo of Gaunt's speech in a similar situation, I. iii. 238-44.'[23] For York, principle is so much an absolute that he does not even see the need to reconcile principle and affection, let alone attempt it. Shakespeare clearly does mean to contrast the stiffness of York's medieval couplets with Gaunt's Renaissance urbanity.

The presence, then, of a good deal of couplet writing is not without dramatic point, both for the purpose of characterization and for the significance of the plot. It represents an experiment in style that was essential to Shakespeare's intention. It is not at all conclusive evidence for the existence of 'an old play written entirely in rhymed verse and belonging to a period when the English drama was not yet using blank verse'. Rather more likely is the notion that Shakespeare himself introduced rhyme into his play as a way of modifying the Marlovian verse line. It may indeed be true, as Feuillerat concludes, that 'the historical events essential to a play on Richard II' are to be found in the sections of couplet writing comprising over 500 lines of rhymed verse, though there seems little reason to suppose that these represent the 'skeleton' of a more 'primitive play' when they so clearly are, in Shakespeare's hands, an economical way of alluding to the historical significance of his plot without distracting attention from the primary focus on individual action. If some couplets are inferior in quality to others, there is no need to invent a predecessor 'who may have understood something of the theatre but who was not a poet'.[24] Stretches of inferior poetry may be something the dramatist can hardly escape, since some of his characters must be inferior in intelligence to others and some must be more and less intelligent in different parts of the play.[25] The same basic motive that led Shakespeare into his exciting experiments with the couplet in I, i; V, vi; and I, iii led him into the mannered stiffness of V, iii.

Moreover, the experiment is not unique to *Richard II.* Attempting to accommodate history and tragedy, Shakespeare tested the couplet as early as *Henry VI, Part I* and drew on the resources he had discovered as late as *King Lear.* The figure most nearly approaching tragic stature in the earlier play is Talbot, whose death, immediately following the death of his son, marks the decline of the English fortunes in France. A. S. Cairncross remarks that the style of these scenes is 'deliberately made more formal (cf. the rhymed couplets, stichomythia, and word patterns) as fitting the more poetic emotion and treatment.'[26] Shakespeare uses stichomythia tied together by closed couplets as Talbot tries to persuade his son to escape, and John Talbot, imitating his father's sense of honour and courage, avows his intention to remain, making his point with the emphasis of couplet closure (IV, v, 18–21 and 34–43). In the next scene, Talbot tells of rescuing his son:

> The ireful Bastard Orleans, that drew blood
> From thee, my boy, and had the maidenhood
> Of thy first fight, I soon encountered,
> And, interchanging blows, I quickly shed
> Some of his bastard blood, and in disgrace
> Bespoke him thus: 'Contaminated, base,
> And misbegotten blood I spill of thine,
> Mean and right poor, for that pure blood of mine
> Which thou did force from Talbot, my brave boy'.
>   (IV, vi, 16–24)

The threat to social and political order, implicit in the Bastard's parentage and in his allegiance to the wrong side, and explicit in his wounding of John Talbot, is heavily underscored by this powerful series of enjambed couplets. While continuing to suggest the stable values of proper lineage, English patriotism, and family affection, the heroic couplet allows Talbot to lay claim to the vaunting, energetic style appropriate to his fighting spirit. Father and son then proceed to reaffirm their mutual concern and essential unity in a series of closed couplets (IV, vi, 28–57). And in the final scene, Talbot recounts the death of his son in four enjambed couplets (IV, vii, 9–16) before submitting to his own death. He apprehends his own end, beginning with the phrase 'thou antic Death' that seems to anticipate *Richard II*, III, ii, 162, in a speech that returns to the closed couplet norm (IV, vii, 18–32), as he is re-united with his son in death.

In *King Lear*, the closed couplet is made to stand for the same sort of proper alignment among personal feeling, social duty, and political order. Following his banishment for attempting to redress Lear's rage in the opening scene, Kent, like Gaunt in *Richard II*, rebukes the king as well as Goneril and Regan and offers solace to Cordelia in a speech composed in closed couplets (I, i, 179–86). The King of France adopts the same form later in the scene when he takes up the castaway Cordelia.[27]

> Gods, gods! 'tis strange that from their cold'st neglect
> My love should kindle to inflam'd respect.
> Thy dowerless daughter, King, thrown to my chance,
> Is Queen of us, of ours, and our fair France:
> Not all the dukes of wat'rish Burgundy
> Can buy this unpriz'd precious maid of me.
> Bid them farewell, Cordelia, though unkind:
> Thou losest here, a better where to find. (I, i, 253–60)

The stately and emphatic rhythm of the closed couplet, along with the choice diction of this passage, helps to affirm Cordelia's proper station as: 'Queen of us, of ours, and our fair France.' Lear's answer, by contrast, violates the closed couplet norm and simultaneously violates the deepest feelings that create *human* nature.

> Thou hast her, France; let her be thine, for we
> Have no such daughter, nor shall ever see
> That face of hers again; therefore be gone
> Without our grace, our love, our benison.
> Come, noble Burgundy. (I, i, 261–5)

The radical deviation from the hierarchy of pauses in these two couplets underlines the radically deviant judgment and feeling. The heroic couplet, holding out the promise of order in its closed couplet form, becomes an instrument for measuring precisely the violation of that order: in the drama 'the deepest effect is produced, when the fate is represented as a higher and intelligent will, and the opposition of the individual as springing from a defect'. Even Lear's triplet 'our grace, our love, our benison' holds in confused potential, as it were, the primal elements – personal, social, political – that when morally and spiritually well-ordered, as in France's couplets, make for human life.[28]

The heroic couplet, then, provides a synthesis of individual energy and political order and, therefore, helps to lay the basis for the great tragedies that follow *Richard II*. It alludes to the powerful connections between personal acts and universal significance and, therefore, helps to make possible the presentation of character and action in the Aristotelian sense. We may say that Coleridge's intuition about the near alliance of historical drama and tragic drama is not without cause and reason; and we may say that Shakespeare's discovery of this truth is, in part, made possible by his experiment with the heroic couplet in *The Tragedy of King Richard the Second*. Some of the findings of this mode are available for exploitation in blank verse.

9 · Astounding terms: bombast and wonder

> Beatrice began to speak pleasantly and softly . . . and this is well said, for the divine style is sweet and plain, not lofty and proud as that of Virgil and the poets.[1]

Valuable though the experiment with the heroic couplet is, there is no denying that Shakespeare's main instrument is blank verse.[2] And blank verse, in drama, as it developed in England in the latter part of the sixteenth century is predominantly bombastic and arouses primarily the kind of wonder or astonishment appropriate to bombast. It is axiomatic that this development leads to the great achievements of Elizabethan tragedy; but despite the excellent work done by critics such as Howard Baker in *Induction to Tragedy* and Wolfgang Clemen in *English Tragedy Before Shakespeare*, it is not clear how the wonder appropriate to bombast becomes finally (to give what in some sense is a definition of tragedy) a kind of wonder fully appropriate to woe. For this, something more than the bombastic style is needed. In much of the blank verse of *Richard II*, Shakespeare can be seen creating out of the methods of his predecessors a new high style that incorporates the sweet and the plain.[3]

For many of those predecessors, one of the main attractions of blank verse is the chance it gives the author himself to be wondered at, to be admired. The most noticeable thing about the high style is that it is noticeable; it was, like free verse in our time, a technique on which to build a reputation. As Baker points out, George Gascoigne gives this reason for choosing the medium 'at least ten years before the prologue to *Tamburlaine*'.[4] In his prefatory poem to 'The Steel Glas', Gascoigne asserts that '. . . there is a sort of fame . . . The walles whereof are wondrous harde to clyme:/ And much to high, for ladders made of ryme.' He must therefore use another technique: 'Such battring tyre, this pamphlet here bewraies,/ In rymeless verse, which thundreth mighty threates'.[5]

168

And similarly, Robert Greene's famous remarks in the *Groatsworth of Witte* testify to the prestige of blank verse. His castigation of Shakespeare as 'an upstart Crow, beautified with our feathers, that with his *Tygers hart wrapt in a Players hyde*, supposes he is as well able to bombast out a blanke verse as the best of you' gives us our first glimpse of Shakespeare's reputation in London. And his advice to Peele and the others is primarily aimed at protecting their own reputations: 'never more acquaint them with your *admired* inventions' (my italics).[6] The wonder of blank verse was clearly at a premium at a time when other elements of literature and theatre (characters, plots, ideas, songs, and scenes) were often regarded as common property. These remarks concerning reputations also indicate the overriding effect blank verse was thought to produce in 1576 and 1592.

But the noticeable style does not have a monopoly on wonder, and to see this is to see more clearly the developing complexity of Elizabethan tragedy. J. V. Cunningham explains the general principles most lucidly.

The effect of astonishment or wonder is the natural correlative of unusual diction, as it is of the unusual event. The proper word satisfies by its exactness; the unusual pleases or displeases by its startling effect. Upon this basis, which though obvious is not unimportant, together with the doctrine of the appropriateness of style to subject, rests the whole later theory of the kinds and characters of style in all its elaboration. Hence, the theorists will ascribe to any style which is noticeable as such the quality of wonder. That style which is elaborated for the purpose of charm or pleasure – the *genus floridum* – will evoke the kind of pleasant wonder that the marvellous story does, and will be appropriate to such subjects: for instance, the Milesian style of Apuleius, for the effect of wonder is ascribed in the passage cited above not only to the subject matter but also to the style. The high style, the forceful, the grand – the style of Demosthenes and of Aeschylus – will evoke that wonder which is akin to fear, and will be especially appropriate to tragedy. Yet wonder may be on a lesser scale than this: it corresponds to the displacement, large or small, that initiates internal movement: with respect to the intellect, inference, the processes of logic, and learning; with respect to the irrational part of the soul, feeling and emotion. Hence style can evoke emotion in the audience, and at the same time by the law of decorum the degree of unusual diction should be proportionate to the height and intensity of the feeling inherent in the subject matter. Again, to wonder at style is to regard it highly, to approve of it, to admire in the modern sense, but this attitude, though not unaccompanied by feeling, nevertheless implies no specific shade of emotional coloring. (*CE*, pp. 64, 65)

Cunningham here outlines the three levels of style according to classical rhetoric: the middle style (the *genus floridum*) and the high style are mentioned explicitly, but 'wonder on a lesser scale' is the province of the plain style – of both the native plain style and the classical plain style. It is the province of inference, logic, and learning and also the province of the feeling and emotion that make an intellectual experience an experience.[7] The three levels of style, in other words, may be examined by noting the sort of wonder they evoke, together with the strategies of language by which the evocations work. I have already discussed at length the workings of the plain and the pleasant styles in *Richard II*. It remains to turn our attention to the high style and to its relationship with the other two and thereby to specify the shades of emotional colouring in the play.[8]

First, however, it is useful to look briefly at the high style in some earlier Elizabethan plays where the emotional colouring is often, by contrast, a simple matter. *Gorboduc* may serve as a typical example since, as Wolfgang Clemen observes, 'The history of rhetorical tragedy in England opens with *Gorboduc*.'[9] The unusual event in this play is death: the death of Ferrex at the hands of his brother Porrex, the stabbing of Porrex by his mother, Videna, and the deaths of both Gorboduc and Videna, king and queen, at the hands of the incensed people. The ultimate cause of these deaths is Gorboduc's mishandling of the succession to the throne, and

Sackville and Norton use the obvious results to impress upon a young Queen Elizabeth in 1561 the dire consequences of leaving the succession uncertain.[10]

> Loe here the end of Brutus royall line!
> And loe the entry to the wofull wracke
> And vtter ruin of this noble realme!

The adjectives that fill out the decasyllabic line are here proportionate to the height and intensity of feeling inherent in the subject matter. The repeated exclamation invites us to wonder at the simple fact of woe. *Gorboduc* is presented on a single level of style emphasizing the seriousness of the events, the striking deaths of noble personages with instant implications for the nation, and emphasizing too the authors' didactic intentions.

Two of Shakespeare's more immediate predecessors, Marlowe and Kyd, have more complicated intentions that call for a more complicated version of the high style. Though *Tamburlaine* with its 'astounding terms' contains numerous synonyms for the sort of wonder characteristic of the grand style, there are interesting indications of other influences at work. Clemen has already noted that the panegyric on Zenocrate's death (2 *Tam.*, II, iv, 1ff.) 'exemplifies the ease and naturalness with which lyrical forms could be absorbed by the drama'.[11] Another interesting sign occurs in some lines at the death of Agidas, a very minor figure. Unlike most of the characters in the play, Agidas dies not so much because he opposes Tamburlaine's political ambitions but because he ridicules his amorous ambitions. In a speech overheard by Tamburlaine, Agidas warns Zenocrate that Tamburlaine is one[12]

> Who when he shall embrace you in his armes,
> Will tell how many thousand men he slew.
> And when you looke for amorous discourse,
> Will rattle forth his facts of war and blood.
> Too harsh a subject for your dainty eares.
>
> (1 *Tam.*, III, ii, 42–6)

Agidas dies, one might say, for pointing out the absence of the pleasant style in Tamburlaine. His apprehension of his

impending death outlines the major effects of the grand
style.

> Betraide by fortune and suspitious love,
> Threatned with frowning wrath and jealousie,
> Surpriz'd with feare of hideous revenge,
> I stand agast: but most astonied
> To see his choller shut in secret thoughtes,
> And wrapt in silence of his angry soule.
> Upon his browes was pourtraid ugly death,
> And in his eies the furie of his hart,
> That shine as Comets, menacing revenge,
> And casts a pale complexion on his cheeks.
>   (1 *Tam.*, III, ii, 66–75)

Here the forebodings of woe evoke that wonder which is
akin to fear. Agidas's lines are a good illustration of the
swelling rhetoric that characterizes the play: grandiloquent
adjectives, strong lines with heavy pauses at the end, near
coincidence of metrical and syntactical units, and the strikingly novel expression of ideas that remain essentially the
same through several repetitions. The verse is padded: that is,
it is bombast.

But since in this case Tamburlaine is not threatening
Agidas with astounding terms but with an ominous silence,
Agidas's reaction takes an interesting turn.

> He needed not with words confirme my feare,
> For words are vaine where working tooles present
> The naked action of my threatned end.
> It saies, *Agydas*, thou shalt surely die,
> And of extremities elect the least. (1 *Tam*. III, ii, 92–6)

Here is wonder on a lesser scale corresponding to the displacement that initiates internal movement. The inference
that Agidas makes is only too plain, and the action of his
death is 'naked', that is, unrhetorical. The internal movement
does, however, allow him the possibility of personal choice,
the chance to elect the least of extremities, which as far as
he is concerned is suicide, and it allows him to make that
choice with the appropriate feeling and emotion, which he

hopes will be a kind of *catharsis* of wonder and woe: 'free from feare of Tyrant's rage' (l. 102).

Thus, in this short scene depicting the death of a very minor character, Marlowe alludes to all three styles: the grand, the sweet, and the plain. Agidas is not very important to the overall action of the play, but the verse he is given to utter reveals something Marlowe could have used more extensively. In its simplest terms, *Tamburlaine* is, as Howard Baker says, 'pride oratory',[13] and it is most successful when the aggressive individualism of its hero is on the upswing, making tragedies for other characters and avoiding his own. With the deaths of Zenocrate and of Tamburlaine himself in Part 2, Marlowe has need of a style that can better show the interconnections of the individual and the nation in order to make the tragedy something greater than the mere exhaustion of mechanical energies. Finally, at his own death Tamburlaine is left without a style, since 'pride oratory' is obviously inappropriate.[14]

Thomas Kyd's protagonist in *The Spanish Tragedy*, by contrast, has a style even in the scene of his own death, and it represents an interesting modification of the Elizabethan high style. Both Wolfgang Clemen and Howard Baker have commented on the strongly personal quality of Hieronimo's expression of grief; blank verse seems no longer merely bombastic but is a necessary filling out of an individual sense of grief. Clemen accounts for this primarily as a new flexibility in the use of the set speech. When Hieronimo discovers his murdered son Horatio, for example, his soliloquy is 'not only spoken, but also acted' and the speech 'accurately reflects what Hieronimo is experiencing'.[15] Baker shows that as the disaster of his son's murder takes ever more complete possession of Hieronimo's mind, Kyd is able to turn some of the conventions closely associated with blank verse, such as the Virgilian descent into hell (from Surrey's translation of Book II of *The Aeneid*), or the tragical complaint of a ghost (from Sackville's portrait of Buckingham in *The Mirror For Magistrates*), and make them, in Hieronimo's imagination, lively images of grief.[16] Thus, both Clemen and Baker offer valuable insights into the way in which *The Spanish Tragedy* widens the expressive powers of blank verse.

But bombast remains bombast even if in some ways the stuffing is justified, and Kyd, especially in the resolution of his play, shows some hankerings after another style even to the point of setting up a kind of pretence at the plain style. A brief survey of the word 'resolution' as it is used in the play will help to sketch in something of Kyd's procedure. Shortly after discovering the body of the murdered Horatio, Hieronimo receives a letter written in blood from Bellimperia informing him that Lorenzo and Balthazar are responsible for the murder. But Hieronimo worries that the letter might be a trap laid by the very persons who took Horatio's life: [17]

> Then hazard not thine owne, *Hieronimo*,
> But live t'effect thy resolution.
> I therefore will by circumstances trie,
> What I can gather to confirm this writ. (III, ii, 46–9)

'Resolution' appears to have at least some of the meaning that the *Oxford English Dictionary* says was possible before 1644, that is, 'the removal of a doubt on some point from a person's mind'. The removal of doubt, of course, calls for inference and the processes of logic, though Pedringano's letter indicting the murderers confirms Bellimperia's charge before Hieronimo takes any steps of his own.

Hieronimo's next use of 'resolution' comes in an utterance declaring his firmness or steadiness of purpose.

> Strike, and strike home, where wrong is offred thee;
> For euils vnto ils conductors be,
> And death's the worst of resolution. (III, xiii, 7–9)

The note that Boas offers on line 9 is: 'resolute action can at the worst end in death'; but the word also acquires a peculiar resonance in this context because of its original root, meaning 'death or dissolution, the process by which a material thing is reduced or separated into its component parts or elements'. And something of this meaning lingers in his final use of the word, when he takes Bellimperia into his confidence, even though the primary meaning is 'fixed determination'.

> And heere I vow – so you but giue consent,
> And will conceale my resolution –

I will ere long determine of their deathes
That causles thus haue murdered my sonne. (IV, i, 42–5)

Now although the suggestion of 'solving a doubt or difficulty' in the word 'resolution' might seem to call for the
plain style, the primary meaning of the word, 'fixity of
purpose' or 'unyielding temper', is perfectly congruent with
the high style, and it must be admitted that this is the style
Kyd uses throughout. Our survey might seem without point,
except for the peculiar way that Hieronimo sets up the resolution of his own play about Soliman and Perseda, which
is also used to effect the resolution of *The Spanish Tragedy*.
The peculiarity that Hieronimo insists on is that each actor
must speak his part in a different language, and to Balthazar's
objection, 'But this will be a mere confusion,/ And hardly
shall we all be understood', he replies:

It must be so; for the conclusion
Shall proue the inuention, and all was good:
And I my selfe in an Oration,
And with a strange and wondrous shew besides,
That I haue there behinde a curtaine,
Assure your selfe, shall make the matter knowne:
And all shalbe concluded in one Scene,
For there's no pleasure tane in tediousness. (IV, i, 181–8)

The strange and wondrous show behind a curtain turns out
to be the dead body of Horatio (IV, iv, 88). Hieronimo's
resolution, therefore, makes everything plain, and yet its
effect continues to be one of utter astonishment. Nor is his
style out of keeping with the spectacle he unveils. Through
the device of making the actors speak in 'unknown languages'
Hieronimo elevates the style of his play within a play and
makes his own following oration, explaining among other
things that Lorenzo and Balthazar really have been killed,
appear plain in style even though in fact it is not.

Heere breake we off our sundrie languages,
And thus conclude I in our vulgar tung.
Happely you thinke (but booteles are your thoughts)
That this is fabulously counterfeit,
And that we doo as all Tragedians doo. (IV, iv, 74–8)

175

'Our vulgar tung', following the elevated passions of Hieronimo's play, purports to make everything clear and simple even though the verse remains essentially bombastic: 'The hopeless father of a hapless son/ whose tongue is tun'd to tell his latest tale'. In this way Kyd manages to incorporate some apparently plain-style effects (clarification, the processes of learning, the simple truth) without ever abandoning the grand style. The net effect of the tragedy (its resolution) is just what Hieronimo had earlier predicted it would be.

> Assure you it will prooue most passing strange,
> And wondrous plausible to that assembly. (IV, i, 83, 84)

Drama that would be astounding and at the same time plausible has need of some sort of adjustment between the grand style and the plain style.

The Elizabethan grand style, then, even in two of its purest and most influential instances, *Tamburlaine* and *The Spanish Tragedy*, shows some tendency to accommodate the uses and pressures of other styles. It does so in part, at least, because the development of English tragedy toward something greater than Senecan self-assertion or Stoic resignation needs such an accommodation. In 'Seneca in Elizabethan Translation', T. S. Eliot voiced in 1927 what in some respects remains the accepted view of the subject: 'Dante, for instance, had behind him an Aquinas and Shakespeare behind him a Seneca'.[18] But, whatever is to be said about Dante, Shakespeare had behind him a Seneca *and* an Aquinas. And the influence that we may associate with Aquinas has (like the influence of Seneca) some very important implications for the use of language.

One of the great achievements of Scholasticism, of course, was to assimilate to Christianity some of the best that was thought and known in antiquity, including thought about rhetoric or the art of discourse. Erich Auerbach in his essay, '*Sermo Humilis*', gives a valuable account of the development of the Christian form of the sublime, which modified the classical doctrine of three levels of style:[19]

> the style of the Scriptures throughout is *humilis*, lowly or humble. Even the hidden things (*secreta, recondita*)

are set forth in a 'lowly' vein. But the subject matter, whether simple or obscure, is sublime. The lowly, or humble, style is the only medium in which such sublime mysteries can be brought within the reach of men. It constitutes a parallel to the Incarnation, which was also a *humilitas* in the same sense, for men could not have endured the splendor of Christ's divinity. But the Incarnation, as it actually happened on earth, could only be narrated in a lowly and humble style. The birth of Christ in a manger in Bethlehem, his life among fishermen, publicans and other common men, the Passion with its realistic and 'scandalous' episodes – none of this could have been treated appropriately in the lofty, oratorical, tragic, or epic style. According to the Augustan esthetic, such matters were worthy, at best, of the lower literary genres. But the lowly style of Scripture encompasses the sublime.

As a result, there is often in Christian literature 'a mixture of sublimity, popular rhetoric, and tender *caritas*, forcefully didactic and dramatically alive, addressed to a general and indiscriminate audience'. Auerbach draws out a further consequence of this mixing of the high, the low, and the middle:[20]

> And the *sermo humilis*, as I am trying to describe it here, has other features besides vulgarisms and the like: one is its implication of direct human contact between you and me, a note that was lacking in the sublime style of Roman antiquity; another is its power to express human brotherhood, an intimate bond between men: all of us here and now.

From the Christian *sermo humilis* to Shakespearean tragedy may appear to be a large leap, but there is an intimate connection that helps to illuminate Shakespeare's practice, especially in *Richard II*. Shakespeare's audience is similarly 'general and indiscriminate' in the sense that it contains both masters and servants, the aristocracy and the groundlings. 'Direct human contact' and 'an intimate bond between men' are explored in

177

Richard II with a persistent interest in the religious and moral
sanctions that foster human well-being and with a persistent
interest in the lack of them that thwarts human well-being.
The leap from *sermo humilis* to Shakespeare is not, in fact, so
large, for it was a style available in Renaissance England and
was practised by Spenser in, for example, two of his Foure
Hymnes, 'An Hymne of Heavenly Love' and 'An Hymne of
Heavenly Beavtie'. At any rate, the grand style of *Richard II*
undergoes a number of modifications, some of which are best
understood in terms of Auerbach's description.[21]

The play opens in the grand style without modification.

> Old John of Gaunt, time-honoured Lancaster,
> Hast thou according to thy oath and band
> Brought hither Henry Herford thy bold son,
> Here to make good the boist'rous late appeal,
> Which then our leisure would not let us hear,
> Against the Duke of Norfolk, Thomas Mowbray?
>
> (I, i, 1–6)

The blank verse of Richard's opening speech is essentially
balanced. Howard Baker's general characterization of the
heroic medium fits these lines precisely: 'the mighty line is,
I believe, in its narrowest form a balanced line in which the
first part plays against the last part either verbally or allitera-
tively and often in both ways'.[22] Richard, then, in this opening scene uses this medium in his attempt to set the emotional tone accentuating dignity, gravity, and decorum. As
opposed to 'the *boist'rous* late appeal', proceedings here are
to go 'according to oath and band', that is, in appropriate
language, spoken and written.

And Bolingbroke and Mowbray in their accusations and
counter-accusations at first try to observe Richard's sense of
decorum, Mowbray even making explicit mention of the kind
of wonder that he supposes should govern his speech on this
occasion.

> First, the fair reverence of your Highness curbs me
> From giving reins and spurs to my free speech,
> Which else would post until it had return'd
> These terms of treason doubled down his throat.
>
> (I, i, 54–7)

Impatience with the constraints of a style tied to reverence, or pretending to be so tied, moves Bolingbroke to action and to a widening of the terms of the quarrel. 'Fear,' he says, not 'reverence' is what causes Mowbray to take exception to 'my high blood's royalty', and in order to force this 'guilty dread' out into the open, he challenges Mowbray to arms, discounting in the process his own kinship with the king. The challenge leads directly to Bolingbroke's making clear exactly what his accusations are. Before replying to the explicit accusations, Mowbray bids his sovereign 'a little while be deaf', and Richard in turn grants Mowbray 'free speech and fearless'.

Clearly, the nature of the quarrel demands some modification of the style that Richard tries to establish at the outset. Some of Auerbach's remarks on Augustine help to clarify what modifications are needed and what Shakespeare actually does.[23]

In his conception of the three traditional levels of style (the sublime, the intermediate, and the low, or lowly) he follows Cicero (in particular *Orator* 69ff.). For instruction and exegesis he recommends the low style, which according to Cicero, should be unadorned but neither slovenly nor uncouth; for praise and blame, admonition and dissuasion, the intermediate (*temperatum*), in which rhetorical figures have their proper place; while for arousing the transports of emotion that move men to action, he advises the sublime, lofty style, which does not exclude rhetorical ornament but has no need of it.

In order to blame and admonish Mowbray, Bolingbroke has need of the intermediate style, though since he also wishes to arouse those 'transports of emotion that move men to action', he needs to retain the sublime. That is, to make the point in another way, he needs to arouse wonder at the peculiar facts surrounding the death of the Duke of Gloucester, and, at the same time, he needs to move men with his sense of disinterested allegiance acting out of patriotic motives. Since Richard, using the high style narrowly conceived as an instrument of patriotic fervour (in much the same cast as the style of almost all of *Gorboduc*), has set a tone that encourages only expressions of loyalty to his own person, Bolingbroke is forced to introduce modifications. After charging Mowbray with embezzlement and then general knavery at inciting treasonous plots over a period of eighteen years, he makes his most telling accusation.

> Further I say, and further will maintain
> Upon his bad life to make all this good,
> 100 That he did plot the Duke of Gloucester's death,
> Suggest his soon-believing adversaries,
> And consequently, like a traitor coward,
> Sluic'd out his innocent soul through streams of blood,
> Which blood, like sacrificing Abel's, cries
> 105 Even from the tongueless caverns of the earth
> To me for justice and rough chastisement;
> And, by the glorious worth of my descent,
> This arm shall do it, or this life be spent. (I, i, 98–108)

The balanced half lines and the generous use of alliteration sustain the feeling of the grand style, while Bolingbroke emphasizes the height and transport of his disinterested emotion in the allusion to Abel, reinforcing as it does Gloucester's innocence and the universal implications of his death. At the same time, Shakespeare introduces into the speech with striking effectiveness techniques for avowing and insinuating blame. The image of atrocity in 'Sluic'd out' and the image of desolate pity in 'tongueless caverns' are both, in their contrary ways, an appeal to the poignancy and tenderness appropriate to the event and an arousal of hatred for the cause. Though I have discussed the intermediate style largely in terms of the golden style of love lyrics, it is not too difficult to see that the same style will be effective for expressing hate: the techniques of praise and compliment are near relations to those of blame and admonition.

More important than the direct accusations against Mowbray are the insinuations implicating Richard. The allusion to Abel, as Dover Wilson has noted, carries with it the suggestion that Gloucester's murder, like Abel's, is the responsibility of a near kin.[24] The compact accusation of line 101 'Suggest his soon-believing adversaries' includes a note of contempt for both the person doing the prompting and the persons being prompted. Finally, the syntactic thrust of lines 104 to 106 requires in the handling of metre a kind of subtlety foreign to the heroic medium. The suspension of the verb 'cries' from its object 'to me' plus the strategic placing of these words at the end and beginning of the line create an emphasis that fully justifies Coleridge's comment: 'alarming; pregnant with meaning'.[25] The personal energy in these lines goes with the sense of personal engagement that obtrudes on Bolingbroke's patriotic disinterestedness, even as he attempts to amalgamate the intermediate and the grand style.

That he is not completely successful at retaining the range of feeling appropriate to the grand style is most evident in the oath with which his speech concludes. An oath is a formal declaration calling to witness the bond between the individual and an external order: king, country, God. The oath may be said to be characteristic of the grand style as Richard tries to establish it at the beginning of the scene. It is noteworthy in this opening scene that Mowbray swears by either God (l. 68) or the king (l. 78), whereas Bolingbroke swears by 'mine honour's pawn' (l. 75) or by 'the glorious worth of my descent' (l. 107). The pattern here is similar to the one that W. B. Piper describes so well with respect to the heroic couplet at the end of the scene: that is, Mowbray conforms to Richard's mode of utterance, whereas Bolingbroke does not.

And just as Bolingbroke comes himself to invoke that mode unsuccessfully in the heroic couplets at the end of the play, so the characters at the end of Act IV invoke without success the dignity and gravity of the high style. The first half of Act IV is obviously intended to counterbalance the opening scene of the play, returning as it does to the question of Gloucester's death and breaking down even more quickly into a series of personal vendettas. Shakespeare once more employs 'high astounding terms', but in the absence of any discernible motives beyond pure self-interest, the high style seems curiously etiolated and mean-spirited. The following lines by Fitzwater are typical:

> If I dare eat, or drink, or breathe, or live,
> I dare meet Surrey in a wilderness,

> And spit upon him whilst I say he lies,
> And lies, and lies. There is my bond of faith
> To tie thee to my strong correction.
> As I intend to thrive in this new world,
> Aumerle is guilty of my true appeal. (IV, i, 73–9)

One notes especially the phrase that serves as a substitute for an oath: 'As I intend to thrive in this new world'. Like Bolingbroke in Act I, Fitzwater has a number of substitute oaths: 'By that fair sun which shows me where thou stand'st' (l. 35) and 'Now by my soul' (l. 42), which characterize the use of astounding terms without sanctions. One of the most prominent words in this speech and throughout the hearing (if that is what it is to be called) is 'dare', standing for a pure act of the will. It might be compared with 'courage', a quality of mind that stiffens the resolution. Instead of courage, honour, duty, and allegiance, the high style here conveys bravado, opportunism, and self-serving. The hearing demonstrates Bolingbroke's efficiency and perhaps even his goodwill, but it demonstrates also a narrowing of the range of what can be said that he himself is partly responsible for. Certainly he is no closer here than he was in Act I to making 'justice and rough chastisement' his own personal prerogative, for the announcement of Mowbray's death, which concludes the hearing, suggests that vengeance is the Lord's. Carlisle's account of that death (IV, i, 91–100) attributes to Mowbray the virtues of honour, duty, courage, and allegiance in heroic style.

To return for a moment to Bolingbroke's original accusation with his accompanying vow that the murder cries out 'To me for justice and rough chastisement', Coleridge continues his comment that the 'to me' is 'alarming; pregnant with meaning' by saying 'and so felt by Richard –'

> How high a pitch his resolution soars!

Richard's reaction is, foremost, an expression of wonder – wonder at high astounding terms impregnated with specific accusations and insinuations and with a strong sense of personal engagement – that is, wonder at a high style more resonant than his own. The word 'resolution' here carries some of the same sorts of complexities that it has in *The Spanish Tragedy*. It is not only Bolingbroke's ambition, his fixed determination, but the full act of clarification at which he aims that Richard marvels at. To suggest with Chambers that at this moment 'on stage the actor might raise his hand to the crown as he speaks the line' is to oversimplify.[26] It is true that Richard feels threatened by Bolingbroke, but he is also puzzled, and the nature of his puzzlement can be seen most clearly in the final scene of Act I.

This scene represents a general lowering of tone, consisting largely of snide conversation in the intermediate style. Aumerle, for example, reports using the Petrarchan 'speaking silence' (I, iv, 11–15) to counterfeit grief at his parting with 'high Herford'. And Richard's remarks on the dying Gaunt are positively callous. But at the centre of the scene is still the relationship between Bolingbroke and Richard.

> Ourself and Bushy
> Observ'd his courtship to the common people,
> 25   How he did seem to dive into their hearts
> With humble and familiar courtesy;
> What reverence he did throw away on slaves,
> Wooing poor craftsmen with the craft of smiles
> And patient underbearing of his fortune,
> 30   As 'twere to banish their affects with him.
> Off goes his bonnet to an oyster-wench;
> A brace of draymen bid God speed him well,
> And had the tribute of his supple knee,
> With 'Thanks, my countrymen, my loving friends' –
> 35   As were our England in reversion his,
> And he our subjects' next degree in hope. (I, iv, 23–36)

This is the native English grand style marvelling at the appearance of the Christian *sermo humilis*. Actually, Shakespeare uses some of the techniques of the latter in order to register Richard's astonishment at the way that Bolingbroke combines the high and the low. Peter Ure concludes a long note on this passage by remarking that 'this speech describes how Bolingbroke behaves to the people with a wealth of imaginative detail quite independent of the historical sources'. But it is not only the realistic detail of the 'oyster-wench' and the 'brace of draymen', nor the incongruity of the whole proceeding, 'what reverence he did *throw away* on slaves', that registers the astonishment, but also the inference to be drawn about Bolingbroke's motive. He seems to be doing this in order 'to banish their *affects* with him'. By throwing away reverence on slaves, he invites them to reciprocate in kind and especially to marvel at his patience and endurance in misfortune. Ure's note on line 30: ' "as if he were trying to carry away into exile with him the affections which the people ought to have for me as their king" ', though helpful, needs clarification itself because the emotions Bolingbroke would arouse are wonder on a grand scale as well as pleasant affections. Richard's conclusion, therefore, 'As were our England in reversion his', is not merely a snide comment on pretentious ambition, but a puzzling over this odd combination of the humble and the sublime. He puzzles over Bolingbroke's grand manner, which incorporates 'direct human contact' and 'an intimate bond between men: all of us here and now'.

Shakespeare's interest in the dramatic potential of the *sermo humilis* seems to me indubitable in the scene which mirrors, in some ways, Richard's picture of Bolingbroke's departure from England, namely York's description of the entry of both Richard and Bolingbroke into London at the beginning of Act V, scene ii. York presents in Bolingbroke a picture that combines grandeur and humility simultaneously and in Richard a picture of nobility and magnanimity in the midst of humiliation. He employs vulgarisms – the 'greedy looks of young and old' and the 'tedious prattle' of the unfortunate actor who must follow a well-graced one – and in an earlier attempt to tell the story, he has broken off weeping at the spectacle of Richard's humiliation. In other words, here is that 'mixture of sublimity, popular rhetoric, and tender *caritas*, forcefully didactic and dramatically alive', that Auerbach describes as characteristic of *sermo humilis*. Because of the balanced picture of the two principals, the only didactic message that York is able to infer is something of a deadlock: 'But heaven hath a hand in these events,/ To whose high will we bound our calm contents' (V, ii, 38–9). Shakespeare has not yet begun to use the *sermo humilis* to explore the deep interconnections of human action and human responsibility.

In fact, neither of the principals is ever given a speech that could be accurately described as *sermo humilis*. The only major speech worthy of the name is by the Bishop of Carlisle at the moment Bolingbroke offers to ascend the throne.

> Marry, God forbid!
> 115 Worst in this royal presence may I speak,
> Yet best beseeming me to speak the truth.
> Would God that any in this noble presence
> Were enough noble to be upright judge
> Of noble Richard! then true noblesse would
> 120 Learn him forbearance from so foul a wrong.
> What subject can give sentence on his king?
> And who sits here that is not Richard's subject?
> Thieves are not judg'd but they are by to hear,
> Although apparent guilt be seen in them,
> 125 And shall the figure of God's majesty,
> His captain, steward, deputy elect,
> Anointed, crowned, planted many years,
> Be judg'd by subject and inferior breath,
> And he himself not present? O forfend it, God,
> 130 That in a Christian climate souls refin'd
> Should show so heinous, black, obscene a deed!
> I speak to subjects, and a subject speaks,
> Stirr'd up by God thus boldly for his king.
> My Lord of Herford here, whom you call king,
> 135 Is a foul traitor to proud Herford's king,
> And if you crown him, let me prophesy –
> The blood of English shall manure the ground,
> And future ages groan for this foul act,
> Peace shall go sleep with Turks and infidels,
> 140 And, in this seat of peace, tumultuous wars
> Shall kin with kin, and kind with kind, confound.
> Disorder, horror, fear, and mutiny,
> Shall here inhabit, and this land be call'd
> The field of Golgotha and dead men's skulls –
> 145 O, if you raise this house against this house,
> It will the woefullest division prove

That ever fell upon this cursed earth.
Prevent it, resist it, let it not be so,
Lest child, child's children, cry against you woe.
(IV, i, 114–49)

The force and grandeur of Carlisle's utterance is the result
in large part of its strict adherence to the form of the classical oration.[27] It is worthwhile to sketch in briefly its
structure. Lines 115 and 116 are an *exordium*, catching the
audience's attention and setting out the speaker's right to be
heard. The *narratio* (ll. 117–20) outlines in general the facts
of the case, or rather, since the verbs are in the subjunctive
mood, the facts that would be necessary for the case to proceed and, being absent, present an impediment. The *explica-
tio* defines the terms of the case in the rhetorical questions of
lines 121 and 122 and opens the issue in the analogy of lines
123–9. By stating exactly what is to be proved, the *partitio*
clarifies the points at issue (ll. 129–31); it is what we would
today call the 'thesis', and Carlisle states it here in the form
of a prayer, though he has also stated it succinctly in his
opening line as an imperative: 'Marry, God forbid!' In the
amplificatio (ll. 132–5), he sets forth the proof by a definition of his own character and the character of his audience
generally and by a specific characterization of Bolingbroke,
whom he mentions explicitly for the first time. The *refutatio*
(ll. 136–47) is devoted wholly to the prophecy of civil war,
the probable consequences of ignoring Carlisle's thesis. Lines
148 and 149 offer a *peroratio* intended to stir the audience
by means of a compact and forceful restatement of the thesis
and the prophecy.[28]

Yet, in addition to the obvious force and the impassioned
tone, the style is also lowly. Carlisle begins by deprecating his
own worthiness to speak and yet avowing his dedication as an
ecclesiastic to speak the truth. His speech exhibits not only
that wonder which is akin to fear, but also wonder on a lesser
scale corresponding to the displacement that initiates internal
movement. In fact, he uses many of the preacher's devices for
instruction and exegesis: he plays on the various senses of the
word 'noble' in order to bring out the true meaning of nobility; he conducts an imaginary dialogue with his audience

in his series of three questions, in order that they may see clearly the precise stages of the action they are about to take or to condone; he draws an analogy, which, in the great disparity between 'thieves' and 'the figure of God's majesty', clarifies how momentous the action is; and he shifts easily from an address to God in the prayer or thesis 'O forfend it, God' to 'I speak to subjects' in order that his hearers may feel the full interconnections from high to low.

Here, finally, is a high style capable of evoking the grandeur of momentous political action while registering simultaneously the subtleties of thought and feeling in the individual sentience that is the indispensable focus of political action. The significance of the Christian *sermo humilis* for Shakespearean drama is not necessarily that it is Christian, but that it allows for the depiction of a character whose sense of nationality *'quoad* his country, is equal to the sense of individuality *quoad* himself – i.e., subsensuous, central, inexclusive, etc.'. Carlisle's speech, as Derek Traversi remarks, represents 'a community of style with the patriotic utterances of Gaunt'.[29] Carlisle is a portrayal of man in his 'causative character', even though he is arrested immediately following his speech by Northumberland. In fact, he is man in his 'causative character' especially because he is arrested, for his arrest shows that he puts reasoned judgment ahead of personal safety. Northumberland is represented very early in *1 Henry IV* in the kind of paralysis that is the antithesis of 'causative character.'

The relationship of Carlisle's prophecy to the later history plays, in fact, has suggested to some commentators 'that Shakespeare had already conceived the whole series as one drama.'[30] And it is true that the prophecy is one of the strongest links between *Richard II* and the following plays of the second tetralogy as well as, in a general way, the later events dramatized in the first tetralogy. In addition, it is also true that the sentiments of Carlisle's speech are very close to the sentiments expressed in Tudor homilies warning against the evils to be expected from rebellion.[31] It might seem, then, as we reconsider the relation between tragedy and history with which we opened our discussion of *Richard II*, that Shakespeare is thinking primarily of history and thinking of historical drama as a separate genre, possibly as a 'mirror' of

Elizabethan policy in the special sense of 'mirror' defined so
well by Lily B. Campbell. Arguing for the classification provided by the editors of the First Folio, who designate several
of Shakespeare's plays, including *Richard II*, as 'histories',
Miss Campbell concludes her chapter 'What are "Histories"?'
as follows:[32]

> a history play must be regarded as a literary medium
> for history. If it is understood that a history play is con-
> cerned with politics, furthermore, the point of its diver-
> gence from tragedy becomes clear, for the divisions of
> philosophy known as *ethics* and *politics* were familiar
> from the very titles of Aristotle's works and represented
> the accepted approaches to the study of human con-
> duct. . . . Tragedy is concerned with the doings of men
> which in philosophy are discussed under *ethics*; history
> with the doings of men which in philosophy are dis-
> cussed under *politics*.

Miss Campbell buttresses these remarks with a qualification
that W. D. Ross applied to Aristotle and she applies to
Shakespeare: 'he does not forget in the *Ethics* that the individual man is essentially a member of society, nor in the
Politics that the good life of the state exists only in the good
lives of its citizens.'[33]

But however much we may wish to applaud the idea that
Shakespeare deals with both ethics and politics, Professor
Campbell's 'accepted approaches to the study of human conduct' fails to recognize poetic drama as an approach that is
distinct from both history and philosophy. The distinctive
feature of that drama is its poetry, its measured language, its
styles – the means by which the dramatist creates thought,
character, and action. And in *Richard II*, in each of the styles
that we have considered: the moral and the golden, the metaphysical and the Shakespearean, the heroic couplet, and the
grand style, Shakespeare's intention is to represent a sense of
individuality and of nationality at the same time. Even the
reductions and deflections associated with the characters of
Bolingbroke and Richard are not really different in kind in
this respect. Men have their being, their specifically *human*
being, in language, and it is the aim of poetry to measure that

being, to apprehend as many aspects of reality as possible, simultaneously. It is because the poetic approach to the study of human conduct is to grasp the ethical and political life together, and to evoke the feelings appropriate to both, that *Richard II* is an apprenticeship in poetic tragedy.

Even Carlisle's prophecy, where the political implications are strong, has a balancing sense of ethical responsibility. In fact, the prophecy, Carlisle's *refutatio*, consists of essentially two parts, (ll. 136–44) 'And if you crown him' and (ll. 145–9) 'O, if you raise this house against this house', in which the emphasis falls first on ethics and then on politics. The two parts make contrasting use of the verbs 'shall' and 'will'. In the second and third persons, 'shall' expresses determination; it is also used, according to the *Oxford English Dictionary*, in all persons, for prophetic or oracular announcements of the future, and for solemn assertions of the certainty of a future event. 'Will' in the second and third persons is used as an auxiliary expressing mere futurity. On a personal level ('And if you crown him . . . / The blood of English shall manure the ground/ And . . . Peace shall go sleep . . .'), Carlisle speaks of necessary consequences, of what must follow; on the national level of the houses of York and Lancaster ('O, if you raise this house against this house,/ It will . . . prove . . .'), he speaks simply of what will happen. Nationality in each individual is equal to the sense of individuality.

The whole of Carlisle's speech exhibits this interplay of the personal and the extra-personal. As a set speech, it illustrates the flexibility that Wolfgang Clemen describes as characterizing the development of drama in England in the late sixteenth century. By having Carlisle speak at precisely the moment that Bolingbroke ascends the throne, Shakespeare sets up a resonance not only with the distant future but with the immediate, dramatic present. For one thing, Carlisle's arrest the instant he concludes provides at once a piece of evidence confirming the prophecy. For another, 'in Holinshed, Carlisle's speech occurs after the abdication and is directed against the plan that Richard should be tried for his crimes';[34] by having him speak before the abdication and against both the trial and the coronation of Henry, Shakespeare makes the speech comment on the whole proceeding –

a fact emphasized when Carlisle repeats part of his *peroratio* at the end of the scene.

> *Abbot.* A woeful pageant have we here beheld.
> *Car.* The woe's to come; the children yet unborn
>   Shall feel this day as sharp as any thorn. (IV, i, 321–3)

These choric comments following the 'pageant' of the abdication suggest the emotional effects of woe and wonder that the play as a whole seems to be striving for.

As a representative of the perspective consciousness that was earlier in the play associated with John of Gaunt, Carlisle also provides a standard against which to measure the utterances of Bolingbroke and Richard in the deposition scene. Bolingbroke's first words after Carlisle's arrest are:

> Fetch hither Richard, that in common view
> He may surrender; so we shall proceed
> Without suspicion. (IV, i, 155–7)

Who, one might ask, could be more suspicious than Carlisle has just been? Would Bolingbroke, in this style, recognize a suspicion if he saw one? The plain, blunt manner is once more being used to evade moral issues.

With Richard the case is more complicated because Shakespeare endows him with a grand manner that at times seems to approach *sermo humilis*. The public ceremonial nature of the deposition calls for the grand style, or some variation of it, and Richard, upon entering, seems to promise as much.

> Alack, why am I sent for to a king
> Before I have shook off the regal thoughts
> Wherewith I reign'd? I hardly yet have learn'd
> To insinuate, flatter, bow, and bend my knee.
> Give sorrow leave awhile to tutor me
> To this submission. (IV, i, 162–7)

In addition to some bitterness of feeling and some realistic penetration, Richard seems to offer that combination of 'regal thoughts' and 'submission', of sublime subject matter and humble bearing, that is typical of *sermo humilis*. Like Carlisle, he attempts to imbue his utterances with religious significance, especially in the allusions to Judas, Pilate, and

Christ, finding himself analogous to Christ, who was also betrayed, and to Judas and Pilate, 'myself a traitor with the rest'. Indeed, at this most crucial point in the plot of *Richard II*, Shakespeare has portrayed Richard in such a variety of styles and attitudes that the scene reads like a pastiche of several of the styles we have considered in the play. The incongruity of the pastiche probably explains why so many readers have found the scene to be an odd combination of exquisite suffering, realistic understanding, and histrionic indulgence. The attempt to bring the styles together probably represents an intention to develop something like the *sermo humilis*, which in its final development will become the Shakespearean style.[35]

I have already commented on the moral style which expresses forcefully Richard's reply to Northumberland's request that he read out a list of his 'grievous crimes'. The golden style is present throughout the scene and is especially evident at the very moment of abdication, introduced by paradoxical statements that register the ambivalence of Richard's feelings and his near despair: 'Ay, no; no, ay; for I must nothing be./ Therefore no "no", for I resign to thee.' Throughout, the speech employs balanced lines that evoke the formality and gravity of the high style but are at the same time full of tender *caritas*. For example:

> With mine own tears I wash away my balm,
> With mine own hands I give away my crown,
> With mine own tongue deny my sacred state,
> With mine own breath release all duteous oaths.
>
> (IV, i, 207–10)

The Petrarchan conventions that are ordinarily used to pledge allegiance to a loved one are here used to undo a pledge, as the personal pronouns, the repetitions, and the intimate items record the intense feeling of the moment. 'Regal thoughts' and 'submission' are both almost wholly preoccupied with exquisite feeling.

Elsewhere in the abdication scene, at least three images have a metaphysical or a Shakespearean look about them, though the promise is not finally fulfilled. The comparison of the golden crown to a deep well that 'owes two buckets' seems to offer heterogeneous ideas yoked by violence together, but the ideas do not stay together because there is no necessary relationship. Though modern commentators attempt to justify the figure by explaining that buckets and well derive from the medieval figure of Fortune's buckets, Samuel Johnson's comment is still essentially correct: 'This is a comparison not easily accommodated to the subject, nor very naturally introduced.'[36] The figure does not clarify the nature of the crown, and it does not evoke wonder about what is causing the exchange of the crown on this particular occasion. Its *raison d'être* is once more the expression of almost pure feeling, as the moralistic device of Fortune's buckets allows Richard a sentimental comparison. 'That bucket down and full of tears am I,/ Drinking my griefs'. Johnson's comment on the development of the figure (l. 186) is again worth quoting: 'The best part is this line, in which he makes the usurper the "empty" bucket.'

The figure of the 'mockery king of snow' and the figure of the 'looking-glass' do raise metaphysical questions of essence, the latter especially, in a speech showing how nearly Richard approaches *sermo humilis*.

> Give me that glass, and therein will I read.
> No deeper wrinkles yet? hath sorrow struck
> So many blows upon this face of mine
> And made no deeper wounds? O flatt'ring glass,
> 280   Like to my followers in prosperity,
> Thou dost beguile me. Was this face the face
> That every day under his household roof
> Did keep ten thousand men? Was this the face
> That like the sun did make beholders wink?
> 285   Is this the face which fac'd so many follies,
> That was at last out-fac'd by Bolingbroke?
> A brittle glory shineth in this face;
> As brittle as the glory is the face,
>   [*Dashes the glass against the ground.*]
> For there it is, crack'd in an hundred shivers.
> 290   Mark, silent king, the moral of this sport –
> How soon my sorrow hath destroy'd my face.
> *Bol.* The shadow of your sorrow hath destroy'd

The shadow of your face.
Rich.   Say that again.
The shadow of my sorrow? ha! let's see –
295   'Tis very true, my grief lies all within,
And these external manners of lament
Are merely shadows to the unseen grief
That swells with silence in the tortur'd soul.
There lies the substance. And I thank thee, king,
300   For thy great bounty, that not only giv'st
Me cause to wail, but teachest me the way
How to lament the cause. (IV, i, 276–302)

This passage evokes wonder on a grand scale, exciting admiration and sympathy, and wonder on a lesser scale, pointing a moral and drawing inferences. The repeated questions recall the grand manner of Christopher Marlowe, especially in the echo of the speech about Helen from *Doctor Faustus*, and there are certain signs of padding out the bombastic line: 'Was this face the face', for example, or 'Say that again'. At the same time, the lines display a syntactical and metrical fluidity that far surpasses the early English grand style and surpasses Marlowe as well. The rhetorically parallel questions, which if kept strictly parallel in form would seem more purely bombastic, deployed at various places in the line and in syntactical units of varying length represent a genuine effort of thought and emotion to come to understanding. And in the movement from the past tense of '*Was* this the face/ That like the sun did make beholders wink?' to the present tense of '*Is* this the face which fac'd so many follies,/ That was at last out-fac'd by Bolingbroke' Richard comes very close to holding 'the mirror up to nature; to show virtue her own feature, scorn her own image, and the very age and body of the time his form and pressure'. He is helped in this effort, of course, by the traditional uses of the looking-glass, 'the double edged symbol of vanity and truth-telling',[37] which explain in part the movement from 'O flatt'ring glass' to 'the moral of this sport'. But the structure of this movement is more closely governed by one of the typical devices of *sermo humilis*, as Auerbach describes it: 'At an early date the Christian sermon began to develop on the model of the diatribe, or moralistic declamation, in which the speaker replies, the whole thus forming a dialogue.'[38] Richard's diatribe has significance both for his own personal case and for the new public, which is his audience, as represented especially by the 'silent king'.

Yet even as one notes the signs of *sermo humilis* in this passage – the concern for public and private well-being, the concern with moral truth and with rhetorical heightening – one is aware of a histrionic quality that seems to undermine it. Unlike Carlisle's, Richard's oration is not governed by any very stable external form or purpose, and, as his use of Bolingbroke's interruption makes clear, he proceeds mainly by way of association. Peter Ure offers a fair enough paraphrase of lines 294–9:[39]

> Richard develops the well-loved Shakespearian contrast between *shadow* and *substance* (cf. II, ii. 14 and note), implicit in Bolingbroke's remark, and in l. 297 deliberately alters the meaning which Bolingbroke had given to his first *shadow*: 'The shadow (= darkness) cast by my sorrow? Let's see – 'tis very true; my sorrow – these external ways of lamenting – are simply shadows (= unreal images) of the grief within . . .'

That is, at this crucial moment of the action of *Richard II*, Richard resorts once more to the libertine golden style and, furthermore, resorts to claiming that the range of feeling and attitude provided by that style, by that way of looking at the world, is the only reality. The true 'substance', according to Richard, lies in the real images of grief that 'swell with silence' in his free imagination. As a result, the moral with which he attempts to conclude – not how to understand the cause but 'how to lament the cause' – is deflected from moral purposes. By using the libertine golden style and the moral style deflected at this moment, Shakespeare empties the *sermo humilis* of its public import and replaces it with the vice of histrionic action, the definition of which is: acting out feelings and attitudes in public while at the same time claiming that their significance is wholly private.

The *sermo humilis*, in order to be truly successful at this crucial stage in the development of plot and character in

Richard II, would probably have to draw upon the diction and thought available in the styles that I have described as metaphysical and Shakespearean. The presence of these styles in the utterances by John of Gaunt and in a related way by the Bishop of Carlisle indicates that Shakespeare has the resources. The experiments with various styles in the utterances by Richard and Bolingbroke indicate that he has the desire to employ these resources at the key points of his drama. It remains to bring desire and resources together. As apprentice work, *The Tragedy of King Richard the Second* offers a clear prognosis of a dramatist whose mature style will be at once grand and sweet and plain.

10 · *Macbeth:* style and form

I

The analysis of style in drama is a way of cultivating attentive reading, of increasing fidelity to the author's intention as that is realized in language. Both *Mustapha* and *Richard II* reveal a vigorous use and development of the styles available, especially the poetic styles, in late sixteenth-century England, and both Greville and Shakespeare disclose their intentions to evoke the emotions of woe or wonder, the two aspects of the single emotional effect of tragedy, the most fully human response to death. Greville's intention is more explicit, Shakespeare's more subtle. The analysis of style is, in the first instance, a way of emphasizing the reader's point of view. Whatever aspect of the drama the writer first considers, he must finally embody his intention in language, and the reader must realize that intention from language – even actors must first read their lines. Yet speech is not merely a technique or a method subordinate to other things; it is also, as George Whalley remarks, 'one of the principal resources of human action'.[1] It should be possible, therefore, to shift the analysis of style to emphasize the writer's point of view. What implications do Shakespeare's styles have for the form of his drama? To what extent does poetic style determine other elements of the dramatic action? In order to open these questions and in order to test the approach that I have developed for *Mustapha* and *Richard II*, I wish to consider certain crucial moments in one of Shakespeare's greatest and most mature plays, *The Tragedy of Macbeth*.

II

My remarks do not presuppose an Ideal Form of drama, or of tragedy, and even the claim that the emotional effect of tragedy is 'single' does not suppose that the effects of any two tragedies will be precisely the same. Yet the persistent

196

attempt in tragedies to work out an adjustment of woe and wonder has a universal element that makes the Aristotelian analysis perennially relevant. As George Whalley argues in 'On Translating Aristotle's *Poetics*', Aristotle is not merely classifying tragedies known to him, deducing rules for the correct or successful composition of tragedies; he is in the *Poetics* exploring 'the activity of man as a moral creature' and the ways in which that activity comes to be 'final and normative':[2]

> A tragic action correctly traced will lead to the end of recognizing at least something about the nature of man, the values that are paramount, the vulnerable centres that we must at all costs preserve – which is the law, our law. Here, it may be, the old debate about what happens according to nature (*physei*) and what according to law (*nomōi*) comes into ironic coincidence in Aristotle's mind when he sees the form of tragedy, when the inner law simply *is* our nature – not 'natural law' or 'the law of Nature' but the law of *our* nature.[3]

The law of *our* nature is not a dispensation: it is neither a system of management nor an exemption from any obligation or fate. It is a responsibility. It is a law that is created or discovered in the actions of individuals and that exists nowhere else and has no existence in the drama prior to the unfolding of the action. The absolute need to have it recognized is what causes Aristotle to regard plot as first in importance.[4]

> When Aristotle says that 'the first principle of tragedy – the soul, if you like – is the plot, and second to that the characters' he means this quite specifically, not rhetorically: the soul is the 'form' of the person, and prior to the body – the plot is the 'form' of the tragedy, and prior to the action – the characters are the 'body' of the action (will body forth the action) and are shaped by, as well as generating the action. The person acting does not disclose or externalize his character in action, as though the character existed before the action: the character (in Aristotle's view) is *shaped by* his actions,

197

and in tragedy we see the protagonist, as character, being shaped by his choice and his actions.

One of Whalley's central goals for achieving the right translation of the *Poetics* is to get for English-speakers an appropriate sense of the word *mimesis*. *Mimesis*, he argues, is emphatically not the same as 'imitation', as if tragedy were something merely copied out of nature and the theatre a kind of showcase where characters display themselves for a time. *Mimesis* should mean the activity or process by which the action and the poem, or tragedy, are brought into being. Since the nature in question is our nature, the process is conducted in language and is fundamentally exploratory.

Our peculiarly modern difficulty in trying to imagine the protagonist as one who has character only in so far as it is shaped by his choice and his actions is related to the problem of defining individuality. Ian Robinson in *The Survival of English* has some lucid remarks on this topic, and what he says helps us to get a clearer view of the relationship between plot and style.[5]

> Partly the difficulty in thinking about the question of individuality and speech is that our individuality isn't quite of the kind we like to believe. From the fact that we are all unique it does not follow that our uniqueness always expresses itself (as we may fall into assuming) as difference from other human beings. 'When she knew that: $x^2 - y^2 = (x+y)(x-y)$ then she felt she had grasped something, that she was liberated into an intoxicating air, rare and unconditioned.' Ursula's knowledge is here an intensely individual experience which depends, however, on precisely the same knowledge being available to other individuals.
>
> Further, our individuality itself has to develop within a common verbal language which we share with others (however individually we use it) and which differs from other languages in ways not explicable by individual whim on the one hand or the prescribed physical limits of human beings on the other.

Robinson puts his point in a more emphatic way, and in some sense a more old-fashioned way, near the end of his book: 'The common language enters so deeply into us that it becomes part of the material of which the soul is made; conversely, when we manage to speak from the soul we make the common language.'[6] The activity of 'making' that Robinson refers to here corresponds closely to what Whalley understands by *mimesis* because both are concerned with recognizing at least something about the essential nature of man. In tragedy, the concern may become more sharply defined because it confronts the death of those individuals who have best learned how to speak from the soul. Tragic action, like the individuality of Ursula in *The Rainbow*, depends upon knowledge that is intensely individual and yet widely available to others. Language is an indispensable resource of human action because it is our most highly developed way of finding and recording knowledge.

Actually, the language provides several ways, for, as Robinson also argues, the 'common language' comprises several levels of style. These are related both to the emotional effect and to the form of tragic action, which is shaped crucially by the interplay of recognitions and mistakes, the interplay of the known and the unknown. George Whalley makes clear this interplay and its relation to form and feeling when he comments on Aristotle's central definition of tragedy.[7]

'Tragedy is a *mimēsis* (process) not of men simply but of an action, that is, of life.' To achieve the precise end, a precise action is needed. We could think of the tragic action as a sort of trajectory traced by a projectile, implying a certain amplitude, direction, velocity, momentum, target, and that in every moment of flight all these terms are implied; and the nature of the projectile matters very much, because it is a man who, being morally strong, makes choices, determines the flight, is not simply propelled, is not a mere victim. Aristotle, I suggest, is showing us the tragic action as though it were a pure abstract motion traced out with exquisite precision, the precision that is needed to impart the force of necessity to an action that can at no point be altered or deflected: it will at once feel both inevitable and free.

The plot, the sequence of events that specifies the action, Aristotle says, has to be conceived as a *schēma*, an abstract motion, and you put in the names afterwards; but the *schema* is not simply a locus of dramatic points or a flight plan, for the points are not so much intersections in time and space as events, each momentous, crucial, chosen, formative. Yet the tragedy is *inside* the protagonist and is of his own doing; and if he did not know, he could have known, perhaps should have known – which is why knowing and not-knowing is crucial to the tragic action. Recognition (*anagnōrisis*) is not a device of plot structure, but an essential crisis in the action; and *hamartia* a mistake rather than a sin, a distinction that was clearer to Peter Abelard and other subtle Fathers than it seems to be to us – *hamartia* is an *ignorant* act, and in tragedy (as in *The Ancient Mariner*) ignorance is no excuse, for in these matters the plea is made not to a court of external law, but is argued in the inner dialogue of moral choice according to the law of our nature. And these things have to be declared outwardly, presented openly in action, so that they strike us not only with the *frisson* of horror and pity but with the shock of recognition; we too must be drawn into that intricate web of knowing and not-knowing. And that is the peculiar pleasure of tragedy.

'That intricate web of knowing and not-knowing' is what we mean by 'wonder'. Like Cunningham, Whalley finds it necessary in his account to include 'the shock of recognition', the wonderful, as part of the emotional effect of tragedy along with pity and horror. And the various kinds of wonder, the various modes of knowing and not-knowing, are especially related to language, for, as we noted earlier in our discussion of Cunningham, the several levels of style are different strategies for evoking different kinds of wonder. Thus, even if the plot 'has to be conceived as a schema, an abstract motion, and you put in the names afterwards', the names and the language will determine the exact particular motion by specifying the kinds of wonder that culminate in the essential crises in the action. The range of styles a dramatist has at his disposal, the richness of style he is able to bring to bear on the tragic action, defines the action to this extent. Even if, as Aristotle and Whalley say, the plot is prior, and if, as Ian Robinson suggests, language and individual character are co-existent, the styles of the dramatist determine the other elements of dramatic action to the extent that they shape the recognitions; they create the contours of knowing and not-knowing that are crucial to tragic action.

III

Having thus borrowed from the most impressive argument available on behalf of the Aristotelian analysis of tragedy, I wish now to turn to the most serious challenge to the prestige of tragic drama. In 'Problems for the Modern Critic of Literature', Yvor Winters devotes a good deal of his attention to considering the potentialities of various literary forms, including poetic drama. Using *Macbeth* as a test case for the very reason that its greatness as a play and as a work of literature makes it possible to consider problems due neither to carelessness and haste nor to limitations in subject matter, but which 'may be unavoidable in the medium', Winters concludes that the form of poetic drama is inherently flawed.[8] His conclusion is especially relevant to consider here because it follows upon a close scrutiny of the verse of the play; and Winters's analysis of poetic style in general is one of the important models I have used in developing an approach to *Mustapha* and *Richard II*.

Winters's argument is roughly as follows. Although *Macbeth* is not merely an imitation of an action, but also a moral judgment of the action, and although what makes the play a living simulacrum and a living judgment is the emotion resulting from the rational grasp of the theme, the demands of imitation present almost insoluble problems. We might grant that the principle of imitation is not simple because the poetry of *Macbeth* sharpens, accelerates, and heightens the perceptions and thoughts of all the characters. We might also grant that this sharpening, accelerating, and heightening introduces the intelligence of Shakespeare beyond the intelligence of his characters and that, therefore, the imitation stands at one remove at least: not a literal imitation, but 'a plausible imitation of an imitation'. Nevertheless, the principle of imitation demands that at various points in the action the dramatist must represent 'the speech of a character of moderate intelligence in a situation of which the character does not in any serious sense understand the meaning'.

> If a poet is endeavoring to communicate his own best understanding of a human situation, that is one thing. If he is endeavoring to communicate approximately a plausible misunderstanding of a situation on the part of an imaginary character much less intelligent than himself, that is quite another. He can only guess at the correct measure of stupidity which may be proper to such a character in a given situation, whether the character is offered as an imitation or as a plausible imitation of an imitation; and whether he is successful or not, he will still be writing poetry which as poetry will be of an inferior kind.

Dramatic form demands that the dramatist make particular characters speak as they ought to speak at particular points in the action, and this demand produces inferior verse in two major ways: the poet is forced either to express an understanding of the subject far inferior to the understanding he is capable of expressing, or to surrender the form of his statement to the formlessness of his subject matter.

In the dagger speech, according to Winters, shortly before the murder of Duncan, Macbeth is a competent but rough opportunist, somewhat more intelligent than most men of his kind but far less intelligent than he is destined shortly to become. Because Macbeth's feelings are terribly aroused but his understanding is imperfect, the situation calls for a powerful statement made by a defective intelligence. The first seven lines of the speech, Winters says, are fine lines, plain in style, and definitive of Macbeth's perplexity, but they are somewhat quiet and speculative, and Macbeth is on the brink of murder. Winters then comments on the way the speech continues (II, i, 40–9):

The subsequent lines about the dagger add little to what has been said in the lines just quoted [II, i, 33–39], but they come closer to 'imitating' the distraught state of mind and they give the actor an opportunity to 'ham' it. The imitation resides partly in the redundancy, partly in the broken rhythm, partly in the violent detail at the end, the gouts of blood. Now these lines may transform the passage into a plausible imitation of an imitation of a second rate intelligence in a distraught condition, or it is possible that they fail to do this – I confess that I am unable to say. But they are not very good poetry.

In the redundancy, the broken rhythm, and the violent detail, Shakespeare surrenders the form of his statement to the formlessness of his subject matter. It is no use replying that this procedure is an essential part of drama and is there-fore justified, for that is to grant Winters's argument: drama-tic form sacrifices form in the interests of drama.

Towards the end of the dagger speech, Macbeth shifts abruptly from the dagger to the theme of 'midnight horror'. Winters comments as follows on the seven lines beginning 'Nature seems dead, and wicked dreams abuse/ The curtain'd sleep' (II, i, 50–6):

> It seems unlikely that Macbeth in real life would have spoken anything so elaborate, but had he done so it would doubtless have been violent; and it would cer-tainly have been composed of stereotypes, because at this stage of his development he had only a stereotyped understanding of what he was doing: he would probably have found this speech satisfactory in a play. But the fact remains that it is a more or less standard huffing speech, containing something of Marlowe and a little of Pistol; and although it contains a little of Shakespeare in addition, it is far below the great speeches in the play. . . . , once again, it is not very good poetry.

And here again Winters's criticisms are unanswerable within the terms of his argument: the bombastic style of the latter part of the dagger speech is far inferior to the styles of the great speeches in the play. Dramatic form is inherently flawed to the extent that it imposes such inferiority on the dramatist and to the extent that it imposes the surrender of form.

IV

One might begin to answer Winters's criticisms by challenging the terms of his argument. The argument rests too heavily on the supposedly Aristotelian notion of 'imitation.' Winters discusses the Chicago critics, R. S. Crane and Elder Olson, in 'Problems for the Modern Critic of Literature', and his views of imitation are very close to theirs. But the Aristotle of Crane and Olson is less satisfactory than the Aristotle of George Whalley. Here is Olson, for example:[9]

> Since the actor is imitating an action, it is obvious that a play is, first of all and essentially, an imitation of an action. In order to contrive such an imitation, the playwright himself must be an imitator, assuming the persons of the characters of his play and speaking as if he were they.

Mr Olson's 'assuming' assumes that the characters already have persons before the playwright comes along. It is as if the nature of the characters is already given in the story and the playwright is limited to duplicating that nature adequately. Winters's 'plausible imitation of an imitation', which introduces the intelligence of Shakespeare, avoids this mistake, but the emphasis on imitation still does not allow enough scope to the way in which the playwright *makes* his characters. It is not for nothing that George Whalley insists on replacing 'imitation' with *mimesis*.

How, then, does Shakespeare *make* the character and the action of *Macbeth*? The plot, of course, opens with a rapid succession of events: messengers report Macbeth as performing frightful deeds of war in the service of his king, they commend his valour, and Duncan honours him with the title, Thane of Cawdor. The witches then make their prophecy, a 'strange intelligence', with no explanation of where it comes from or why they offer it, and Macbeth learns of

the honour that Duncan has conferred on him. This conjunction of events precipitates the first crisis in the action as
Macbeth and Banquo ponder what to make of the 'strange
intelligence'; Macbeth asks Banquo if its partial fulfilment
does not raise in him a hope that his children shall be kings.[10]

120 *Ban.*   That, trusted home,
  Might yet enkindle you unto the crown,
  Besides the Thane of Cawdor. But 'tis strange:
  And oftentimes, to win us to our harm,
  The instruments of Darkness tell us truths;
125   Win us with honest trifles, to betray's
  In deepest consequence. –
  Cousins, a word, I pray you.
 Macb.   [*Aside.*] Two truths are told,
  · As happy prologues to the swelling act
  Of the imperial theme. – I thank you, gentlemen. –
130   [*Aside.*] This supernatural soliciting
  Cannot be ill; cannot be good: –
  If ill, why hath it given me earnest of success,
  Commencing in a truth? I am Thane of Cawdor:
  If good, why do I yield to that suggestion
135   Whose horrid image doth unfix my hair,
  And make my seated heart knock at my ribs,
  Against the use of nature? Present fears
  Are less than horrible imaginings.
  My thought, whose murther yet is but fantastical,
140   Shakes so my single state of man,
  That function is smother'd in surmise,
  And nothing is, but what is not.
 Ban. Look, how our partner's rapt. (I, iii, 120–43)

Banquo's last remark is a guide to the emotional effect of
Macbeth's thought. Macbeth was also 'rapt' immediately
after hearing the prophecy (I, iii, 57), and in the letter to his
wife he says, 'I stood rapt in the wonder of it' (I, v, 5–6).
In Banquo's opening remarks, the two words 'strange' and
'harm' suggest the emotional effects of wonder and woe. The
relevance of Banquo's warning both to Macbeth's immediate
predicament and to the entire play is obvious, but it is not
mere perverse ambition that prevents the warning from

taking effect. It is not 'that Macbeth hears but prefers to reject Banquo's assessment because it is not convenient to him',[11] but that the warning, uttered in a plain style that borders on the proverbial, is too brief and too general to be immediately persuasive. Even if one grants that the powers of Darkness win us with honest trifles to betray us in deepest consequence, one still must decide whether the truths offered are trifles, and if they are, whether they are the sort that will lead to betrayal. In attempting to decide whether 'this supernatural soliciting' is good or ill, Macbeth is, in fact, taking up Banquo's warning.

The first sentence of Macbeth's speech is in the swelling rhetoric of the grand style as Macbeth aspires to 'the sweet fruition of an earthly crown'. But although this first aside does convey some of the wonder of bombastic ambition, the second aside is wonder on a lesser scale attempting to follow through the processes of logic and inference: 'If ill, why . . .? If good, why . . . ?' Logic and inference, however, soon give way to 'suggestion' and 'imaginings', and the following sentence 'Present fears/ Are less than horrible imaginings' is not a conclusion or an answer to the parallel logical questions 'If . . . why?', but a statement saying that the logical questions, the 'present fears' that the supernatural soliciting might not be good, lead only to the yet more fearful suggestion of murdering Duncan. 'My thought' in the next sentence echoes 'present fears' as 'fantastical murther' echoes 'horrible imaginings'. Shakespeare is clearly employing the libertine golden style, the method of induced imagination showing forth the movements of a mind discovering images as it goes, fantasizing while it speaks. If it seems inapposite to call images as fearful as Macbeth's 'golden', it should be remembered that the goal of his desire is, as Lady Macbeth puts it, 'the golden round,/ Which fate and metaphysical aid both seem/ To have thee crown'd withal'. The imagination is *induced* in the same sense that it is when Bacon speaks of *induced* knowledge. The members of Macbeth's periods from line 134 and following violate at will the predetermined plan of his logical investigation, and the images they introduce, though they arise in his imagination and are therefore his responsibility, also seem to come from something outside of him, beyond his control.

Macbeth's speech, in other words, offers a fairly clear example of all three styles, the grand, the plain, and the intermediate, registering his high aspirations, his morals, and his desires. Shakespeare brings the styles together in this way in order to outline the contours of knowing and not-knowing that are crucial to the action of *Macbeth*. The conclusion of this first crisis in the action is really a statement of the central problem in the play. The word 'function' (l. 141), as Kenneth Muir explains, is 'the intellectual activity which is revealed in outward conduct: but the word is applied to action in general, whether physical or mental'.[12] Macbeth's intellectual being and his conduct, his action, are 'smother'd in surmise' – suspended, we might also say, between the conflicting claims of various kinds of wonder. It is premature to speak of Macbeth's character at this point, for even though we know a number of important things about him, his character is, in an important sense, still in the process of being shaped, of being made. The crucial question to ask, then, of Shakespeare's *mimesis* is, 'What kinds of wonder accompany the action?'.

Some of the most profound kinds of wonder make up Macbeth's soliloquy at the opening of Act I, scene vii.

> If it were done, when 'tis done, then 'twere well
> It were done quickly: if th'assassination
> Could trammel up the consequence, and catch
> With his surcease success; that but this blow
> 5   Might be the be-all and the end-all – here,
> But here, upon this bank and shoal of time,
> We'd jump the life to come. – But in these cases,
> We still have judgment here; that we but teach
> Bloody instructions, which, being taught, return
> 10   To plague th'inventor: this even-handed Justice
> Commends th'ingredience of our poison'd chalice
> To our own lips. He's here in double trust:
> First, as I am his kinsman and his subject,
> Strong both against the deed; then, as his host,
> 15   Who should against his murtherer shut the door,
> Not bear the knife myself. Besides, this Duncan
> Hath borne his faculties so meek, hath been

So clear in his great office, that his virtues
Will plead like angels, trumpet-tongu'd, against
20   The deep damnation of his taking-off;
And Pity, like a naked new-born babe,
Striding the blast, or heaven's Cherubins, hors'd
Upon the sightless couriers of the air,
Shall blow the horrid deed in every eye,
25   That tears shall drown the wind. – I have no spur
To prick the sides of my intent, but only
Vaulting ambition, which o'erleaps itself
And fall on th'other – (I, vii, 1–28)

This speech, of course, has commanded an enormous volume of commentary, much of it devoted to interpreting its extraordinary imagery. J. Dover Wilson regards the soliloquy as the supreme expression of Macbeth's 'visual imagination'.[13] A. C. Bradley, discussing what he takes to be the 'key to Shakespeare's conception' of the character, conferring on him the imagination of a poet, explains that[14]

> Macbeth's better nature – to put the matter for clearness' sake too broadly – instead of speaking to him in the overt language of moral ideas, commands, and prohibitions, incorporates itself in images which alarm and horrify. His imagination is thus the best of him, something usually deeper and higher than his conscious thoughts; and if he had obeyed it he would have been safe.

And Kenneth Muir, though quite clear about not confusing 'the powers of expression possessed by Macbeth with the powers of Shakespeare himself', remarks that 'the imagery of the speech shows that Macbeth is haunted by the horror of the deed, and impresses that horror on the audience. . . . we may say his imagery expresses his unconscious mind.'[15]

But the most important analysis along these lines is offered by F. R. Leavis, who wants to get, for literary criticism, a more complex sense of 'imagery' and to define, for poetry, a kind of thought that is antithetic to the logic and clarity of good exposition. Shakespeare's imagery includes 'tactual effects' evoking different kinds of effort and movement not adequately to be described under a heading such as 'visual imagination'. After quoting lines 2–4 ('if th'assassination . . .'), Leavis comments on the 'incredulity' of the 'if':[16]

> The incredulity is conveyed in the vigour of the imaginative realization: the assassination can't conceivably trammel up the consequence, and the impossibility is expressed in the mocking sense of an instantaneous magic that turns the king's 'surcease' into assured final 'success'. No one would call this kind of more-than-stated 'as if' (an effect much used by Hopkins) an 'image', but, in its evocative immediacy of presentment, it replaces mere prose statement or description with a concreteness intimately related to that of 'trammel up the consequences', which anyone would describe as metaphor.

In addition to effects such as this, the speech exhibits shifts of imagery which are 'logically non-sequential' but which complete 'dramatically relevant' perceptions and thoughts. The closing lines ('I have no spur . . .'), for example, move from suggesting a rider mounted on a horse to suggesting one who is vaulting towards the saddle. In doing so they convey to us that Macbeth, though without a sense of purpose or will to spur him on and, indeed, without a sense of any other control, nevertheless still entertains his 'appallingly dangerous' ambition. Macbeth's 'perverse self-contradictions' are thus vividly exposed in Shakespeare's poetry. In such 'non-logical' shifts and in such concrete effects of effort and movement, Leavis discovers a mode of thought he believes is peculiar to poetry.[17]

> If we say that the complex tension has had its analysis in Macbeth's speech, that is to recognize that Shakespeare's poetry is the agent and vehicle of thought. That Shakespeare so obviously can't have first stated his thought explicitly, 'clearly' and 'logically' in prose, and then turned it into dramatic poetry doesn't make it any the less thought.

By concentrating on the poetry, on the way the language works, Leavis is able to show the distinction between Macbeth's character and Shakespeare's analysis of it, the persistent contemplation of the horrid deed even though contemplation is repelled at every point. In this way, the wonderfully vigorous exploration of theme is attributed not to the poetical imagination of the character or to his unconscious mind but to the quality of the author's *making.*

Yet, though one might agree that Shakespeare's language in Macbeth's soliloquy is fundamentally exploratory, it is not exploratory in quite the way that Leavis says it is. To begin with, the structure of the soliloquy as a whole is not only clear and logical, it is syllogistic.

> If it were done, when 'tis done, then 'twere well
> It were done quickly
>
>   – But in these cases,
> We still have judgment here
>
>   – [Therefore] I have no spur
> To prick the sides of my intent

The incredulity of the 'if', though it is supported by the sort of 'imagery' that Leavis talks about, is primarily the kind of wonder appropriate to the syllogism. The speech opens with a plain statement, an explicit condition contrary to fact, which by all grammatical rules amounts to the assertion that it will not be done when 'tis done. In other words, by means of the subjunctive, the major premise offers not a more-than-stated 'as if' but a mere statement in plain style, and we are led from the beginning to expect a conclusion that denies the possibility conditionally asserted in the opening.[18]

The conclusion, of course, is not introduced by the word 'therefore', but the complex metaphorical development of the soliloquy and the absence of the clear syntactical pointer must not be allowed to obfuscate its force. The syllogistic structure will carry a certain momentum however the conclusion is expressed. Furthermore, the force of the syllogism, an emphatic recoil from the idea of murder, carries over beyond the soliloquy into the first few exchanges with Lady

Macbeth, where Macbeth twice expresses himself in plain, emphatic language.

> We will proceed no further in this business. (1. 31)

>   Pr'ythee, peace.
> I dare do all that may become a man;
> Who dares do more, is none. (ll. 45–7)

And the middle section of the syllogism is also stated in plain language. The Arden editor glosses 'have judgment' as 'receive sentence', which makes it seem that Macbeth is only developing the note of expediency, and, in the metaphors following, 'bloody instructions' raises the fear of further rebellion and 'even-handed Justice' the fear of the reprisals that might be taken by legitimate authority. But the plain style lines which continue the development of the minor premise make it clear that 'have judgment' does not mean simply 'receive sentence' but is an emphatic recognition of the human foundations upon which sentences are based.[19]

>   He's here in double trust:
> First as I am his kinsman and his subject,
> Strong both against the deed; then as his host . . .

The sanctions here are all-inclusive: personal, political, and social; and Macbeth himself is presented as capable of judging from a truly human perspective, a moral perspective. To reply to Bradley in his own terms, Macbeth's better nature clearly does speak to him in the overt language of moral ideas, commands, and prohibitions.

Part of the difficulty of perceiving this overt language lies in perceiving correctly the rhythm of the first line and a half.[20] The nervous energy accompanying Macbeth's meditation is brought out by the powerful compression and by the rhythmic organization – by the quick monosyllables, by the use of repetition, and by the caesuras. The metre is regular except for the standard inversion in the first position (the fourth foot is iambic despite the caesura and the heavy stress of the unaccented syllable).

If it̄/wēre doṅe,/whēn 'tĭs/dōne, thén/'twēre wéll

It̄ wēre/dōne quiċk/ly

The accent falls on the syntactical pointers, If, then; and the word 'done,' though it appears three times in short space, receives the accent only in the first instance. The more narrowly circumscribed actions that are referred to in the second and third appearances of the verb 'to do' are thus made subordinate to action in the fullest sense, embracing the complete range of moral and spiritual sanctions.[21] It is this rhythmical subtlety, characteristic of the classical plain style developed in England in the 1590s, that allows Shakespeare to register Macbeth's complicated attitude within the framework of the logical structure. At any rate, the plain style is fundamental to the exploratory nature of Shakespeare's *mimesis.*

But Macbeth's soliloquy is not simply in the plain style, and some account of the other elements is needed. In fact, a fundamental part of Shakespeare's procedure involves quick alternations between the plain and the eloquent styles. The customary complaint brought against the syllogism, of course, is that the conclusion is so absolutely predetermined by the premises that the language seems not at all exploratory, especially if the premises do not take sufficient account of the flux of human experience. By having Macbeth utter the major premise twice, once in plain language, and then in an elaborately metaphorical way ('if th'assassination/ Could trammel up the consequence ... We'd jump the life to come'), Shakespeare portrays him as trying to get out from under the constraints of his logic. The procedure seems to be something similar to what we noticed in Macbeth's earlier speech where the libertine golden style violates at will the predetermined plan of logical investigation. Certainly images and metaphors such as 'our poison'd chalice', 'bear the knife myself', and 'trammel up the consequence' keep the idea of murdering Duncan emphatically present in Macbeth's mind. But the imagery, instead of violating the premises, works mainly to support and develop them, making them richer and deeper. Whether he pursues the wonder of his own imaginings or the wonder of logical connectives, he arrives at the same conclusive moral prohibitions.

This coincidence of styles produces, in the last half of the speech, the metaphysical style, as two alternative ways of looking at the world, of discovering or creating reality, are brought together in violent union. The plain realization that in these cases we still have judgment *here* is yoked to the imaginative realization that such judgment is also, and at the same time, eternal. The libertine period beginning in the middle of line 16 with the loose connective 'Besides', introduces a moral description of Duncan's character and suggests essential religious qualities. Duncan's faculties or powers which are yet borne meekly and the greatness of his office in which he has yet been clear, or free from stain, demonstrate the integrity and vitality of a 'self' subservient to larger purposes in a way that is essentially religious. In the succeeding metaphors, the 'trumpet-tongu'd angels' and 'heaven's Cherubins', Macbeth's attention veers from the essence of religion to the paraphernalia of religion. But the heart of the matter lies in the justly famous Shakespearean figure:

> And Pity, like a naked new-born babe,
> Striding the blast . . .

Whatever this figure is, it is not primarily an image. It has, in fact, several of the characteristics that James Smith discerns in the metaphysical conceit: it seems impossible that pity should possess both the innocent vulnerability of the babe and the awesome power implicit in 'striding the blast'; it seems impossible that it should not possess both. The difficulty, in other words, springs from essence. F. R. Leavis, commenting on the oddity of the figure, remarks 'that "pity," whatever part it may play in the total effect, is certainly not at the centre – certainly doesn't represent the main significance'.[22] The explanation for this, I believe, is that the figure brings together two things, pity and fear, and makes us feel that they are one. The result is a problem either deriving from, or closely resembling in the nature of its difficulty, the problem of the Many and the One.

What Macbeth discovers at this point is that sympathy and judgment are terms of the same order. 'Judgment here', founded on the bonds of kinship and on political and social obligations, is also eternal judgment because it springs from nature – not 'the law of Nature' or 'natural law' but the 'law of *our* nature', the law which discloses the vulnerable centres that we must preserve at all costs. The *murder* of Duncan would bring simultaneously the *birth* of a fearfully avenging pity; that it would be *done* when 'tis done is absolutely impossible. The emotional effect of pity and fear that would spring from such an act of woe could not be more emphatically present to Macbeth's wonder. The emphasis is the creation of wonder at every level. By having Macbeth describe Duncan as 'so clear in his great office' that at the report of his murder 'tears shall drown the wind', Shakespeare is obviously intent upon 'stirring the affects of admiration and commiseration'. At the same time, it is also true that he has made a character who understands human nature profoundly and who understands, as well, the full implications of the action he contemplates.[23]

But if this is so, we may well want to raise, along with Robert Bridges, the common-sense objection that a man with such 'magnificent qualities of mind, extreme courage, and poetic imagination' would not have perpetrated the crime.[24] As Macbeth himself recognizes, there is nothing in his thought – logical, imaginative, or metaphysical – that can provide him with a motive or a reason to act, but only 'vaulting ambition'. It is the part of Lady Macbeth in the exchange following the soliloquy to suppress and supplant the wonder of Macbeth's thought in order to release this ambition. That she succeeds despite his searching scrutiny of the whole problem is a measure of the terrible intensity of his desire to be king. She succeeds by undermining logic, imagination, and metaphysics. Following a specious argument on the distinctions between cowardice and courage and between beast and man, she offers a shockingly imaginative repudiation of the pity owing to the babe nursing at her breast. In so doing she denies that pity and fear are part of the essential nature of humankind. Macbeth's response at this point signifies the precise instant of his fall from grace (I, vii, 59):

If we should fail?

This question, so apparently close in form and meaning to the phrase that opens the scene ('If it were done'), is in reality far more simple-minded, far less full of wonder. Allowing his wife's false reasoning to supplant his true reasoning, he re-opens the question in a way which suggests that reason has already proposed a legitimate goal and that what remains to do is to find appropriate means. The means once found, Shakespeare shows Macbeth rapt in wonder and admiration for the bombastic ambition that he sees in his wife and settles for in himself.

> Bring forth men-children only!
> For thy undaunted mettle should compose
> Nothing but males.

It is a powerful statement, but it excludes from the nature of men everything but fearlessness.

If the common language 'enters so deeply into us that it becomes part of the material of which the soul is made', then Macbeth murders his own soul by cutting off or denying almost all of the ways of knowing and not-knowing what human nature is.[25] When his protagonist is at the point of murdering Duncan, Shakespeare has only one style left in which to show Macbeth being himself, and that style is the bombastic style. The criticism that Yvor Winters brings against dramatic form, then, is justified to this extent: at certain points the dramatist will be compelled to use a style less rich, less wonderful, than the styles he is capable of using elsewhere. There is no inherent reason, however, why, using the style that remains to him, the dramatist should not write the best poetry he is capable of in that style. The converse of Ian Robinson's argument is that 'when we manage to speak from the soul we make the common language'. Macbeth at the most crucial moment of the action, though his soul is frighteningly narrow, displays what Robinson calls elsewhere a 'monstrous creativity in murder'.[26]

> Now o'er the one half-world
> 50   Nature seems dead, and wicked dreams abuse
> The curtain'd sleep: Witchcraft celebrates
> Pale Hecate's off'rings; and wither'd Murther,

Alarum'd by his sentinel, the wolf,
Whose howl's his watch, thus with his stealthy pace,
55 With Tarquin's ravishing strides, towards his design
Moves like a ghost. (II, i, 49–56)

In some respects Winters's criticism of this passage as a
'More or less standard huffing speech, containing something
of Marlowe and a little of Pistol', is correct. It also contains,
as Howard Baker argues, something of Sackville and a little of
Kyd, and by combining 'huffing' with mental anguish brings
the heroic medium to perfection. The repeated combination
of adjective plus noun that is characteristic of the bombastic
style is everywhere evident: 'wicked dreams', 'curtain'd
sleep', 'Pale Hecate's off'rings', 'wither'd Murther', 'stealthy
pace', 'ravishing strides'.[27] This is the medium of mighty
threats. (The other important commentator to agree with
Baker and Winters is Macbeth himself – 'Whiles I *threat*, he
lives'.) But the 'little of Shakespeare' that Winters concedes
to it as well is worth further attention. In the first place, it
is a matter of syntax: one long period divided into three
major elements separated by the colon and semi-colon. By
placing the idea of murder last in a series of three, Shakespeare gives it a sense of inevitability, a sense that is streng-
thened by the long suspension of the subject 'wither'd Murther' from its final predicate 'Moves like a ghost.' Murder is
here given phrase and being.

The deadness of nature is not merely a theme of midnight
horror, but a deadness in Macbeth's own nature, causing him
to obey his 'wicked dreams' and to repudiate the knowledge
he arrives at in a plain statement referring to the dagger
immediately preceding the passage quoted: 'There's no such
thing./ It is the bloody business which informs/ Thus to mine
eyes.' It is also a deadness in his nature to repudiate the other
senses in favour of the eyes (ll. 44–5). Macbeth is subject to a
kind of mental tyranny that sees what it wants to see and
denies the substantial evidence of the senses and of the mind.
The reference to witchcraft is apposite in that Macbeth, having understood the supernatural sanctions he contemplates
violating in I, vii, here employs the language of superstition
that is a debased and corrupted supernatural in which violation

is the rule. And the allusion to Tarquin and rape has a clinching effect, because rape is the archetype of the mental tyranny that is a lust of the eyes. Murder is indeed 'wither'd' in more than the conventional sense of allegorical personification, and Macbeth's somnambulism is the sign of what his nature has come to. In this way, through Macbeth's speech, Shakespeare makes, for the common language, a language of murder.

Because of the contrast between what Macbeth's soul comes to and what it has been, he is able to feel, in a way commensurate with one of Fulke Greville's greatest short poems, the very depth of his iniquity:

> That ugly centre of infernal spirits
> Where each sin feels her own deformity
> In these peculiar torments she inherits.

Without commenting on the superb recognitions that follow upon the killing of Duncan, I will conclude by examining one small exchange very near the end of the play. Macbeth's most famous speech ends by making a claim about life:

> it is a tale
> Told by an idiot, full of sound and fury,
> Signifying nothing.

Whatever else this claim is, it is a remark about language, about style, and the style to which it applies most fully is the bombastic style, the style adopted at the crucial moment in the action of the play. Macbeth's attitude is immediately placed, for the next words in the text are '*Enter a Messenger*,' and the implication is – with a tale. Macbeth responds: 'Thou com'st to use thy tongue; thy story quickly.' The messenger, however, does not proceed at once to give his story, or its significance, but instead wonders how best to express it, what style to use.

> Gracious my Lord,
> I should report that which I say I saw
> But know not how to do't.

He settles on the plain style.

> *Macb.*   Well, say, sir.
> *Mess.* As I did stand my watch upon the hill,

> I look'd toward Birnam, and anon, methought,
> The wood began to move.

This is wonder on a lesser scale than the wonder of sound and fury, but its implications for Macbeth are very great, and he finds it impossible not to discover significance in such a tale.

> I pull in resolution; and begin
> To doubt th'equivocation of the fiend,
> That lies like truth.

In the end, Macbeth finds it impossible not to wonder (to doubt), to draw inferences, and to distinguish truth and falsity.

Shakespeare's *mimesis* defines character and action in *Macbeth* by drawing, in language, the limits of wonder. This is definition in another sense from the definition of an expository poem such as Greville's 'Down in the depth', but it is equally legitimate. Winters's criticism of dramatic form, then, does not take sufficient account of the fact that drama, in a certain sense, is also expository, and that the distinction between the imitative and the expository is a false distinction.[28] It follows, however, that the appeal to imitative form is bogus, and that Winters's criticism of that aspect of dramatic theory and practice is correct. True art is not an imitation, but a making. On the other hand, Leavis's account of the essentially dramatic or the essentially poetic use of language does not take sufficient account of the part played by the simple tools of exposition: logic, clarity, and mere statement. How shall the dramatist make his art without recourse to these central ways of wondering? Shakespeare's astonishing range of definition in drama, that is, of form, is the achievement of mastering an equally astonishing range of styles – at the centre of which is the plain style.[29]

V

A style is 'a principle of selection and order'. When a dramatist chooses a style, he chooses a way of including and excluding 'certain classes of ideas and expressions, and in

verse of certain meters and metrical practices'.[30] The choice
is a conscious one, but it does not fully determine the dramatist's intention, for he also chooses his subject, his action,
which may be conceived of as a pure abstract motion, or
form. The essence of poetic drama is the presentation of
characters who are shaped by what they do and by what they
say. 'Presentation' does not insist on theatrical performance
(though it does not exclude it either), for it is not the performance of the play by actors, but the performance of the
action by the characters within the play that is essential. And
just as there are several kinds of action, so there are several
styles of language available to the dramatist. The kind of
language he brings to bear on any given act will be a comment on the relation of that act to the alternative acts that
are excluded in the instant of performance. The more complex the language, that is, the more compressed or poetic it
is, the more subtle, numerous, and complex are the alternative acts that give resonance to the plot and make it truly a
mimesis of human life. This process, the interinanimation of
style and form, of language and action, reaches its greatest
precision and scope when the dramatist succeeds in making
verse into drama.

It is through the interinanimation of form and style that
an author embodies his intention. When a dramatist's subject
is a tragic action, his problem is to determine what can be
thought and known about death, and his choice of style,
therefore, rests on deciding which styles are capable of tragic
effect. The grand style and the middle style are capable of
nobility and suffering; but tragedy offers something other
than the nobly suffering self. The plain style is germane to
poetic tragedy because it is a means of registering tragic
impersonality and the emotional effect of woe or wonder.

Certainly, Greville, in *Mustapha*, and Shakespeare, in
Richard II and *Macbeth*, make use of the grand and middle
styles. The grand style is the medium of high aspiring minds
and is well suited to defining the kind of wonder they evince.
But 'horrible periods of exorbitant passions among equals'
are not sufficiently plain by themselves to provide 'a perspective into vice and the unprosperities of it'. For one thing, the
'equals', the leaders of society, are a very narrow segment,

219

and the high style does not show clearly enough how their 'exorbitant passions' affect all of us here and now. The middle style is the medium of praise and blame, love and hate, and, especially as perfected in the golden style of lyric poetry, is well-suited to defining the wonder of private personal feelings. But isolated personalities, however intense the isolation or the personality, are not the whole truth about human nature.

The truth is the province of the plain style. In the native plain style it is emphatic, but limited; in the plain style of Greville and Shakespeare, improved by refinements in the short poem, it is urbane and inclusive, capable of sustaining wonder when confronted with the fact of woe. Sidney provides a clear and succinct statement of the emotional effects appropriate to tragedy, and he also suggests two of the styles available to the poet, but the dramatist, in order to make his play, has to sort out some of Sidney's equivocations on the question of style. Greville and Shakespeare, making 'a *mimesis* not of men simply but of an action, that is, of life', both have to depend more centrally on the images of life than on the images of wit. Both have to be more careful to speak truly than to speak curiously. It is not true that the dramatist 'nothing affirms, and therefore never lieth'. He affirms something central about the true nature of man, the vulnerable centre we must at all costs preserve. He defines the law of *our* nature – the plain truth of our common language.

Notes

1 Verse into drama

1   Yvor Winters, 'The 16th Century Lyric in England: A Critical and Historical Reinterpretation', *Poetry*, Vols 53 and 54, 1939, reprinted in Paul J. Alpers, ed., *Elizabethan Poetry: Modern Essays in Criticism*, Oxford University Press, 1967, p. 95.

2   In *Forms of Discovery: Critical and Historical Essays on the Forms of the Short Poem in English* [Chicago], Alan Swallow, 1967, p. 3, Winters repeats, with only minor alterations, his original 1939 description of the characteristics of a typical poem in the native plain style:

> a theme usually broad, simple, and obvious, even tending toward the proverbial, but usually a theme of some importance, humanly speaking; a feeling restrained to the minimum required by the subject; a rhetoric restrained to a similar minimum, the poet being interested in his rhetoric as a means of stating his matter as economically as possible, and not, as are the Petrarchans, in the pleasures of rhetoric for its own sake. There is also a strong tendency toward aphoristic statement, many of the best poems being composed wholly of aphorisms, or, if very short, being composed as single aphorisms. The aphoristic lyric, like the logical lyric, of which the aphoristic lyric is usually a sub-form, is medieval in its origins, but certain poems by Wyatt, Gascoigne, Raleigh, and Nashe probably represent the highest level to which the mode has ever been brought. The aphoristic structure, however, is not invariable: *Gascoigne's Woodmanship*, for example, is cast in the form of consecutive and elaborate exposition, and so are many poems by Wyatt.

3   Lewis, though he does not exactly intend it, supports Winters when he describes what he calls 'Drab Age Verse': 'The language is very plain. There is little aureation, few metaphors, no stylized syntax, and none of the sensuous imagery loved by the Elizabethans' (*English Literature in the Sixteenth Century Excluding Drama*, Oxford, Clarendon Press, 1954, p. 222). And Hunter, if we make allowance for modern prejudice in the words 'life-style' and

'persona', argues cogently that choosing one of the two styles is a matter of more than literary significance. He comments on two poems:

> A careful reading suggests that neither style is a version of the other; each has as its aim a distinct image of the world, and other features are explicable in terms of this aim. What changes when poets move from one style to the other (if they move) is not only literary style but also the life-style of the persona who emerges from the body of their work. ('Drab and Golden Lyrics of the Renaissance' in *Forms of Lyric*, ed. Reuben A. Brower, New York and London, Columbia University Press, 1970, p. 7)

4 One of the important refinements that Cunningham and Trimpi offer is to show how the native plain style was made urbane not only by assimilating many of the experiments of Petrarchan love poetry but also by absorbing several of the principles of Latin verse as well as Latin prose. As Cunningham says in 'Lyric Style in the 1590s' in *The Collected Essays*, Chicago, The Swallow Press, 1976, p. 323, John Donne and Ben Jonson achieve: 'a style that can handle circumstantiality and detail, can accommodate in poetry what we think of as the material of prose, and yet without modulation of manner can strike through to the heart of human feeling'. This accommodation is something that Trimpi discusses at length, proceeding on the assumption that:

> The application of traditional rhetorical classifications and descriptions of prose style to the poetry of the Renaissance can be more extensively explored in Jonson's case than it has been in the past in those of other poets, since his rhetorical statements are so consistent with his own practise and since he has left sufficient commentary on ancient and modern writers to enable us to apply his theoretical comments to his particular literary judgments. Once such an application proves valuable in describing Jonson's intentions, it can be assumed to be relevant to the interpretation of other writers. Although it will be necessary to find explicit evidence in dealing with their work, the type of evidence to look for and a way of applying it shall have been indicated. (*Ben Jonson's Poems: A Study of the Plain Style*, Stanford University Press, 1962, p. 239)

While Cunningham and Trimpi demonstrate continental and classical influences at work in the development of the native English plain style, Douglas Peterson in his book, *The English*

Lyric from Wyatt to Donne, Princeton University Press, 1967, shows that the courtly verse of medieval England provides many of the origins of the eloquent style and that, in most cases, 'eloquent' is a more apt descriptive term than either 'Petrarchan' or 'golden'.

5 Yvor Winters, *The Function of Criticism: Problems and Exercises*, 2nd edn, Denver, Alan Swallow, 1957, pp. 51–8.

6 *Essays in Criticism*, 22, 1972, pp. 109–30.

7 Jonas Barish, 'Yvor Winters and the Antimimetic Prejudice', *New Literary History*, 2, 1970–1, pp. 419–44.

8 Ibid., p. 426.

9 Andor Gomme's attempts to refute Winters's criticisms of drama are suggestive but undeveloped. For examples, see *Attitudes to Criticism*, Carbondale and Edwardsville, Southern Illinois University Press, 1966, p. 82, pp. 98–9, and p. 164, n. 57.

2 Sidney's *Defence* and Greville's *Mustapha*

1 For example, two recent editors print an outline of the *Defence* indicating that it has the seven parts of a classical oration — even though they do not quite agree on what the seven parts are. See Geoffrey Shepherd, ed., *An Apology for Poetry*, London, Thomas Nelson, 1965 and Jan Van Dorsten, ed., *A Defence of Poetry*, Oxford University Press, 1966.

2 The quotation is taken from Van Dorsten's edition, pp. 71, 72. Subsequent quotations from the same edition will be noted parenthetically in the text.

3 O. B. Hardison Jr, 'The Two Voices of Sidney's *Apology for Poetry*,' *English Literary Renaissance*, 2, 1972, 83–99.

4 Despite the oddity of his conjectures, Hardison's conclusion gives good support to the idea that there are two distinct styles available in sixteenth-century England.

> Close reading of Sidney's *Apology* leads inevitably, I think, to the conclusion that it speaks in two distinct and discordant voices. The first is the familiar voice of humanist poetics. Its basic debts are to Plato, the neo-Platonists, and Horace, and it is heard most clearly prior to Sidney in the writing of Boccaccio, Politian, Daniello, and Tasso. It results not only in a particular content in the *Apology*, but also to some degree in a particular form — the pattern of the forensic oration, using the *poeta, poesis, poema* schema attributed to Horace. Its tone is affirmative and inclusive. It welcomes

classical and medieval poems, mixed forms, allegory and fable, and complex, sometimes obscure diction. Its key ideas are inspiration, the superiority of imagination to reason and nature, and the power of poetry, through its emotional appeal, to cause *praxis* rather than *gnosis*.

The second voice, is that of incipient neo-classicism. Its tone is prescriptive, sometimes satiric or openly scornful. It is exclusive rather than inclusive, for it expects the critic to act as a judge, censuring and even excluding work which is flawed. It is suspicious of allegory and complex diction, and it ridicules mixed forms. Its touchstones are the subordination of imagination to reason and nature, the need for artistic 'rules,' the interpretation of imitation as copying masterpieces, and insistence on verisimilitude — with the corollary of the three unities — in drama. (Ibid., p. 97)

For a discussion of the relationship between poetic styles in drama and the doctrine of imitation see Ch 10, '*Macbeth*: style and form.'

5   J. V. Cunningham, *Woe or Wonder: The Emotional Effect of Shakespearean Tragedy* (1951), reprinted in *The Collected Essays*, Chicago, The Swallow Press, 1976, p. 53. Most references to Cunningham's work are from his collected essays, hereafter abbreviated as *CE*.

6   All quotations from *Mustapha* are taken from Geoffrey Bullough's edition of the *Poems and Dramas*, vol. II, Edinburgh, Oliver and Boyd, 1939, and act, scene, and line numbers will be cited in the text.

7   Joan Rees, *Selected Writings of Fulke Greville, First Lord Brooke*, Athlone Renaissance Library, London, The Athlone Press, 1973.

8   Reprinted in Bullough, op. cit., vol. I, pp. 25, 26.

9   'Introduction' to ibid., vol. II, p. 58.

10   Cunningham, *CE*, p. 10.

11   The change is noted in Bullough's 'Commentary', which collates the four major texts of the play, op. cit., vol. II, p. 245.

12   Cunningham, *CE*, p. 87.

13   Nowell Smith, ed., *Sir Fulke Greville's Life of Sir Philip Sidney*, Oxford, Clarendon Press, 1907, pp. 222–5. The letter 's' has been modernized.

14   Bullough, op. cit., vol. I, pp. 180, 181.

15   Nowell Smith, op. cit., p. 151.

16   See ibid., pp. 155–7. Many of the arguments for and against the claim that the play used by the Essex conspirators on 7 February 1601 was Shakespeare's are summarized by E. M. Albright, 'Shakespeare's *Richard II* and the Essex Conspiracy', *Publications of the Modern Language Association*, vol. 42, 1927, 686–720.

17 'Introduction' to Bullough, op. cit., vol. II, p. 1.

18 Similarly, Constance in Shakespeare's *King John* apostrophizes
death: 'Thou hate and terror to prosperity' (III, iv, 28), and
conversely, Achmat in *Mustapha* decides in the end that he must
defend Soliman, if only for the sake of the prosperity that his
rule has guaranteed in the past: he will '...strive/To save this high
rais'd *Soueraignitie*,/Under whose wings there was Prosperitie'
(V, iii, 112–14). In *Paradise Lost* Milton gives Satan a speech
showing the two meanings of 'prosperity' (success and morality)
pulling against one another. Satan argues that since in Hell there
is 'no good/For which to strive' the fallen angels with this 'advantage' can

> now return
> To claim our just inheritance of old,
> Surer to prosper than prosperity
> Could have assur'd us; and by what best way,
> Whether of open War or covert guile,
> We now debate; who can advise, may speak. (II, ll, 37–42)

Though Satan ends by asking for advice about a 'best way,' which
presupposes the ability to make moral choices, this contradicts his
earlier remarks about their prosperity being more assured because
of the absence of any good for them to choose. Milton's perspective into the unprosperities of vice is, like Greville's, traditional.
The quoted lines are from Merritt Hughes's edition of the *Complete
Poems and Major Prose*, New York, Odyssey Press, 1957.

19 *Aristotle on the Art of Poetry*, trans. Ingram Bywater (1909),
reprinted in *The Works of Aristotle*, vol. XI, ed. W. D. Ross,
Oxford, Clarendon Press, 1924, 1460b23–b26.

20 Cunningham, *CE*, p. 55.

21 W. Trimpi, *Ben Jonson's Poems*, Stanford University Press, 1962,
pp. 68–70.

22 William A. Ringler, Jr, ed., *The Poems of Sir Philip Sidney*, Oxford,
Clarendon Press, 1962, p. 173.

23 Bullough, op. cit., vol. I, p. 78. Thom Gunn has an excellent discussion of this poem in his 'Introduction' to *Selected Poems of
Fulke Greville*, University of Chicago Press, 1968, pp. 21–3.

24 Quoted from Ringler's edition, p. 38.

25 Unless otherwise noted, quotations from Shakespeare are from
Hardin Craig, ed., *The Complete Works of Shakespeare*, Chicago,
Scott, Foresman, 1961.

26 William Empson, *Seven Types of Ambiguity* (1930), reprinted,
Harmondsworth, Penguin, 1973, p. 59.

27 Ringler's edition, p. 148.
28 Neil Rudenstein, *Sidney's Poetic Development*, Cambridge, Mass., Harvard University Press, 1967, p. 127.
29 For definitions of the terms in parenthesis see Cunningham, *CE*, p. 98.
30 Bullough, op. cit., vol. I, p. 84.
31 Agnes M. C. Latham, ed., *The Poems of Sir Walter Ralegh*, Cambridge, Mass., Harvard University Press, 1951, p. 50.
32 Yvor Winters, 'The Audible Reading of Poetry', in *The Function of Criticism*, Chicago, Alan Swallow, 1957, pp. 92, 93.
33 This phrase is offered by J. V. Cunningham as a definition of 'imagery', *CE*, p. 167.
34 See especially Rosemond Tuve, *Elizabethan and Metaphysical Imagery*, University of Chicago Press, 1947, pp. 251–80.
35 'Sidney perfected most of the lyrical graces, and worked out in detail the relationships between elaborate syntax (that is, the forms of reason) and a variety of beautiful stanzaic and linear structures: he thus became the school-master of more than a century of poets.' Yvor Winters, *Forms of Discovery: Critical and Historical Essays on the Forms of the Short Poem in English*, Chicago, Alan Swallow, 1967, p. 28.
36 The phrase is cited in the *Oxford English Dictionary* as an illustration of the use of the word 'equipoise' and is attributed to Samuel Johnson.
37 Ross, op. cit., 1450b18–20.
38 Wotton's remark in a letter to the Queen is quoted by Trimpi, op. cit., p. 190. Trimpi also quotes Edmund Bolton (*Hypercritica*, c. 1618), an admirer of the plain style, who commends especially Sir Fulke Greville for '*his matchless* Mustapha' (p. 115).

3 Tragedy and history in *Richard II*

1 Among the earliest to recognize the sweet style in Shakespeare are Richard Barnfield, John Weever, and Francis Meres. Barnfield's praise in 1598 of Shakespeare's 'honey-flowing vein' (*Poems in Divers Humours*) is echoed by Weever, who in 1599 uses the epithet 'honey-tongu'd' (*Epigrams in the Oldest Cut, and Newest Fashion*). Meres's remark in *Palladis Tamia, Wit's Treasury* (1598) has become the most famous of the three: 'The sweet, witty soul of Ovid lives in mellifluous and honey-tongued Shakespeare, witness his *Venus and Adonis*, his *Lucrece*, his sugared sonnets among his private friends.' All three are conveniently cited in

S. Schoenbaum, *Shakespeare's Lives*, Oxford, Clarendon Press, 1970, pp. 53, 54.

2   Francis Meres again provides an interesting note, for after claiming that, 'As Plautus and Seneca are accounted the best for comedy and tragedy among the Latins, so Shakespeare among the English is the most excellent in both kinds for the stage', he cites *Richard II* as his first example of Shakespearean tragedy. That he also cites *Richard III*, *Henry IV*, *King John*, *Titus Andronicus*, and *Romeo and Juliet* suggests that he saw no sharp division between history plays and tragedies. For a facsimile reproduction of Meres's remarks on Shakespeare see S. Schoenbaum, *William Shakespeare: A Documentary Life*, New York, Oxford University Press in association with Scolar Press, 1975, p. 140.

3   T. M. Raysor, ed., *Samuel Taylor Coleridge: Shakespearean Criticism*, London, Dent, 1960, vol. I, pp. 125, 126. The translation of the Greek phrase is taken from Terence Hawkes, ed., *Coleridge on Shakespeare* (1959), reprinted, Harmondsworth, Penguin, 1969, p. 241.

4   *Aristotle on the Art of Poetry*, trans. Ingram Bywater (1909), reprinted in *The Works of Aristotle*, vol. XI, ed. W. D. Ross, Oxford, Clarendon Press, 1924, 1451a16–a19.

5   Ibid., 1450b8–b12.

6   Raysor, op. cit., vol. II, p. 231.

7   The foregoing paragraph is congruent with an argument put forward by George Whalley, 'The Aristotle-Coleridge Axis', *University of Toronto Quarterly*, vol. 42, 1973, pp. 93–109.

8   Raysor, op. cit., vol. I, p. 126.

9   F. R. Leavis, 'Tragedy and the "Medium"', *Scrutiny*, vol. 12, 1944, pp. 255, 256, and 258.

10 Ibid., p. 260.

11 'Preface to Shakespeare' (1765) in *Johnson on Shakespeare*, vol. I, ed. Arthur Sherbo, The Yale Edition of the Works of Samuel Johnson, vol. VII, New Haven and London, Yale University Press, 1968, p. 71.

4 The standard: the moral and the golden

1   For example, in the second book of 'Of the Dignity and Advancement of Learning' he divides all human learning into history, poesy, and philosophy with reference to the three intellectual faculties, memory, imagination, and reason, but then is forced to dismiss from poesy satires, elegies, epigrams, odes and the like and

refer them to philosophy and the arts of speech. *The Works of Francis Bacon*, vol. VIII, eds James Spedding, Robert Ellis, and Douglas Heath, Boston, Houghton, Mifflin, 1857, pp. 407 and 439.

2 'Answer to Davenant's Preface to *Gondibert*' (1650), in *Critical Essays of the Seventeenth Century*, vol. II, ed. J. E. Spingarn (1908), reprinted, Bloomington, Indiana University Press, 1957, p. 59. In *Leviathan* (1651), ed. Michael Oakeshott, Oxford, Basil Blackwell, 1946, p. 15, Hobbes discusses the 'faculty of invention' in his third chapter, 'of the Consequence or Train of Imaginations', where he asserts that 'we have no transition from one imagination to another, whereof we never had the like before in our senses' (p. 13). The implications for poetry of this argument and its later adumbration in the associationism of John Locke have not yet been fully explained.

3 An interesting defence of this kind of critical approach to literature is found in John Fraser, 'Stretches and Languages: A Contribution to Critical Theory', *College English*, vol. 32, 1971, pp. 381–98.

4 Walter Pater, *Appreciations*, 4th edn, (1901), reprinted, London, Macmillan, 1967. See especially pp. 202, 203.

5 E. Auerbach, *Mimesis*, trans. Willard R. Trask (1953), reprinted, Princeton University Press, 1971, p. 322.

6 Madeleine Doran, 'Imagery in "Richard II" and in "Henry IV"', *Modern Language Review*, 37, 1942, pp. 113–22, discusses the differences in the quality of imagery between *Richard II* and *1 Henry IV*, which she summarizes as the difference between 'enunciation and suggestion'. Her observations support the idea that 1595–7 is a crucial stage in Shakespeare's poetic and dramatic growth.

7 Unless otherwise noted, quotations are from *Richard II*, ed. Peter Ure, The Arden Shakespeare, 5th edn, London, Methuen, 1961. Act, scene, and line numbers will be given in parentheses after the quotation.

8 Ibid., Notes, p. 48.

9 Ben Jonson restates this Aristotelian principle succinctly in 'Discoveries' after outlining the main qualities of epistolary style: brevity, perspicuity, vigour, and discretion: 'The last is; Respect to discerne, what fits your selfe; him to whom you write; and that which you handle, which is a quality fit to conclude the rest, because it doth include all.' *Ben Jonson*, vol. VIII, eds C. H. Herford and Percy and Evelyn Simpson, Oxford, Clarendon Press, 1947, p. 633.

10 Ure, op. cit., Appendices III and IV, pp. 206–7.

11 Richard D. Altick, 'Symphonic Imagery in *Richard II*', *Publications*

of the Modern Language Association, vol. 62, 1947, pp. 339–65.
This article takes as its starting point Walter Pater's claim that:

> the play of *Richard the Second* does, like a musical composi-
> tion, possess a certain concentration of all its parts, a simple
> continuity, an evenness in execution, which are rare in the
> great dramatist. With *Romeo and Juliet*, that perfect sym-
> phony (symphony of three independent forms [The Sonnet:
> the Aubade: the Epithalamium] set in a grander one which it
> is the merit of German criticism to have detected) it belongs
> to a small group of plays, where, by happy birth and consis-
> tent evolution, dramatic form approaches to something like
> the unity of a lyrical ballad, a lyric, a song, a single strain of
> music. Pater, op. cit., pp. 202, 203.

Altick combines these musical analogies with the idea that poetry
is essentially a matter of association: 'In *Richard II* we see the
crucial intermediate stage in the development, or perhaps more
accurately, the utilization of Shakespeare's singular associative
gift' (op. cit., p. 364). Where *Richard II* is concerned, his article is
more immediately relevant than Wolfgang Clemen's *The Development of Shakespeare's Imagery*, Cambridge, Mass., Harvard
University Press, 1951, and in fact Clemen, when discussing this
play, is indebted to Altick throughout. Several critics have followed
Clemen and Altick in ascribing a dramatic and/or a musical function to the imagery of the play. See Arthur Suzman, 'Imagery
and Symbolism in *Richard II*', *Shakespeare Quarterly*, vol. 7, 1956,
pp. 355–70 and K. M. Harris, 'Sun and Water Imagery in *Richard II*:
Its Dramatic Function', *Shakespeare Quarterly*, vol. 21, 1970,
157–65. Karl Felsen adds a 'fugue' to Altick's 'symphony' (both
variations on a theme from Pater), '*Richard II*: Three-Part Harmony',
Shakespeare Quarterly, vol. 23, 1972, 107–11.

12   Altick, op. cit., p. 341, n. 6.
13   Ibid., pp. 341, 342.
14   Ibid., p. 342.
15   E. H. Kantorowicz, *The King's Two Bodies*, Princeton University
Press, 1957, p. 24. Kantorowicz argues that *Richard II* 'is the
tragedy of the King's Two Bodies', and that, at some points,
Shakespeare may have been influenced directly by Edmund
Plowden's *Reports* of a dispute over the Duchy of Lancaster, tried
in the fourth year of Elizabeth I. In Plowden's account, the crown
lawyers rely heavily on the argument that the king has in him a
'Body Natural' and a 'Body Politic'.

16 Howard Baker, *Induction to Tragedy* (1939), reprinted, New York, Russell & Russell, 1965. See especially pp. 56, 57.

17 E. M. Tillyard, *Shakespeare's History Plays* (1944), reprinted, Harmondsworth, Penguin, 1969, p. 268. Matthew Black, commenting on Gaunt's speech, makes nearly the same claim: 'the true protagonist in Sh.'s history plays is England,' *The Life and Death of King Richard the Second*, ed. Matthew Black, A New Variorum Edition of Shakespeare, Philadelphia and London, J. B. Lippincott, 1955, p. 102.

18 Quoted in Ure, op. cit., Notes, p. 50.

19 Cunningham, *CE*, p. 97.

20 Cunningham, *CE*, p. 19.

21 L. A. Cormican, 'Medieval Idiom in Shakespeare', *Scrutiny*, vol. 17, 1950, p. 186.

22 Ibid., p. 188.

23 Ibid., p. 200. L. C. Knights's chapter on Shakespeare in *Public Voices*, London, Chatto & Windus, 1971, uses Erich Auerbach's term to support an argument that is something like Cormican's: 'Perspective consciousness, then, is not simply a matter of opening up and filling in something we can safely think of as "background"; it is a steady reminder that what political and social questions are, ultimately, about is the ways in which one person or group of persons affects another person or group of persons' (p. 37).

24 Cormican, op. cit., p. 187.

5 The standard: the metaphysical and the Shakespearean

1 'A Discourse Concerning the Original and Progress of Satire' (1693), in *Essays of John Dryden*, vol. II, ed. W. P. Ker, Oxford, Clarendon Press, 1900, p. 19.

2 'Cowley', in *Lives of the English Poets*, vol. I, ed. George Birkbeck Hill, Oxford, Clarendon Press, 1905, p. 20.

3 James Smith, 'On Metaphysical Poetry', *Scrutiny*, vol. 2, 1933, pp. 226, 227.

4 Ibid., p. 228.

5 Ibid., pp. 231–235.

6 Odette de Mourgues, *Metaphysical, Baroque and Precieux Poetry*, Oxford, Clarendon Press, 1953.

7 Thom Gunn, ed., *Selected Poems of Fulke Greville*, University of Chicago Press, 1968, p. 113.

8 *Poems and Dramas*, ed. Geoffrey Bullough, vol. I, Edinburgh, Oliver & Boyd, 1939, p. 133.

9 Smith, op. cit., p. 237.

10 M. C. Bradbrook, *Shakespeare and Elizabethan Poetry*, London, Chatto & Windus, 1951, p. 37.

11 'Introduction', to *The Poems*, The Arden Shakespeare, ed. F. T. Prince, London, Methuen, 1960, p. xliv.

12 Ibid., p. xliv.

13 Cormican, 'Medieval Idiom in Shakespeare', *Scrutiny*, vol. 17, 1950, p. 192.

14 *Lectures and Conversations on Aesthetics, Psychology and Religious Belief*, ed. Cyril Barrett, Berkeley and Los Angeles, University of California Press, 1972, p. 8.

15 Smith, op. cit., pp. 235, 236.

16 See, for example, Donald Guss, *John Donne, Petrarchist*, Detroit, Wayne State University Press, 1966, and F. R. Leavis, *Revaluation*, (1936), reprinted, London, Chatto & Windus, 1962, pp. 11–14.

17 Cunningham, *CE*, p. 324.

18 C. H. Herford and P. and E. Simpson, eds, *Ben Jonson*, vol. VIII, Oxford, Clarendon Press, 1947, p. 216. Cf. the last line of 'To Penshvrst': 'their lords have built, but thy lord dwells' (p. 96). Cf. also, for an interesting account of the metaphysical content of the distinction between 'built' and 'dwells', Martin Heidegger's discussion of Holderlin, 'Poetically Man Dwells...', in *Poetry, Language, Thought*, trans. Albert Hofstadter, New York, Harper & Row, 1971.

19 Cunningham, *CE*, p. 168.

20 T. M. Raysor, ed., *Samuel Taylor Coleridge: Shakespearean Criticism*, vol. II, London, Dent, 1960, p. 144.

21 Smith, op. cit., p. 235.

22 John Donne, *The Elegies and The Songs and Sonnets*, ed. Helen Gardner, Oxford, Clarendon Press, 1965, p. 80.

23 Richard D. Altick, 'Symphonic Imagery in *Richard II*', *Publications of the Modern Language Association*, vol. 62, 1947, p. 350.

24 Inga-Stina Ewbank, 'Shakespeare's Poetry', in *A New Companion to Shakespeare Studies*, eds Kenneth Muir and S. Schoenbaum, Cambridge University Press, 1971, p. 104.

25 E. H. Kantorowicz (*The King's Two Bodies*, Princeton University Press, 1957), in discussing this passage, puts the point somewhat tendentiously in favour of Richard: 'The fiction of the oneness of the double body breaks apart' (p. 31). The word 'fiction' over-simplifies the problem of the king's two bodies, and Kantorowicz, looking at the play alongside more pedestrian historical documents, overrates Shakespeare's treatment of it in *Richard II* when he calls it one of Shakespeare's 'greatest plays' (p. 26). For an interesting

modern defence of the monarchy as a poetic and religious institution see Donald Davie, 'Editorial', *PN Review*, vol. 5, no. 1, 1977, pp. 1, 2.

26 *Wilson's Arte of Rhetorique* (1560), ed. G. H. Mair, Oxford, Clarendon Press, 1909, p. 204. The letter 's' is modernized.

27 C. T. Onions, *A Shakespeare Glossary*, 2nd edn (1919), reprinted, Oxford, Clarendon Press, 1941.

28 P. Ure, ed., *Richard II*, The Arden Shakespeare, 5th edn, London, Methuen, 1961, Notes, p. 56.

29 *A Defence of Poetry*, ed. J. Van Dorsten, Oxford University Press, 1966, p. 70. Demetrius's definition is quoted in W. Trimpi, *Ben Jonson's Poems*, Stanford University Press, 1962, 'frigidity "overshoots the expression appropriate to the thought"' (p. 84).

30 J. V. Cunningham, 'Tragic Effect and Tragic Process in Some Plays of Shakespeare, and Their Background in the Literary and Ethical Theory of Classical Antiquity and the Middle Ages', Dissertation, Stanford, 1945, p. 37. Ruth Wallerstein presents a similar view of intuition when she says that images in Milton and Donne are 'the substance of a concentrated intuition that draws thought and feeling inward to a center'. *Studies in Seventeenth Century Poetic* (1950), reprinted, Madison and Milwaukee, University of Wisconsin Press, 1965, p. 140.

31 Stanley Wells, ed., *King Richard the Second*, Harmondsworth, Penguin, 1969, p. 193.

32 F. R. Leavis, *Education and the University*, 2nd edn (1948), reprinted, London, Chatto & Windus, 1965, p. 81.

33 Cunningham, 'Tragic Effect and Tragic Process...,' pp. 31, 32.

34 A. Sherbo, ed., *Johnson on Shakespeare*, vol. I, The Yale Edition of the Works of Samuel Johnson, vol. VII, New Haven and London, Yale University Press, 1968, p. 431.

35 A. C. Partridge, *Tudor to Augustan English*, London, Deutsch, 1969, p. 123.

36 Partridge's discussion of some of the difficulties of the subjunctive in general opens up in part the question of to what extent the plain style is inherently moral. He begins by quoting H. W. Fowler.

> The modern situation of the subjunctive mood, especially its relevance to style, has been summarized by Fowler, in *Modern English Usage*, pp. 574–8. Here are the more important of his findings:

> > ...subjunctives met with today, outside the few truly living uses, are either deliberate revivals by poets for legitimate enough archaic effect, or antiquated survivals

as in pretentious journalism, infecting their context with dullness, or new arrivals possible only in an age to which the grammar of the subjunctive is not natural but artificial....They diffuse an atmosphere of dullness and formalism over the writing in which they occur; the motive underlying them, and the effect they produce, are the same that attend the choosing of FORMAL WORDS... That two verbs whose relation to their surroundings is precisely the same should be one subjunctive, and one indicative, is an absurdity that could not happen until the distinction had lost its reality...

The situation, as Fowler depicts it, was clarified only in the eighteenth century, despite the gradual decline of the inflectional subjunctive since the sixteenth. To express non-factual relationships between subject and predicate a device is indispensable, no matter what modal form it takes. Conditional, concessive and final clauses, among others, contain wish-fulfilling statements of a non-factual kind, which, since the Tudor period, have been communicated by the periphrastic subjunctive substitute, with modal auxiliaries, such as *may, might, have, shall, will, should* and *would*. These became necessary because there was so little distinction between the indicative and subjunctive forms of most verbs, except *be*. (Partridge, op. cit., p. 123)

Despite his agreement with Fowler on modern usage, Partridge goes on to give numerous examples of the varied and rich use of the subjunctive in Chaucer, Spenser, Shakespeare, and Jonson. One has little difficulty agreeing that some such device is 'indispensable'. The notion that the subjunctive is limited to expressing non-factual relationships, however, is open to some qualifications, even though the writers of textbooks in logic agree with the grammarians on this point: propositions in the conditional tense, or subjunctive mood, or hypothetical syllogisms are called, 'counter-factual'. But, in truth, the subjunctive can be used with striking effect to set up a point of view, a way of looking at things, that makes possible a more accurate perception of the 'facts'. For example, Richard, when asked to 'confess' his crimes during the deposition scene, speaks to Northumberland:

> Gentle Northumberland,
> If thy offences were upon record,
> Would it not shame thee, in so fair a troop,
> To read a lecture of them? If thou woulds't,

> There shoulds't thou find one heinous article,
> Containing the deposing of a king,
> And cracking the strong warrant of an oath,
> Mark'd with a blot, damn'd in the book of heaven.
>   (IV, ii, 229–36)

These lines are essentially plain in style. The subjunctive is here remarkably effective in declaring flatly what is the case. Northumberland's offences *are* on record (in Shakespeare's history plays, not to mention the numerous historical records; or, if this is thought to be anachronistic from the perspective of the speaker, the deposition ceremony itself must be a kind of record or it would lack the formality necessary to effect the transfer of the crown). Those records do indeed contain the article Richard mentions. That Northumberland ought to be shamed is, of course, no guarantee that he is or will be shamed. But subsequent events in the history plays confirm Richard's remarks.

The point is that for Shakespeare, as for a good many of his contemporaries, questions of 'fact' on any subject of truly human concern, are mostly inseparable from questions of moral and spiritual value. The Renaissance plain style, in the time preceding the influence of Francis Bacon and the establishment of the Royal Society, is dedicated to expressing as definitively and literally as possible the full significance of any given aspect of reality. It is, therefore, inescapably moral. It is also deeply committed to the use of the subjunctive. (An interesting thesis, though it would require a good deal of historical investigation to support, would be that the decline and banishment of the subjunctive is intimately connected to the rise and triumph of empiricism.) Shakespeare's use of the plain style is not a way of describing isolated empirical facts, but of describing that widespread communal agreement about what the facts are and what their value or importance is that we call literal truth.

37 A. L. French, '*Richard II* and the Woodstock Murder,' *Shakespeare Quarterly*, vol. 22, 1971, pp. 341, 342.

38 Ibid., p. 341.

39 Ibid., pp. 338, 339.

40 A. P. Rossiter, *Angel With Horns*, ed. Graham Storey, New York, Theatre Arts Books, 1961, pp. 23–39, argues that because too much information is left behind in one of Shakespeare's sources, the anonymous Elizabethan play *Woodstock*, *Richard II* is deeply flawed. French is right to reply (op. cit., p. 344) that this kind of reliance on an earlier play is not in itself a flaw — though we still

need to ask how good an understanding Shakespeare offers in his treatment of similar matter.

6 Reductions: style and the character of Bolingbroke

1 Kenneth Muir, 'Shakespeare Among the Commonplaces', *Review of English Studies*, vol. 10, 1959, pp. 283–6, points out just how proverbial Gaunt's consolations are and cites possible analogues in Erasmus and Cicero.

2 The phenomenon of a plain style emptied of moral content suggests, perhaps, a character who is at least capable of acting in accordance with Machiavellian principles. A useful article by Irving Ribner, 'Bolingbroke, a True Machiavellian', *Modern Language Quarterly*, vol. 9, 1948, 177–84, lists some twelve or thirteen ways in which Bolingbroke's actions are a manifestation of the 'actual Machiavellian philosophy' (in contrast to the 'burlesque stage "Machiavel"'). Ribner, however, offers no interpretation of how Shakespeare judges those actions. D. A. Traversi, speaking in a similar vein, does tackle this larger issue: 'the development of a political capacity that recalls, in its various aspects, the Machiavellian conception of the Prince...increasingly poses for Shakespeare, whose thought was at once more traditional and less limited to the political than that of the great Florentine, wider problems more definitely moral, even religious, in kind'. *An Approach to Shakespeare*, vol. I, 3rd edn, New York, Doubleday, 1969, p. 263. Bolingbroke's narrowing of the plain style can be seen for what it is because other stretches of the play exhibit a plain style that *is* moral.

3 D. A. Traversi, *Shakespeare From 'Richard II' to 'Henry V'*, Stanford University Press, 1957, p. 29, remarks that Bolingbroke's indictment of Bushy and Green reveals two essential aspects of his nature: 'his separation of spiritual and political responsibilities' and 'his anxiety to seek public justification for his necessary ruthlessness.'

4 A. L. French, '*Richard II* and the Woodstock Murder', *Shakespeare Quarterly*, vol. 22, 1971, p. 343.

5 Kenneth Muir, ed., *The Tragedy of King Richard the Second*, New York, New American Library, 1963, p. 91.

6 R. F. Hill, 'Dramatic Techniques and Interpretation in *Richard II*', in *Early Shakespeare*, Stratford Upon Avon Studies, vol. III, London, Edward Arnold, 1961, p. 110. Coleridge says: 'Bolingbroke had an equivocation in his mind, and was thinking of the

king, while speaking of the castle.' T. M. Raysor, ed., *Samuel Taylor Coleridge: Shakespearean Criticism*, vol. II, London, Dent, 1960, p. 148.

7 Quoted in P. Ure, ed., *Richard II*, The Arden Shakespeare, 5th edn, London, Methuen, 1961, Notes, p. 108.

8 S. Wells, ed., *King Richard the Second*, Harmondsworth, Penguin, 1969, p. 224.

9 T. M. Raysor, ed., *Samuel Taylor Coleridge: Shakespearean Criticism*, vol. II, London, Dent, 1960, p. 149.

10 Since Bolingbroke, silent or very nearly silent at certain crucial moments of the play, does not present a great deal to work with for an analysis of style, this chapter is accordingly brief. Brents Stirling, 'Bolingbroke's "Decision"', *Shakespeare Quarterly*, vol. 2, 1951, p. 30, comments pointedly on this aspect of Bolingbroke's character: 'opportunism, of which [Bolingbroke] becomes the living symbol, is essentially a tacit vice'. And Wilbur Sanders, *The Dramatist and the Received Idea*, Cambridge University Press, 1968, p. 66, summarizes nicely some of the implications of the silences for an understanding of Bolingbroke:

> We have seen that Shakespeare's treatment of the man is largely a series of vast lacunae, so that the understanding of his character is dependent on the tricky business of interpreting his silences. But they are silences of a definite shape and outline and they are filled out by the overt acts of state which separate them, or — sometimes more revealingly — by the garrulity of his comrades-in-arms. In fact there is a good deal on which to build an estimate of the man. His silences are, to put it sharply, the void where moral consciousness should be at work.

This section, discussing very briefly Bolingbroke's moral consciousness, or lack of it, and the concomitant narrowing of the plain style, is supplemented by material in chapters 8 and 9.

7 Deflections: style and the character of Richard

1 Quoted in P. Ure, ed., *Richard II*, The Arden Shakespeare, 5th edn, London, Methuen, 1961, Notes, p. 115.

2 The emotional effects of wonder and woe are mentioned more or less explicitly by a number of characters who serve something of a choric function in the play. Consider the Queen's forebodings after Richard leaves for Ireland: 'I know no cause/Why I should

welcome such a quest as grief' (II, ii, 6, 7): and, 'But what it is that is not yet known what,/I cannot name: 'tis nameless woe, I wot' (II, ii, 39, 40). York, who confirms some of her misgivings, expresses similar feelings in the same scene: 'what a tide of woes/ Comes rushing on this woeful land at once!/I know not what to do' (II, ii, 98–100). As woe becomes more specifically identified, not-knowing (or wondering) becomes more directly concerned with what action should be performed or with what thought is appropriate. Thus, the Welsh Captain, in the first of the two most obviously choric scenes in the play, argues:

> 'Tis thought the king is dead; we will not stay.
> The bay trees in our country are all wither'd,
> And meteors fright the fixed stars of heaven,
> The pale-fac'd moon looks bloody on the earth,
> And lean-look'd prophets whisper fearful change. ...
> (ii, iv, 7–11)

For those who have not the opportunity to try to escape their fears, the only relief from woe is wonder, as the Queen discovers in the second of the choric scenes. Her lady is unable to devise any 'sport' in their 'garden' that will drive away 'the heavy thought of care' (III, iv, 1, 2), and the Queen rejecting her suggestions, turns to wonder what the gardeners will say about the present state of affairs.

3   E. M. W. Tillyard comments on the readiness of an Elizabethan audience to look for a symbolic, political meaning in the garden scene and claims, moreover, that, 'the gardener gives both the pattern and the moral of the play' (*Shakespeare's History Plays*, (1944), reprinted Harmondsworth, Penguin, 1969, p. 256).

4   P. Ure, op. cit., Notes, p. 151.

5   Yvor Winters, 'The 16th Century Lyric in England: A Critical and Historical Reinterpretation', *Poetry*, vols 53 and 54, 1939, p. 122.

6   M. Croll, *Style, Rhetoric, and Rhythm*, eds, J. Max Patrick *et al.*, Princeton University Press, 1966, p. 221.

7   Winters, op. cit., p. 120.

8   Ibid., p. 121.

9   Or to put the point in the terms of F. R. Leavis, cited in chapter 3: the enclosed self, the nobly suffering self, or the ready defined will is radically untragic.

10 Florio's translation of Montaigne appeared in 1603 and is generally thought to have influenced Shakespeare in the writing of *King Lear*. Most of the commentators focus on the influence of Montaigne's

philosophy or his vocabulary; the influence of his principles of style may have even broader implications.

11 Quoted in M. Black, ed., *The Life and Death of King Richard the Second*, A New Variorum Edition of Shakespeare, Philadelphia and London, J. B. Lippincott, 1955, p. 182.

12 Quoted in ibid., pp. 180, 181. The square brackets are Black's.

13 See Charlton Hinman, ed., *Richard the Second: 1597*, Shakespeare Quarto Facsimiles, no. 13, Oxford, Clarendon Press, 1966, III, ii, 6–26.

14 Quoted in Ure, op. cit., Introduction, p. xv.

15 Croll, op. cit., p. 221.

16 E. Auerbach, *Mimesis: The Representation of Reality in Western Literature*, trans. Willard R. Trask (1953), reprinted Princeton University Press, 1971, p. 288.

17 Ibid., p. 298.

18 Clemen, for example, remarks that: 'In the full consciousness of his kingly dignity, the king frequently compares himself with the sun...these sun images underline the majestic splendour of the king.' *The Development of Shakespeare's Imagery*, Cambridge, Mass., Harvard University Press, 1951, p. 59. Peter Ure suggests that, 'Oscar Wilde seems to have been the first to note the connexion between Richard's sun-badge...and the sun-imagery' ('Introduction' to *Richard II*, p. lxxi). See also, Paul Reyher, 'Le Symbole du Soleil dans la tragedie de *Richard II*', *Revue de l'Enseignement des Langues Vivantes*, vol. 40, 1923, pp. 254–60; Caroline Spurgeon, *Shakespeare's Imagery and What It Tells Us*, Cambridge University Press, 1934, pp. 233–5; J. Dover Wilson, ed., *King Richard II*, Cambridge University Press, 1939, pp. xii, xiii; Samuel Kliger, 'The Sun Imagery in *Richard II*', *Studies in Philology*, vol. 45, 1948, pp. 196–202; and S. K. Heninger, Jr, 'The Sun-King Analogy in *Richard II*', *Shakespeare Quarterly*, vol. II, 1960, pp. 319–27. As part of his argument that in *Richard II* Shakespeare for the first time is 'wholly successful' in developing the tension between the ideal and the actual, Heninger claims that the figure of the sun-king is also wholly successful:

> the sun-king image unifies the other expressions of ideal government that appear throughout *Richard II* and draws the political issue into focus, thereby increasing the intensity of the climactic action. The image embodies, develops, and tests the basic political theme that the personal conduct of both king and subject must subsist congruously within the framework of God's natural order. The sun-king concept is an

ideal, an absolute, a fixed-point, the hub of Fortune's wheel about which Richard and Bolingbroke turn, the well-pulley around which the buckets of the adversaries rise and fall. (p. 325)

In this way an 'image' becomes a 'key' to the play.

19 Quoted in Black, op. cit., p. 184.
20 Ure, op. cit., Notes, p. 96.
21 A. Sherbo, ed., *Johnson on Shakespeare*, vol. I, The Yale Edition of the Works of Samuel Johnson, vol. VII, New Haven and London, Yale University Press, 1968, p. 439. A. R. Humphreys, *Shakespeare: Richard II*, Studies in English Literature, no. 31, London, Edward Arnold, 1967, p. 46, gives a representative modern response that, even while seeing through Richard's complacency, is enchanted by his powers of expression: 'His sudden lyric devotion to England and the Divine Right of his office is an indulgence the fantasy of which the practical Carlisle rebukes, but its sentiment and extravagance are compelling, even though every phrase shows his assumptions to be volatile and gratuitous.' Similarly, M. M. Reese, *The Cease of Majesty*, London, Edward Arnold, 1961, p. 237: 'The words are splendid, but they bring short comfort to the speaker.'
22 Newbolt's suggestion, quoted in Black, op. cit., p. 187.
23 *Ben Jonson*, vol. VIII, eds, C. H. Herford and P. and E. Simpson, Oxford, Clarendon Press, 1947, p. 584.
24 J. Smith, 'On Metaphysical Poetry', *Scrutiny*, vol. 2, 1933, p. 235.
25 Sherbo, op. cit., vol. I, p. 441.
26 The Variorum ed. quotes Ivor John who points out that 'the title page of the additional part of [*The Falls of Princes*] added in 1554 read "A memorial of suche Princes as since the tyme of King Richard the Seconde have been unfortunate in the Realme of England"'.
27 G. Wilson Knight, *The Imperial Theme*, 3rd edn (1951), reprinted London, Methuen, 1965, pp. 351, 355. E. K. Chambers is in general agreement with Wilson Knight about the character of Richard: 'in Shakespeare's psychology, he stands for the type of artist'. *Shakespeare: A Survey* (1925), reprinted New York, Hill & Wang, 1958, p. 91.
28 Knight, op. cit., p. 351.
29 W. S. Howell, *Logic and Rhetoric in England, 1500–1700*, Princeton University Press, 1956, p. 73.
30 Rosemond Tuve, *Elizabethan and Metaphysical Imagery*, University of Chicago Press, 1947, p. 12.
31 Howell, op. cit., p. 70.

32 'Immunity' in this sense is discussed by F. R. Leavis in his last book, *Thought, Words and Creativity*, London, Chatto & Windus, 1976. See, for example, pp. 70 and 78. Leavis is preoccupied with a saying of D. H. Lawrence's: 'At the maximum of our imagination we are religious.' The 'immunity' of the enclosed self is finally an immunity from religious questions.

33 Terence Hawkes, *Shakespeare's Talking Animals*, London, Edward Arnold, 1973, pp. 73–104.

34 'Jane Austen: Poet', in *Jane Austen's Achievement*, ed. Juliet McMaster, London, Macmillan, 1976, p. 115.

35 S. Wells, ed., *King Richard the Second*, Harmondsworth, Penguin, 1969, p. 262.

36 Derek Traversi, for example, suggests that these lines are 'a serious attempt to make expression respond to feeling, in something like a tragic statement about life'. *Shakespeare From 'Richard II' to 'Henry V'*, Stanford University Press, 1957, p. 47.

8 Tragic doings, political order and the closed couplet

1 J. W. H. Atkins, *English Literary Criticism: The Renascence* (1947), reprinted, London, Methuen, 1968, p. 239.

2 *The Complete Works of Christopher Marlowe*, vol. I, ed. Fredson Bowers, Cambridge University Press, 1973, p. 79. In the epistle addressed 'To the Gentleman Readers', R. J. Printer speaks of both tragedy and history ('*the two tragical Discourses of the Scythian Shepheard*, Tamburlaine' and '*so honorable and stately a historie*') suggesting that he saw no radical distinction between the two. In both references the emphasis falls on Marlowe's having achieved an appropriately dignified style. See Bowers, p. 77.

3 Joseph Quincy Adams, ed., *Chief Pre-Shakespearean Dramas*, Boston, Houghton Mifflin, 1924, pp. 664 and 638.

4 Madeleine Doran, *Endeavors of Art*, Madison, Milwaukee, and London, University of Wisconsin Press, 1954, p. 120.

5 J. C. Maxwell, ed., *Titus Andronicus*, The Arden Shakespeare, 3rd edn (1961), reprinted, London, Methuen, 1968, p. 128; E. A. J. Honigman, ed., *King John*, The Arden Shakespeare, 4th edn (1954), reprinted, London, Methuen, 1967, p. 3. Subsequent references to *Titus Andronicus* and *King John* are from these editions.

6 Maxwell, op. cit., p. xxxviii.

7 Ibid., p. xxx.

8 R. M. Sargent, quoted in ibid., p. xxix.

9 E. M. Waith, 'The Metamorphosis of Violence in *Titus Andronicus*', *Shakespeare Survey*, vol. 10, 1957, p. 49, comments briefly on the 'rhetoric of admiration' in *Titus Andronicus*.

10 Excerpts from these various sources and a discussion of their possible relations with Shakespeare's *Richard II* are found in Geoffrey Bullough, ed., *Narrative And Dramatic Sources of Shakespeare*, vol. III, London, Routledge & Kegan Paul, 1966, pp. 351–491.

11 *Aristotle on the Art of Poetry*, trans. Ingram Bywater (1909), reprinted in *The Works of Aristotle*, vol. XI, ed. W. D. Ross, Oxford, Clarendon Press, 1924, 1453a8–1453a9.

12 A. P. Rossiter, *Angel With Horns*, ed. Graham Storey, New York, Theatre Arts Books, 1961, p. 219.

13 Since the following argument attempts to make a case for regarding the passages of heroic couplets in *Richard II* as a special sign of Shakespeare's hand in the play, it is well to mention that other students of the play have regarded them in just the opposite way, as a special sign of someone else's hand. Feuillerat, for example, claims that the rhymed verses 'are too mediocre to make us suppose that they were meant to raise the dialogue in moments of particularly poetic tension. Unquestionably they are the remnants of an old play written entirely in rhymed verse and belonging to a period when the English drama was not yet using blank verse.' He concludes that 'the historical events essential to a play on Richard II were to be found in the play in rhymed verse'. Feuillerat's argument is summarized in M. Black, ed., *The Life and Death of King Richard the Second*, a New Variorum Edition of Shakespeare, Philadelphia and London, J. B. Lippincott, 1955, pp. 398–400.

14 Yvor Winters, *In Defense of Reason*, 3rd edn, Chicago, The Swallow Press, 1947, pp. 141, 142.

15 W. B. Piper, *The Heroic Couplet*, Cleveland and London, Case Western Reserve University Press, 1969, p. 5.

16 A. Sherbo, ed., *Johnson on Shakespeare*, vol. I, The Yale Edition of the Works of Samuel Johnson, vol. VII, New Haven and London, Yale University Press, 1968, p. 451.

17 E. M. W. Tillyard, *Shakespeare's History Plays* (1944), reprinted Harmondsworth, Penguin, 1969, p. 251.

18 Piper, op. cit., pp. 203, 204.

19 Sherbo, op. cit., vol. I, p. 431.

20 The quotations are from J. V. Cunningham's description of the early Elizabethan moral style, *CE*, pp. 314 and 315. For an account of the medieval couplet see Piper, op. cit., pp. 31, 32.

21 Ibid., p. 32.

22 T. M. Raysor, ed., *Samuel Taylor Coleridge: Shakespearean Criticism*, vol. II, London, Dent, 1960, p. 143. Wilbur Sanders's estimate of York's character is also worth quoting.

> (The later developments of York's character seem to me to be on a much smaller scale, like an unfinished sketch. One senses an overall intention − perhaps to show how bad conscience sets its teeth and hardens into doctrinaire inflexibility, even to the denial of that very love of kindred which first brought him in behind Bolingbroke − but it is fitfully executed and does not engage our sympathies on the same level as the York of the first three acts.)
>
> I suggest, then, that in Bolingbroke, Richard and York, we are confronted with three attempts to solve the problem of responsible, morally sensitive behaviour in a world torn by political strife. And each attempt Shakespeare leads us to see as seriously defective in some direction. (p. 185)

Sanders seems not to consider the character of Gaunt (perhaps because he dies so early in the play) as another attempt. The title of his chapter on *Richard II* is 'Shakespeare's Political Agnosticism'.

23 Quoted in Black, op. cit., p. 315.

24 Feuillerat's phrases throughout this paragraph are quoted from ibid., p. 398. See note 13.

25 Winters discusses the problems inherent in dramatic form in *The Function of Criticism: Problems and Exercises*, 2nd edn, Denver, Alan Swallow, 1957, pp. 51–8. For more on this matter see chapter 10.

26 A. S. Cairncross, ed., *The First Part of Henry VI*, The Arden Shakespeare, 2nd edn (1930), reprinted, London, Methuen, 1969, p. 99. Quotations from the play are from this edition.

27 The edition cited is Kenneth Muir, ed., *King Lear*, The Arden Shakespeare, 8th edn (1952), reprinted, London, Methuen, 1973.

28 The enjambed couplet is also used in *Macbeth* to record Macbeth's misunderstanding of the three apparitions (IV, i, 94–103).

9 Astounding terms: bombast and wonder

1 Benvenuto da Imola, quoted in Erich Auerbach, *Literary Language and Its Public in Late Latin Antiquity and in the Middle Ages*, trans. Ralph Manheim, Princeton University Press, 1965, p. 66.

2 Even Samuel Daniel, the defender of rhyme, thought that 'a Tragedie would indeede best comporte with a blank Verse, and

dispence with Ryme, saving in the *Chorus* or where a sentence shall require a couplet.' *Poems and a Defence of Ryme*, ed. Arthur Colby Sprague (1930), reprinted, Chicago and London, University of Chicago Press, 1965, p. 156.

3 Although it is usual to suppose that the high style is the central style of tragedy, there may be good reasons for arguing that it is the plain style that lays the groundwork for the greatest achievements in English drama. Trimpi makes a similar claim with reference to non-dramatic blank verse when he argues that: 'if one traces the changes in prosody between Gascoigne and Milton, it will appear that the most elevated style in English poetry owes perhaps its most fundamental characteristics to the innovations of the plainest' (*Ben Jonson's Poems: A Study of the Plain Style*, Stanford University Press, 1962, p. 119). See the whole of chapter 6, pp. 115–35 and especially the comparison of metrical practices in Jonson and Milton, pp. 129–34. The issue in Shakespearean drama, however, rests not solely on describing the mechanics of blank verse, but also on seeing how each of the various styles contributes to the creation of Shakespearean blank verse. In this section, as in the preceding one on the heroic couplet, I attempt to give an account of the sort of accommodation Shakespeare works out between the two styles of lyric poetry, the golden and the moral, and the three styles of classical theory, the high, the middle and the low.

4 Howard Baker, *Induction to Tragedy* (1939) reprinted New York, Russell & Russell, 1965, p. 93.

5 *The Complete Works of George Gascoigne*, vol. II, ed. John W. Cunliffe, Cambridge University Press, 1910, p. 140.

6 Robert Green, *Groats-Worth of Witte, bought with a million of Repentance*, The Bodley Head Quartos, ed. G. B. Harrison, London, John Lane, The Bodley Head, 1923, pp. 45, 46.

7 See Cunningham, *CE*, p. 97.

8 The passages in *Richard II* that remain to be discussed include the two most important actions in the play: the initial action, Bolingbroke's attempt to impeach Mowbray; and the climax, the deposition or abdication of Richard. (It is worth noting that the word one chooses to describe the climax implies a judgment about whether Bolingbroke or Richard is most to blame.) Shakespeare appears to want the mixed style for both of these important events.

9 Wolfgang Clemen, *English Tragedy Before Shakespeare*, trans. T. S. Dorsch (1961), reprinted, London, Methuen, 1967, p. 56.

10 *Gorboduc*, V, ii, 180–2, in J. Q. Adams, ed., *Chief Pre-Shakespearean Dramas*, Boston, Houghton Mifflin, 1924, p. 533.

11 Clemen, op. cit., p. 122.
12 This and subsequent quotations from *Tamburlaine* are from F. Bowers, ed., *The Complete Works of Christopher Marlowe*, Cambridge University Press, 1973.
13 Baker, op. cit., p. 54.
14 'For *Tamburlaine*, the Scourge of God must die' (2 *Tam*, V, iii, 248). The irony of the bombastic epithet, of course, is very heavy, but there is little evidence that Tamburlaine himself understands the irony.
15 Clemen, op. cit., p. 109.
16 Baker, op. cit., pp. 99–103.
17 Quotations from *The Spanish Tragedy* are taken from *The Works of Thomas Kyd*, ed. Frederick S. Boas, Oxford, Clarendon Press, 1901.
18 T. S. Eliot, *Selected Essays*, 3rd edn (1951), reprinted, London, Faber & Faber, 1972, p. 96.
19 Auerbach, op. cit., pp. 51, 52.
20 Ibid., p. 57.
21 The problem of documenting any direct connections between *sermo humilis* and Shakespeare's style is similar to the general problem of connections that Trimpi outlines (*Ben Jonson's Poems: A Study of the Plain Style*, Stanford University Press, 1962):

> In describing the similarities between the attitudes of the native and the classical traditions of the plain style I am in no sense suggesting that the ancient writers were the direct and formative influence on the attitudes of English poets. The qualities of language are characteristic of most didactic intentions, and the medieval poetic tradition was overwhelmingly didactic. Despite the structural elaborations of the allegorical method, which the sixteenth-century plain stylists were to abandon, the diction and syntax of the greatest medieval poets remained remarkably plain and beguilingly intimate. Chaucer's simplicity of statement offers a model of purity to the English language that is comparable to the one Terence gave to Latin, and their intention to represent the real concerns of ordinary people was the same. Dante writes Can Grande that one of the reasons he is calling his intricate allegory a comedy is that it is written in the *genus humile* appropriate to comedy, in a vernacular style in which even women converse. The attitudes toward experience and the stylistic qualities appropriate to them, therefore, were quite as available in the medieval tradition as they were in the

classical. Jonson, then, in the late 1590's is not reacting against the native plain style in the sense that he was against the high and middle styles. He is simply returning to the classical statement of his position and adapting certain techniques of prose rhythm, derived from the very origins of the *sermo* itself, to the rhythmical structure of English verse. Once adapted, these techniques of variation gradually became principles of good prosody in general and are no longer restricted to the plain style. (p. 119)

22 Baker, op. cit., p. 57. One might call the heroic medium 'the native English grand style': first, because the balance of the line recalls the balance of the early English alliterative line; and second, because the emphatic metre (heavy stresses, end-stopped lines, regular caesuras) is very much like the metre of the native English plain style. See Cunningham, *CE*, pp. 313–16. On the connections between alliterative verse and the iambic pentameter see, in addition to Baker, Ian Robinson's discussion of balanced pentameter lines in *Chaucer's Prosody*, Cambridge University Press, 1971.
23 Auerbach, op. cit., p. 33.
24 J. Dover Wilson, ed., *King Richard II*, Cambridge University Press, 1939, p. 124.
25 T. M. Raysor, ed., *Samuel Taylor Coleridge: Shakespearean Criticism*, vol. I, London, Dent, 1960, p. 132. Coleridge's phrase is actually in Greek. I have taken the translation supplied by Terence Hawkes, ed., *Coleridge on Shakespeare* (1959), reprinted, Harmondsworth, Penguin, 1969, p. 246.
26 Quoted in M. Black, ed., *The Life and Death of King Richard the Second*, A New Variorum Edition of Shakespeare, Philadelphia and London, J. B. Lippincott, 1955, p. 26.
27 The seven parts of an oration are discussed in Richard A. Lanham, *A Handlist of Rhetorical Terms*, Berkeley and Los Angeles, University of California Press, 1968, pp. 112, 113.
28 Though Carlisle is very clearly expressing didactic sentiments, and though his style is certainly not loose or rambling, his speech exhibits a flexibility and an urbane poise wholly unlike the metrical stiffness and heavy-handed insistence of the heroic medium. In this speech, in fact, Shakespeare employs the two rhythmical principles that Trimpi says were introduced most explicitly into English by the classical plain style: 'No recurring pattern of caesural placement appears, and the caesura is free to fall in any position in the line, odd or even' (op. cit., p. 131).

29 D. Traversi, *Shakespeare From 'Richard II' to 'Henry V'*, Stanford University Press, 1947, p. 39.

30 Tucker Brooke, quoted in Black, op. cit., p. 261.

31 See ibid., p. 261.

32 Lily B. Campbell, *Shakespeare's 'Histories': Mirrors of Elizabethan Policy*, 3rd edn (1963), reprinted, London, Methuen, 1977, pp. 16 and 17.

33 Ibid., p. 16.

34 P. Ure, ed., 'Notes' to *Richard II*, The Arden Shakespeare, 5th edn, London, Methuen, 1961, p. 132.

35 The similarities between the mature style of Shakespeare and the style of the Christian *sermo* have been suggested by Matthew Arnold in one of his best critical essays, 'On Translating Homer', in *Matthew Arnold on the Classical Tradition*, The Complete Prose Works of Matthew Arnold, vol. I, ed. R. H. Super, Ann Arbor, University of Michigan Press, 1960, pp. 155–6:

> the idiomatic language of Shakespeare...should be carefully observed by the translator of Homer, although in every case he will have to decide for himself whether the use, by him, of Shakespeare's liberty, will or will not clash with his indispensable duty of nobleness. He will find one English book and one only, where, as in the *Iliad* itself, perfect plainness of speech is allied with perfect nobleness; and that book is the Bible....But the grand instance of the union of idiomatic expression with curious or difficult thought is in Shakespeare's poetry.

36 Dover Wilson and H. R. Patch are both cited in Black, op. cit., p. 266. For Johnson's remarks see A. Sherbo, ed., *Johnson on Shakespeare*, vol. I, The Yale Edition of the Works of Samuel Johnson, vol. VII, New Haven and London, Yale University Press, 1968, p. 447.

37 Ure, op. cit., Introduction, p. lxxxii.

38 Auerbach, op. cit., p. 31.

39 Ure, op. cit., Notes, p. 142.

10 *Macbeth*: style and form

1 George Whalley, 'On Translating Aristotle's *Poetics*', *University of Toronto Quarterly*, vol. 39, 1970, p. 101.

2 Ibid., p. 97.

3 Ibid., p. 100.

4 Ibid., p. 102. The same emphasis is evident in Whalley's translation of Aristotle's definition: 'For tragedy is a *mimesis* not of men [simply] but of an action, that is, of life. That's how it is that they certainly do not act in order to present their characters: they assume their characters for the sake of the actions [they are to do] ' (p. 96). The square brackets are Whalley's.

5 Ian Robinson, *The Survival of English*, Cambridge University Press, 1973, pp. 6, 7.

6 Ibid., p. 226.

7 Whalley, op. cit., pp. 100, 101.

8 Yvor Winters, *The Function of Criticism: Problems and Exercises*, 2nd edn, Denver, Alan Swallow, 1957, pp. 51–8. In summarizing Winters's argument here and in the following three paragraphs, I have often borrowed his phrasing but have put only the most pertinent comments in quotation marks. The discussion of *Macbeth* is concentrated on pp. 51–5, though see also pp. 26–8.

9 Elder Olson, *Tragedy and the Theory of Drama* (1961), reprinted, Detroit, Wayne State University Press, 1972, p. 12.

10 This and subsequent quotations from the play are taken from Kenneth Muir, ed., *Macbeth*, 9th edn (1962), reprinted, London, Methuen, 1973.

11 D. J. Enright, *Shakespeare and the Students*, London, Chatto & Windus, 1970, p. 126. Enright's discussion of the early part of the play, however, is well worth consulting, especially his remarks comparing Lady Macbeth's early euphemistic (and euphuistic) style with Macbeth's language. See pp. 130–5.

12 Muir, op. cit., Notes p. 21.

13 Notes to *Macbeth*, ed. J. Dover Wilson, Cambridge University Press, 1947, p. 112.

14 A. C. Bradley, *Shakespearean Tragedy*, 2nd edn (1905), reprinted, London, Macmillan, 1967, p. 352.

15 Muir, op. cit., Introduction, pp. liii and li.

16 F. R. Leavis, *The Living Principle: 'English' as a Discipline of Thought*, New York, Oxford University Press, 1975, p. 95. Leavis has used Macbeth's speech repeatedly as an example of the essentially poetic use of language. See also *Education and the University: A Sketch for an 'English School'*, 2nd edn London, Chatto & Windus, 1948, pp. 78–83; and 'Education and the University: III Literary Studies', *Scrutiny*, vol. 9, 1941, pp. 315–19.

17 Leavis, *The Living Principle*, p. 97.

18 The structure of Macbeth's speech is modelled on the type of syllogism known as hypothetical.

- If the act (of murder) is something that can be absolutely complete in itself, it should be performed at once.

- But the act is not something that can be absolutely complete in itself.

- Therefore the act should not be performed at once (or ever).

The structure is similar to the structure of Andrew Marvell's poem 'To His Coy Mistress', the major premise of which is: 'Had we but world enough, and time/This coyness, lady, were no crime.' See Cunningham, *CE*, pp. 164–71. Barbara Herrnstein Smith points out that Marvell's syllogism is 'an excellent example of a textbook fallacy known as "denying the antecedent"'. *Poetic Closure*, University of Chicago Press, 1968, p. 134. Macbeth's syllogism, however, is not guilty of this fallacy because although the rule is that in hypothetical inferences 'the antecedent must be affirmed or the consequent denied', there is one exception. Ralph M. Eaton, *General Logic*, New York, Charles Scribner's Sons, 1931, p. 162, explains both the fallacy and the possible exception:

> Denying the antecedent is also a frequent source of error. We tend to believe that if the conditions under which a certain consequent is true are not fulfilled, this proposition cannot be true. But there are usually other conditions from which it would follow. A believer in economic determinism in history might argue: 'If one nation exploits another economically, we can expect to have wars; but if nations do not economically exploit one another, then we shall have no wars.' The inference is plainly unjustified, for economic exploitation is not the only condition of war. There are religious wars, wars of national unity, and of many other kinds. Such an argument could be correct only if economic exploitation were the sole condition under which wars arise.

In other words, it is permissible to deny the antecedent if the antecedent carries the sole condition under which the consequent is true. The antecedent must have the sense of 'if and only if.' This is the case in Macbeth's speech because of the emphasis of the line.

19 The *Oxford English Dictionary* records a logical meaning for the word 'judgment' that is relevant here: 'The action of mentally apprehending the relation between two objects of thought; predication, as an act of the mind' (*s.v.* 9).

20 For a sampling of suggestions about how the rhythm of this line goes see H. H. Furness, ed., *Macbeth*, A New Variorum Edition

of Shakespeare (1883), reprinted, New York, American Scholar, 1963, pp. 94, 95.

21 The metrical subordination of the second and third instances of the word 'done' and the heightening of the first and most important instance help to give the antecedent clause of Macbeth's major premise the sense of 'if and only if'. See note 18.

22 Leavis, *Education and the University*, p. 79.

23 The depth of Macbeth's understanding before he commits the murder has baffled readers, and it is in dealing with this part of the play that two of the major kinds of Shakespearean criticism in the twentieth century have faltered. One begins with an emphasis on poetry and the other on character; both make an inappropriate appeal to imitative form in order to explain Macbeth. Derek Traversi argues that:

> The supernatural sanctions against which Macbeth has rebelled in conceiving the murder of his king make themselves felt, in a broken form indeed, because they are reflected in a mind already irretrievably shattered, but with the power to impose their validity in his own despite....even his efforts at logical expression are caught up in the incoherence, the broken continuity, which has dominated his thought ever since he first considered the revelation of the Witches. The breathless confounding, so superbly echoed in the sound of his words, of 'assassination' with 'consequence,' 'surcease' with 'success,' reflects a mind involved in the incoherent flow of its own ideas, while the force of 'trammel' and 'catch,' each stressing with its direct impact a break in the rhythm of the phrase, conveys perfectly the peculiar disorganized intensity which Macbeth will bear with him to the final extinction of feeling. (*An Approach to Shakespeare*, 3rd edn, New York, Doubleday, 1969, vol. II, pp. 122, 123)

J. I. M. Stewart, though he does not focus so specifically on the speech in question, comes to a similar conclusion about Macbeth's character in the early part of the play:

> But Shakespeare not only neglects conscious motives; he blurs them — as Bridges, going deeper, discerns. And the explanation must lie, I think, in the fact that an intellectual as well as emotional confusion attends such a deed as the killing of Duncan. The 'veiled confusion of motive' to which Bridges points, the indefiniteness as to when and in whose mind the idea of the crime first started up, echoes this. The

blurring is indeed deliberately put into the play, and is achieved by devices that would be impossible in a naturalistic drama. Thus when Shakespeare secures the effect of their having been, and not been, a previous plot between Macbeth and his wife, he is certainly deserting nature for artifice. Why? In order to secure, I would suppose, by a non-realistic device such as he is always prepared to use, a dramatic correlative to the confusion in Macbeth's mind. If the audience can be made to grope among motives which are insubstantial, phantasmagoric and contradictory they will be approximating to the condition of the protagonist. (*Character and Motive in Shakespeare*, (1941), reprinted New York, Barnes & Noble, 1969, p. 96)

But the point of Macbeth's soliloquy is that he has *no* motive. In so far as Stewart and Traversi refer to I, vii, 1-28 when they appeal to imitative form, they are mistaken in a fairly simple way. The deeper mistake lies in supposing that imitative form should be invoked in defence of the play.

24 Robert Bridges, *The Influence of the Audience on Shakespeare's Drama* (1927), reprinted, New York, Haskell House, 1966, p. 13.

25 Winters, in fact, says something very close to this when he gives an account of the end of the play, and the account explains why despite his criticisms, he regards *Macbeth* as the greatest play with which he is acquainted.

Macbeth has murdered Duncan, Banquo, and the family of Macduff; and he has murdered sleep. But he has murdered more than that, and he knows it — knows it not merely in theory, now, but in fact: he has murdered his own soul. This is the speech [V, v, 17-28] of a man who sees himself as a walking dead man, to whom his own life has lost all meaning. These speeches, in which the general implications of Macbeth's sin are indicated, give greater precision to our understanding of the sin and greater scope to the play: the play is not merely an account of the tragic consequences of a particular irrational passion, as in *Phèdre*; it is an account of the tragic consequences of irrational passion. It is thus the greater play. (op. cit., p. 28)

26 Robinson, op. cit., p. 198.

27 Howard Baker quotes this passage at the end of his essay 'The Formation of the Heroic Medium,' in *Induction to Tragedy* (1939) reprinted New York, Russell & Russell, 1965, p. 104. The need for bombast to pad out the iambic pentameter line sometimes

produced curious results — the frequent appearance of the adjective 'hugie' in *Gorboduc*, for example. The bombastic side of the dagger speech can be seen in the ease with which the lines can be rewritten as iambic tetrameter.

> Now o'er the one half-world
> Nature seems dead, and dreams abuse
> Our sleep: Witchcraft celebrates
> Pale Hecate's off'rings; and Murther,
> Alarum'd by his sentinel,
> Whose howl's his watch, thus with his pace,
> With Tarquin's strides, towards his design
> Moves like a ghost.

This is the medium of mini-threats. Any attempt to re-write the 'If it were done' soliloquy in this way will bring out the difference in the quality of Shakespeare's verse in the two passages.

28 In view of the stringency of Winters's criticism of drama in *The Function of Criticism*, published in 1957, it is worthwhile to note his comments on the subject nearly twenty years earlier in *Maule's Curse*, first published in 1938.

> The extremes of prosaic and of poetic language, each at a high level of excellence, might be illustrated by the prose of *The Age of Innocence*, on the one hand, and by one of the best sonnets of Shakespeare on the other: the extreme of prose is the recounting of individual facts; the extreme of poetry is the lyrical, in the best sense; that is, the expository concentration of a motivating concept, in language such that motivating concept and motivated feeling are expressed simultaneously and in brief space. Between these extremes, but a little nearer to the sonnet than to Mrs. Wharton, is the language of the great epic or dramatic poem: in *Macbeth*, or in *Paradise Lost*, the individual passage is never self-sustaining in the same measure as the poetry of the great sonnet by either author; even the greatest passages are dependent upon the structure and upon the total theme for their greatness, and must be read in their context if they are not to seem inferior in quality to the shorter poems. This does not mean that they are an inferior kind of poetry; it means that they are a different kind of poetry. (*In Defense of Reason*, 3rd edn, Chicago, The Swallow Press, 1947, p. 219)

The recognition here that individual passages in drama are an inextricable part of a larger whole points to the way in which poetic drama goes about its work of exposition. The parts and their relationships define the whole. Macbeth's losses are defined precisely as they are measured against what he had to lose. The dramatist may be forced to employ a greater range of styles in order to differentiate his characters, and among that range, some styles will be necessarily less wonderful than others, and he may have to develop an inferior style at greater length than would the lyric poet (though the lyric poet no less than the dramatist, it must be remembered, has to choose to write in one style or another); but his purpose is finally no different in kind. Poetic drama, no less than the short poem, is dedicated to defining questions of human value – that is, of human nature. It is true that many dramatists (and others) use idiosyncratic styles merely to depict idiosyncratic characters rather than to explore the human potentiality of such styles. The achievement of a perfectly idiosyncratic style would be the defeat of language, because for a style to be a style, its principles of selection and order must be recognized by more than one speaker (See Winters's comments on Joyce and Flaubert in *The Function of Criticism*, p. 37). But in the hands of a dramatist capable of realizing the potential inherent in each style, the drama is a powerful instrument of definition. It is Shakespeare's genius with each of the styles that he takes up in *Macbeth* that gives the play such intensity and scope and that makes it, in Winters's own words, 'an account of the tragic consequences of irrational passion' (*The Function of Criticism*, p. 28).

29 Joel B. Altman, *The Tudor Play of Mind: Rhetorical Inquiry and the Development of Elizabethan Drama*, Berkeley University of California Press, 1978, shows how much of sixteenth-century literature grows from the attempt to dramatize philosophical and rhetorical questions and statements. Altman's findings corroborate the argument that the plain style is central to Elizabethan drama.

30 Cunningham, *CE*, p. 311.

Index

Index